A Handbook
of Catholic Sacramentals

*From left: top, Lourdes Water in decorative vial (see "Water")
and Byzantine Chatky; below, Ladder Rosary (see "Chaplets,
Rosaries, Crowns, and Beads") and St. Joseph's Cord (see
"Girdles, Cinctures, and Cords").*

A Handbook
of Catholic Sacramentals

Ann Ball

Our Sunday Visitor Publishing Division
Our Sunday Visitor, Inc.
Huntington, IN 46750

Nihil Obstat:
Rev. Frank Rossi
Censor Librorum

Imprimatur:
+ Joseph A. Fiorenza, D.D.
Bishop of Galveston-Houston
July 10, 1991

Our Sunday Visitor Publishing Division
Our Sunday Visitor, Inc.
200 Noll Plaza
Huntington, Indiana 46750

International Standard Book Number: 0-87973-484-5
Library of Congress Catalog Card Number: 91-60013

Cover design by Monica Watts
Photographs by John Zierten

PRINTED IN THE UNITED STATES OF AMERICA

484

CONTENTS

Preface-Dedication

As a Protestant child growing up in a small East Texas town, I misunderstood a great deal about the Catholic Church and its devotional practices.

From the time of the Texas Revolution until the 1970s, most of East Texas was a mission field for the Catholic Church. When I was growing up during the '50s and early '60s, there was only a small Catholic congregation in my home town. Sturdy LaSalette Fathers were mission priests here. On Sundays, the priest traveled well over one hundred miles in order to serve Mass in a number of towns. There were no Catholic schools, and in my public school classes there were few Catholic children. The only sisters I saw as a child were nursing sisters at the hospital thirty-five miles away — Daughters of Charity of St. Vincent de Paul. I was surprised when I went away to college and learned that all Catholic sisters did not wear such intriguing large hats!

The first rosary I ever saw belonged to my friend Susan. I thought it was a necklace. Susan explained that the rosary was a set of beads to remind her of her daily prayers. The thought of saying that many prayers daily horrified me.

The Catholics had lovely chili suppers once a year, and we always attended. These were fund-raisers to help build a new church to replace the old wooden one. At last, enough chili had been served and the new church was built, then dedicated. Half the town turned out to walk through the new building. I went with my friend Louisa, whose mother knew enough of Catholic protocol to pin a lace handkerchief on our heads before we entered the sanctuary. There, in irrefutable proof of all the tales about the Catholics that I had heard, they stood — the idols! Being greatly outnumbered, I decided the better part of valor was to keep my mouth shut (a rarity for me!). At least, I kept silent, although I expect my mouth was hanging open in total shock at the temerity of the Catholics in having idols in a church dedicated to God! Creeping close for a good view, I noticed that one of the idols looked a great deal like the picture of Jesus we had in our Sunday school at church. Another appeared similar to the statue of Mary we had in our manger scene at Christmas. And I must admit, the actions of the people all seemed quite silent and reverent, even when they were making strange motions after dipping their fingers in the water in a large bowl at the back of the church. I briefly wondered if they were rebaptizing themselves. Even the strange smell seemed to lend a special air to this unusual place. In the car on the way home, Louisa's mother explained to me that the Catholics did not consider their statues idols. With great logic she paralleled our pictures with the Catholic statues . . . reminders of Jesus, His family, and His friends.

In high school, for a time, my special date was a Catholic boy. Christmas of my senior year I agreed to go with his family to midnight Mass. The singing was lovely. Most of the beautiful carols were ones I was familiar with. However, when the priest stood in front of the congregation, I was totally unprepared for the fact that I could not understand a word of what he said. Or rather, sang! Jimmy's older brother opened what I assumed to be a hymnal, and without speaking he pointed to a page. On the left, the words were written in Latin. On the right, in red and black, the words were printed in English. I am afraid that I missed a great deal of the service in attempting to read every word on the page. I remember he kept turning the pages faster than I could read — and I was a rapid reader. Additionally, with all the standing, sitting, and kneeling, I got more exercise in that one service than I normally did in a week of physical education classes. A later visit to an Episcopal service convinced me that we Methodists were the sluggards among ecclesiastical exercisists.

My best friend in college was Catholic. Our Friday midnight hamburger dashes were notorious. My dates questioned, "What do you mean, you have to be home at midnight when curfew is 12:45? You and JoAnn have to go for hamburgers at this hour?" I assumed that all Catholic college students ate fish on Fridays until midnight, after which it was regulations to "pig out" on Whataburgers.

There are many more humorous misunderstandings I had about Catholic devotional practices, especially as regard the "trappings" of their faith. My natural curiosity has always impelled me to investigate things — and the sacramentals of the Church have provided me with a rich field for research.

One day, when I was in one of the local Catholic bookstores, I noticed a chaplet I had never seen before. The little card said how to pray it, but gave no further information about it. When I asked the store's owner about it, he said he didn't know and suggested I write a book about some of the sacramentals, including their history. This book is the outcome of Rocky's suggestion.

This work is dedicated, as are my previous works, to Our Lady of Sorrows, my gentle mother. It is also written for my mother, my brother and sister, my extended family, my children, and all my Catholic friends, religious and lay, who have helped to form and encourage in me the curiosity that prompted the research for this book.

The Author

Sacramentals in Catholic Theology

J. Michael Miller, C.S.B.

Vice President for Academic Affairs

University of St. Thomas

Over a five-year period at the outset of his papal ministry, Pope John Paul II developed a "theology of the body" in his weekly addresses. By doing so the Holy Father confronted head-on today's false spiritualism. As contrary to conventional wisdom as it might seem, the Church does not need a "more spiritual" Christianity but precisely the opposite. Catholics must develop a less spiritual, but more bodily, more incarnational, and more sacramental vision in living their faith.

In this collection of popular devotions, Ann Ball develops the Pope's theology of the body by addressing a topic often relegated to the fringes of professional theological concern — the sacramentals. If the Holy Father is right, that the Incarnation places the body and material creation at the center of our faith,[1] then sacramentals deserve our serious attention.

The very fact of the Incarnation tells us that the material cosmos is not evil. It is the means through which God has chosen to share his life with us. Through the Eternal Son's taking flesh, "the terrible and tragic rip in the fabric of Creation is being reknit."[2] The Incarnation is an act of reversal of the Fall, bringing spirit and flesh together again. In God's redemptive hands, created realities can once more serve as instruments of grace.

Right from her beginning, the Church denounced those who held that we are saved independently of anything created. These early heretical dualists believed that God was hostile to creation. Christians answered this pessimism with a ringing affirmation of creation as "very good." Not establishing an abyss between God and humanity, the created world is a "sign" of God's presence. His plan is for *salus carnis:* salvation *through* the flesh of Jesus' passion and death and salvation *for* our flesh through the resurrection of the body.

Because of this strongly incarnational perspective, the Catholic tradition has cultivated a sense that human beings should feel "at home in the world."[3] Likewise fundamental to this vision is the law of sacramentality: that bodily and created reality can mediate the divine. "The whole world is a sacrament," writes Peter Kreeft, "a sacred thing, a gift."[4] Since we cannot hear or see God directly, we rely on created realities to bring him first to us and us back to him.

According to the Old Testament, the chosen people's access to God was always mediated — through the prophetic word, the priesthood, the Temple, the prescriptions of the Law. With the coming of Christ, God's love became palpable, humanly visible. In the Incarnate Son the Trinity revealed Its love, mercy, faithfulness, simplicity, and openness. God's own way of saving us is therefore sacramental. He uses His creation to share with us His divine life, the foremost of which was the Son's human nature. By becoming brothers and sisters of the Word made flesh, humanity likewise returns to God in a similar bodily and visible way.

Since Jesus' ascension into heaven, the seven sacraments of the Church are the primary means we have of encountering God. Through these visible signs of invisible and life-giving grace, the human person encounters Christ in His Body, the Church. Instituted by Christ, who is the principal celebrant of every sacrament, each rite confers the unique grace it signifies when celebrated in the Church.

Prior to the high middle ages, the term "sacrament" *(sacramentum)* was also used for rites, prayer, and objects other than the seven sacraments. Not until the thirteenth century did the Church draw a clear distinction between "sacraments" and "sacramentals." Theologians then defined sacraments as those seven actions instituted by Christ that cause what they signify. Sacramentals, they maintained, resembled the sacraments, but were instituted by the Church and prepared the participants to receive grace.

These sacramentals or "little sacraments" are as integral to an incarnational-bodily Christianity as are the seven major sacraments. Not just optional "add-ons," they are essential to experiencing the world through Catholic eyes and, even more importantly, with a Catholic heart. All creation speaks to us of God. Times and seasons will have their place in our devotion since we are beings who live in history. Spaces, places, and special clothing are also indispensable. That's why we build beautiful cathedrals, set aside sanctuary areas, wear religious habits, and buy our children First Communion outfits.

Material objects and blessings enfold Catholic life as reminders of the mysteries of creation and redemption. "There is hardly any proper use of material things," declared Vatican II, "which cannot thus be directed toward the sanctification of men and women and the praise of God."[5] The variety of sacramentals is endless: blessing fields, walking the way of the cross, saying rosaries, venerating crucifixes and statues in churches and homes.

What Is a Sacramental?

After discussing the sacraments in their document on the sacred liturgy, the Fathers at Vatican II defined sacramentals as "sacred signs that bear a resemblance to the sacraments; they signify effects, particularly of a spiritual kind, which are obtained through the Church's intercession."[6] By making holy various occasions of life, the sacramentals dispose believers to receive divine life. They are "any object or prayer or action that can put us in touch with God's grace in Christ."[7] Like sacraments, sacramentals make available to us the stream of "divine grace which flows from the paschal mystery of the passion, death, and resurrection of Christ, the fountain from which all sacraments and sacramentals draw their power."[8]

From ancient times, the Church has pronounced her blessings over men and women, their activities, and the objects they use in everyday life. The minister of the sacramental action expresses the Church's faith in divine providence and prays that God grant a special grace to the person either directly or through correctly using the object blessed.

First among the Church's sacramentals are blessings that invoke God's protection and beneficence. Praise of the God "who has blessed us in Christ with every spiritual blessing in the heavenly places" (Eph 1:3) is necessary to every sacramental blessing. Sacramentals are primarily blessings or actions using the Church's prayer. Through simple gestures and prayer the Church implores God's blessing on persons or things — from making the sign of the cross on the brow of your children, to wearing scapulars, to honoring holy pictures, to lighting blessed candles.

An object is sacramental only because it has been so blessed by this intercessory prayer. Sacramentals are primarily prayers directed to God and secondarily, through his response, a sanctification of persons or objects.

When a blessing sets apart a particular object exclusively for God, we commonly call it a "consecration." These blessings withdraw certain persons, or more commonly, certain objects, from the everyday world and consecrate them totally to God and his service. The prayer offered asks that the objects be the bearers of a blessing for those who use them, occasions for encountering God.

Origin of Sacramentals

In Christianity believers sanctify their everyday life primarily by presenting their bodies "as a living sacrifice, holy and acceptable" to God, their "spiritual worship" (Rom 12:1). But they accompany their bodily gift with other visible signs, reminding themselves that God blesses every dimension of their life. These sacred signs allow created realities to reveal the eternal by directing us heavenward. They saturate and sanctify human life "with divine energy."[9]

The Church has no definitive list of sacramentals. She multiplies them according to need. In medieval Europe ecclesiastics threw a net of blessings over every dimension of life: from food to animals, from throats to vines. As the Church moves through history we can look forward to a continual unfolding of new sacramentals that help to restore all things in Christ.

All authentic sacramentals are dependent on the seven great sacraments with which we are familiar. The Eucharist, as the summit and source of Christian worship, is, for example, the reason why all food and meals are holy. Each commemorates the Eucharistic banquet. In the same way, all sacramentals that involve the sprinkling of water recall the cleansing power of Baptism. The sacramentals are "the small change, as it were, of the sacraments, the fringes (often picturesque) of sacramental life."[10] Intrinsically linked to the major sacraments, these "little sacraments" prepare us for their celebration and prolong their effects. That is their primary purpose.

Unlike the sacraments instituted by Christ, the Church herself creates sacramentals for another purpose: to sanctify everyday life. Although indirectly, even these sacramentals come from the Incarnate Word, who by his taking flesh consecrated the world, thereby making human activity a sign of his creative and redemptive presence. The Church gives us the sacramentals in service of the sacraments, of which they are imitations. As her actions, they express the Church's desire to sanctify humanity on its pilgrim journey. Through the sacramentals all created reality comes into the orbit of God's blessing, making all manner of people, situations and objects occasions of grace.

Celebrating Sacramentals

For sacramentals closely connected to the Church's public worship, it is appropriate that her minister, whether deacon, priest, or bishop, perform the blessing. The bishop presides at the most solemn blessings, and the priest presides over the more ordinary ones in the community to which he ministers. That the 1983 Code of Canon Law allows the laity to administer certain sacramentals reflects Vatican II's recognition of the faithful's common priesthood.[12] Because of their special responsibility, parents may bless their children and catechists bless their students. In these and other situations laymen and laywomen may bless, thereby ministering certain sacramentals.

The right to establish official sacramentals belongs to the Holy See.[13] Without hesitation, however, the Pope grants requests to individual bishops and bishops' conferences to institute sacramentals appropriate to specific cultures and situations.

Whereas the seven sacraments confer sanctifying grace because they are actions of Christ himself, the sacramentals prepare us to cooperate with it. In traditional theological language, the sacramentals are efficacious *ex opere operantis Ecclesiae;* that is, they bring forth spiritual fruits by virtue of the Church's intercessory prayer and the recipient's willing cooperation in faith and love.

When a medal or a scapular is blessed, it does not itself become a cause of grace. What happens is that God responds to our petition to give special graces when the faithful use these things with the proper dispositions.[14] The sacramentals provide actual graces that prepare the soul to receive an increase of sanctifying grace, an intensification of friendship between God and the individual. Although sacramentals have primarily a spiritual purpose, they are directed towards the whole person, body and soul. Through them we are often aided in our temporal needs: restored health, pleasant weather and abundant harvests.[15]

The use of sacramentals obliges the participants to continue deepening their relationship with God. Without such a commitment, sacramentals become objects or practices that people manipulate to extort divine help without submitting to conversion. Sacramentals are not charms adopted to protect us from physical and spiritual harm but means by which we are to grow in faith, hope and love.

Pastoral Concerns

Contemporary society is uncomfortable with religious ritual because of its connection with the magical. Why bother to bless a person or a thing? Christian worship, they say, is essentially a spiritual matter. Sacramentals, with their embarrassing tangibility and emphasis on externals, seem far removed from Jesus' demand for worship "in spirit and in truth" (Jn 4:23). No wonder sacramentals are marginalized, merely folkloric or colorful holdovers from a bygone era.

Non-Catholics, and even some Catholics, object as well that sacramentals and devotional practices contribute to a kind of "automatism" in our relationship with God. These challengers accuse us of holding that by just doing something, going somewhere, or reciting fixed prayers we imagine ourselves to be saved. Critics think that this focus on "little sacraments" in Catholicism does not promote interior conversion of heart but settles for a set of pious exercises that supposedly guarantees its users spiritual and temporal results. Everything from lighting candles to sprinkling holy water to visiting Fátima are frowned upon. These gestures are too easy, too external and too worldly to be taken seriously as truly religious practices! For the critics, sacramentals are superstitious at best and idolatrous at worst.

13

It is perhaps true that in earlier days a mistaken worldview led some people to think that a blessed object contained the power of the person who blessed it. Nowadays the same attitude sometimes shows up in the use of medals, rosaries, Lourdes water, and so on. Who could deny that they *might* "represent a superstitious quest of an effectiveness unconnected with faith"?[16] On the other hand, these practices more often reveal a spirit of genuine faith and trust in God's providence. Those who love and use the Church's sacramentals should never forget their real purpose: to lead us to praise and love of God. If we use them only to secure benefits, usually of a temporal kind, then, indubitably, we are abusing the sacramentals.

Guidelines for Using Sacramentals Wisely

The Fathers at Vatican II expressed their hope that the Church would adapt her sacramentals to present-day needs. Accordingly, they recommended that "the sacramentals are to be revised, account being taken of the primary principle of enabling the faithful to participate intelligently, actively and easily."[17]

Sacramentals feed popular piety, those forms of religious expression not part of official Catholic worship. These nonliturgical practices can lead to a distortion of true religion and a sterile piety. A good Lent is not one in which the priest has smeared your forehead with ashes at its outset. The Church must root out what is obviously superstitious or false from her use of sacramentals.

In renewing our use of sacramentals, Catholics would do well to attend to the following five guidelines.[18] By doing so they will avoid either exaggerating or diminishing their significance to Catholic life.

Every form of Christian devotion ought to have a *biblical imprint*. As the Bible becomes increasingly familiar to Catholics, the sacramental blessing prayers should draw their inspiration, even their wording, from the Word of God. That is why in all her blessings the Church encourages reading from the Sacred Scriptures. In addition, the activities or objects "sacramentalized" should be intimately related to the great events of salvation history, and not just our private, temporal needs.

The Second Vatican Council extolled the practices of piety and devotion that have nourished Catholic life for centuries. But it also wisely advised that we use sacramentals *in harmony with the sacred liturgy*. In order to conform to the norms of Vatican II, we should make a special effort so that sacramentals "harmonize with the liturgical seasons, accord with the sacred liturgy, are in some way derived from it, and lead the people to it"[19] Ann Ball's arrangement of some sacramentals and devotional practices into those associated with the Advent-Christmas cycle and others with the Lent-Easter cycle follows this guideline. Furthermore, we ought not treat the principal acts of the liturgy as mere occasions for using sacramentals. Christ's Eucharistic Sacrifice remains the heart of all worship. Would it be true devotion to go to Mass on Palm Sunday just to get blessed palms to braid for the crucifix over the bed?

Not all sacramentals appeal to every person, culture or age. They must be *pertinent to the life-situation* of the believer. Blessing the fields is not likely to appeal to an urban attorney. Except for those sacramentals most intimately tied to liturgical celebrations — holy water, ashes, palms, crucifixes, candles, etc. — the Church does not favor any particular sacramentals.

Certain sacramentals, valid in themselves, may be very suitable for one period of history or culture and less suitable for another. Many of our present sacramentals will undoubtedly remain. Holy water and the rosary are not likely to fall into disuse. Other sacramentals, such as the use of incense, may be more widely revived in the future. Yet others remain to be discovered.

Removal of the scandal of division and the restoration of full communion among Christians is the goal of the ecumenical movement. To achieve this, we should now be more *ecumenically sensitive* than we were before Vatican II. Without in any way minimizing or discouraging use of sacramentals, the Church asks us to avoid any exaggeration in our devotional practices that could mislead other Christians about true Catholic doctrine. How others understand the sacramental blessings and practices that we celebrate must always be taken into account if we are to be responsible evangelizers.

Sacramentals should bespeak a *noble simplicity*. The Council Fathers thought that certain practices had made "the nature and purpose" of the sacramentals "far from clear."[20] If cluttered by repetitious prayers, individualistic piety and lack of participation, they should be eliminated. Sacramentals that demand complicated formulas, odd practices or difficult duties to perform are best abandoned. As signs of the sacred, sacramentals should find a clear echo in believers' hearts and minds. They are not a trickster's guide to heaven.

Following the lead of John Paul II, parents, teachers, and pastors ought to encourage the use of appropriate sacramentals within their families, schools and parishes. Catholic life and devotion, which takes all its energy from God's betrothal of humanity in Christ, rests on the firm foundation of the incarnation and its spillover effects. Ann Ball has unearthed for us a treasure trove of devotional and sacramental riches. From this vast

Catholic storehouse the wise steward can bring out old sacramentals and dream about new possibilities.

ENDNOTES

1. See John Paul II's writings collected by the Daughters of St. Paul in *Original Unity of Man and Woman* (Boston, 1981); *Blessed Are the Pure in Heart* (Boston, 1983); *Reflections on "Humanae Vitae"* (Boston, 1984); *The Theology of Marriage and Celibacy* (Boston, 1986).
2. Thomas Howard, *Evangelical Is Not Enough* (San Francisco, 1984), 29.
3. Laurence F.X. Brett, *Redeemed Creation: Sacramentals Today* (Wilmington, 1984), 12.
4. Peter Kreeft, *Fundamentals of the Faith: Essays in Christian Apologetics* (San Francisco, 1988), 284.
5. *Sacrosanctum Concilium*, 61.
6. *Sacrosanctum Concilium*, 60. See also the 1983 Code of Canon Law's definition: "Somewhat in imitation of the sacraments, sacramentals are sacred signs by which spiritual effects especially are signified and are obtained by the intercession of the Church" (canon 1166).
7. Patrick Bishop, "Sacramentals," *The New Dictionary of Sacramental Worship*, ed. Peter E. Fink (Collegeville, 1991), 1115.
8. *Sacrosanctum Concilium*, 61.
9. Louis Bouyer, *Rite and Man* (Notre Dame, 1963), 67.
10. *A New Catechism* (New York, 1971), 256.
11. Code of Canon Law (1983), canon 1168.
12. *Lumen Gentium*, 10.
13. Code of Canon Law (1983), canon 1167:1.
14. Cyprian Vagaggini, *Theological Dimensions of the Liturgy* (Collegeville, 1976), 88.
15. J.R. Quinn, "Sacramentals," *New Catholic Encyclopedia* (New York, 1967), vol. 12, 791.
16. Jean Evanou, "Blessings and Popular Religion," in *The Church at Prayer*, vol. 3, *The Sacraments*, ed. A.G. Martimort (Collegeville, 1987), 284.
17. *Sacrosanctum Concilium*, 79.
18. Pope Paul VI applied four of these guidelines to renewing devotion to the Blessed Virgin Mary in *Marialis Cultus* (1974) nn. 29-38. They can, however, also serve as an authentic guide for the proper devotional use of sacramentals.
19. *Sacrosanctum Concilium*, 13.
20. *Sacrosanctum Concilium*, 62.

Sacramentals in the Oriental Rites

Rev. Anselm Walker
St. Basil's Byzantine Catholic Center
Houston, Texas

As Pope Pius XI said, "The Church is neither Latin, nor Greek, nor Slav, but Catholic." That this undoubted fact has not penetrated the thought of many Catholic savants, let alone theologians and especially canonists, is so potent that it is useless to comment on its message. It is therefore heartening to see a work such as the present one inviting an exposition of the Oriental perspective on sacramentals alongside of that of the Latin-Western one for the sake of comparison and contrast. By so doing we begin to live up to our name "Catholic," i.e., all-inclusive.

Rites

In the One Holy Catholic and Apostolic Church, in which we profess our faith Sunday after Sunday and feast after feast, there are, besides the predominant Western Latin rite, some nine Eastern or Oriental rites — Oriental here means the Near East, the Balkans, and Eastern Europe. The largest of these rites is the Byzantine, originating in the modern Turkish city of Istanbul, whose ancient name was Byzantion or Byzantium, a Greek fishing village established by Megarans — from Megara on the Gulf of Corinth. In A.D. 320, the Emperor Constantine I moved the capitol of the Roman Empire to Byzantion, christening it "New Rome." It also became known as Constantinople very soon after its foundation. From 320 to 1453 it remained the capital of the Roman Empire, and its liturgical rites became those of the whole Greek-speaking East.

To most of us, "rite" means a ceremony, or a complex of ceremonies, by which a community engages in the concerted action of honoring some person or event. Among Christians, these persons are the Holy Trinity and the mysteries that were wrought through the Incarnation, Life, Death, and Resurrection of Our Lord Jesus Christ. These include the Mass — the Divine Liturgy in the East — the sacraments, and the sacramentals. But "rite" also includes the theology flowing from a given liturgical tradition, its art, architecture, its spirituality and its canon law; i.e., a whole Christian culture. Each rite in the past has produced, when it was allowed to, whole Christian cultures, all of which deserve our respect, our affection, and our study. In Christ, St. Paul says, "are hid all the treasures of wisdom and knowledge" (Col 2:3), and "He is the head of the body, the church" (1:18)

— therefore, in the Church, His body and bride, the same fullness of wisdom and knowledge is found. We must always remember that most Christians who worship according to the Oriental rites are separated juridically from the Catholic Church. Only the Maronites are totally Catholic. The East Syrian Chaldeans may soon become so if they are allowed to continue unhindered. In this treatise we will deal principally with the Byzantine rite, which is followed by some ten million Catholics and some 230 million orthodox.

Sacramentality

Catholic Christianity, both Eastern and Western, is a historical religion; i.e., it takes time seriously but redeems it by celebrating at specific times and dates, thus linking the here and now sacramentally and mystically through celebration with past events in God's economy visibly among His people. At the same time it is linked through eager expectation and divine promises to the consummation of all things — i.e., the life of the world to come. All this is done by, through, and with the Holy Spirit. The key point in this process is the Incarnation of God in Christ. Only historical Christianity takes the Incarnation in all its content, its applications, and its implications seriously. Reformation Christianity, where it has not surreptitiously reclaimed parts of its lost heritage in the name of the "Salvation by Faith Alone" theory, finds in the historic understanding of the Incarnation most of its slanders of "paganism." For example, the term "mother of God," applied to the Holy Virgin to safeguard the divinity of Christ, is reviled as pagan, and so most biblical evangelicals are in effect "Nestorians" because they deny that a woman can give birth in the flesh to God for man's salvation and thus that "God has shed His own blood" to purchase the Church. If Christ is the wisdom and the power of God, in whom dwells the fullness of the Godhead bodily — and in Him we are being filled unto all the fullness of God — and if the Church is the fullness of Christ whom He fills up completely, then Jesus Christ is the first, fundamental, basic, and primordial sacrament and in Him God condescends to us and we ascend to the Father through the Son by the Holy Spirit. In the Church, the body of Christ, we have the sacraments which communicate to us that fullness of Grace that was and is in Christ. So too St. Leo the Great, probably the greatest theologian ever to sit on the throne of St. Peter, tells us, "That which was present in Our Lord has now passed over into the sacraments." Besides the sacraments — the most blessed of which, the Eucharist, signifies and contains and communicates Christ's glorified body and blood substantially, really, and truly along with His soul and divinity — we have a whole complex of sacrament-like

18

entities. These sacrament-like entities are visible things that dispose us through humility, faith, hope, and charity to receive the grace of God and to hear, assimilate, and apply the teaching of Christ to ourselves and to society. As the brilliant Russian philosopher Vladimir Soloviev (1858-1900) said, "the faith of Catholics and Orthodox is the same, for what is holy to one is holy to the other."

The Sign of the Cross

The most obvious and frequently used sacramental is the *Sign of the Cross.* In the Byzantine rite it is made by joining the thumb and the next two fingers to represent the Holy Trinity. The last two fingers are folded down on the palm of the right hand to represent the two natures in Christ. Formerly in Russia, and still among the "Old Believers" (also known as "Raskolniki" or "schismatics" because they split from the state church as a result of the liturgical reforms of the Patriarch Nikon in the mid 1600s), this order is reversed. The thumb and the next finger are joined while the next three fingers are held down over the palm. The symbolism is then reversed. There are over twenty million of these people in Russian today — there are several parishes of them in this country. With the fingers of the right hand so disposed, one touches the forehead, then the upper sternum, then the right shoulder and finally the left. Some believers touch their hearts instead of the left shoulder. While making the Sign of the Cross, the same invocation is made as in the West. At the beginning of the Divine Liturgy it is made while the celebrant intones "Blessed is the Kingdom of the Father and of the Son and of the Holy Spirit." Other offices begin with "Blessed is Our God now and always . . . etc." The sign of the Cross is made continually in the course of Byzantine worship. As often as the Holy Trinity is invoked, which is very often, the Sign of the Cross is made. When the censer is swung in one's direction it is made as well as when one's own devotion prompts it. The East is much more spontaneous in these matters than the West. There are blessings by the celebrant often during the liturgy. In blessing the faithful, he disposes the fingers of his right hand in such way as to form I.C.X.C., Our Lord's initials. He makes the sign of the cross with the Gospel book over the faithful, when he finishes singing the Gospel. He does the same with the chalice and paten at the end of the offertory procession. He makes the same gesture with the chalice over the worshipers twice after Holy Communion. If a Bishop is celebrating, he makes the Sign of the Cross with the *Dikerion*, symbolizing the two natures in Christ, and the *Trikerion*, symbolizing the three persons of the Holy Trinity. This is done at least three times during the course of the liturgy and may be made at least twice more depending on the occasion and the desire of the bishop. These candelabra — the three branches in the right and the two in the left — are then raised over the head of the bishop then brought down paralleling each other then brought up and crossed before his face. Needless to say there are lighted candles in both candelabra while this is being done. Usually this gesture is repeated toward the four points of the compass. While blessing, the bishop chants, "O Lord look down from Heaven and visit this vine which your own right hand has planted." At the end of each of these invocations, the people sing in Greek, "Unto many years, O Master — *Eti polla eti despota.*" These candelabra are borne before the bishop by deacons or lesser clergy who hold them with humeral veils when the bishop is not using them. Otherwise they are placed on the back of the altar alongside the seven-branched candelabra that is always there. One often sees bishops and priests blessing, outside of church, with both hands with their fingers disposed as are the candles on the *dikerion* and *trikerion*, three fingers on the right hand held erect and two on the left. With these they imitate the motions of a bishop when he is blessing liturgically. Needless to say, the Sign of the Cross signifies for them, as for us, the Trinity, the Incarnation, the Redemption, and much else. Among the other Oriental rites, the Sign of the Cross is made as Latin Catholics make it, except that the Syrian Jacobites often make it with the middle finger only to emphasize their monophysitical belief that in Our Lord there is but one person and one nature.

Postures

Historical Christian worship is "Catholic" not only in the sense that it teaches all the truths all the time to all men of sincerity and goodwill, but also in the sense that it engages the whole man in its worship, intellect, will, voice, and body while it emphasizes all man's senses in the adoration process. Where this ancient Christian system and pedagogy have remained in effect, the Church has held her own; where they have disintegrated, her teaching efforts have been fragmented, dispensed, and have become ineffectual. Two modern slogans express this rather pointedly, but accurately: 1) "If it feels good, do it"; and 2) "Do whatever you are comfortable with." This is secularistic humanism at its most blatant. Man worships God for God's glory, not for man's comfort. In Oriental Christian worship, the predominant posture is standing. This is because standing recalls the resurrection of Christ into which the Christian has been initiated by Baptism and continues to participate in by Holy Communion and other liturgical acts. In Byzantine-rite churches, when they are arranged according to tradition, there are no pews. Chairs are available for the elderly and the infirm and one stands every Sunday continuously from Easter to Pentecost to express the resurrection. During Lent, *prostrations* are in order, especially when the beautiful prayer of St. Ephraim for humility is recited. Kneeling is in order at the kneeling prayers for the vespers of Pentecost. The Orthodox now begin to kneel during the Invocation to the Holy Spirit during the Anaphora of the Divine Liturgy to emphasize their rather recently introduced belief that the invocation *Epiklesis* effects the consecration and not the words of consecration as Catholics believe. The layperson in the nave of the church may prostrate or kneel as his or her devotion prompts. Prostration before the holy chalice just before receiving Holy Communion is a common practice. The especially devout may even prostrate every time the Holy Trinity is invoked at the several *ekphoneses* of the Divine Liturgy. A bow from the shoulders and from the waist are also made at such times by all present.

Kissing

Kissing objects of devotion is much more in use in the Byzantine rite than in the West. On entering the church, one kisses the *ikon* and/or ikons on the *Anatogion* to salute the saints in their holy images. One may also touch the ikons with one's forehead as a gesture of reverence and of trying to acquire the mind of Christ from his saints. The Kiss of Peace has long since disappeared for the laity in the Byzantine rite. It is given by the clergy in the *sitar* (sanctuary) at a pontifical liturgy or when two or more priests concelebrate. It is a pious custom for those who communicate to kiss the base of the chalice and the hand of the priest after communicating, they go immediately to kiss the ikon of the Savior to express their Chalcedonian orthodoxy as well as to honor the teaching of the seventh general council on the veneration of the Holy Ikons. At the end of orthos as the great Doxology is being sung, the celebrant brings the book of the Gospels down into the nave of the church, where all present venerate Christ present in his Word by bowing, crossing themselves, and kissing the holy volume. During the entrances of the liturgy with the Gospel book (little) and the chalice and paten (great), the faithful who are within reach often kiss the hem of the priest's *philon* (chasuble) as he passes them in procession. During Lent on weekdays when the liturgy is celebrated, the great entrance is made with the presanctified gifts (body and blood); the devout laity often lay down in the path of the processing clergy, so that these have to step over them. Something of this has been carried over into the regular Sunday and festal liturgies when the faithful kneel down in the entrances, even though at the great entrance the gifts are not yet consecrated. At the end of the liturgy, all come forward to receive the *antidoron* (blessed bread) and to kiss the cross and the hand of the celebrant. It is also a pious custom for those members of the family who have not communicated to kiss the lips of the one who has done so, and thus to participate in Holy Communion. At Byzantine funerals as the beautiful canon of St. John Damascene is being sung all present file by the casket and give a farewell kiss to the departed. Now this is done by placing a small ikon on the chest of the departed, and that is kissed instead of the lips.

Holy Water

Epiphany (Theophany), feast of the Jordan and the feast of Holy Lights, January 6, is devoted to the Baptism of Our Lord. On this day, water is blessed, preferably at streams, lakes, bays and gulfs, to honor this occasion. Thus on this day the Greeks bless the Aegean, the Adriatic, the Mediterranean, the Gulf of Mexico, and holy-water fonts. In Russia, holes in the form of crosses are cut in the frozen rivers, and the blessing is performed over these. The service is rather lengthy and includes the ceremony of tossing the cross into the blessed body of water, to be retrieved by swimmers who receive a prize for their efforts. This ceremony supplies holy water for the coming year. All homes in the parish are blessed after this feast and again after Easter. In Byzantine areas the clergy go in procession to perform these blessings. In some places this blessing in its "lesser" form is repeated on the sixth of every month. The faithful use holy water in much the same way that it is used in the West.

Holy Oil

As in the West, chrisms are of various kinds and grades. The highest is the *Holy Myron*, consisting of almost 100 ingredients, and blessed on various occasions by the various patriarchs of the different Byzantine jurisdictions. Receiving *Myron* from the prelate acknowledges that one recognizes his jurisdiction. Another kind of holy oil is prayer oil, blessed each time the anointing of the sick is celebrated by the chief celebrant. When the liturgical books are followed, it requires seven priests, though one can suffice. At vespers on all great feasts, *Lytia* is celebrated, which includes the blessing of wheat, wine, and oil as food to be consumed at the all night vigil service. The oil is used to anoint all those present either after the *Lytia* or after the Divine Liturgy the next day. On some feasts the faithful may be blessed with oil from the lamp burning before the ikon of the feast. A small mixture of oil and fragrances is poured over the departed just before burial.

22

Holy Foods

At every liturgy the portion of the *Prosphora* (loaf) not placed in the *diskos* (paten) is sliced up and blessed during the Liturgy when the Holy Father and the hierarchs are commemorated. This is the *antidoron* as mentioned above. It is passed out to all comers at the end of the liturgy. On Easter Night a large *prosphora* is blessed and remains on display during Bright Week (Easter Week). On Thomas Sunday (Sunday in White) it is sliced and passed out. On Easter night after the Matins and the Liturgy of the Resurrection a family brings a basket with bread, meat, cheese, and special Easter sweets (*kulich* and *postka*), and these are blessed for the Easter breakfast that follows the liturgical services. On the feast of the Transfiguration *grapes* are blessed and eaten, and on the feast of Our Lady's Falling Asleep (Assumption) *sweet basil* and other herbs are blessed and used in seasoning various dishes.

Other Sacramentals

Every Byzantine-rite Christian should received a blessed *cross* at Baptism which is to be worn for the rest of his life. *Medals* are made of the small copies of ikons and blessed and worn. *Prayer ropes, chatkies,* or *konvoskinous* are made and blessed to be a part of the monastic habit, "swords of the spirit." On those the Jesus prayer is recited. *Flowers* from the *Plachnitza Epitaphios* — Holy Shroud for the lamentations at the tomb of Christ — or from before the ikon of Our Lady for the chanting of the Akathistos Hymn on the last Saturday of Lent are taken by those worshipers, as well as candles from those services and the resurrection procession on Easter morning, and kept as sacramentals in their homes. *Palms* blessed on Palm Sunday are placed over the Holy Ikons. Among the Ukrainians beautiful *towels* of linen are hand-embroidered and draped around the tops of ikons both at home and in the churches. Ikons of Our Lord, Our Lady, and the Holy Mysteries of the Liturgical Year are painted (literally written). The boards and brushes, paints, and painters of these are blessed before the *ikon* is begun. Every Byzantine house should have an ikon corner which holds the family ikons with their towels, a hand censer, holy water, the prayer book, the family Bible, etc., and before it the family conducts its prayers. Ikons are the wedding presents, and on their backs are recorded births, baptisms, and the wedding of the family being founded. Parents bless their children on the first day of school with the family ikon; brides are so blessed, and young men upon entering the armed services and on similar occasions. When entering Byzantine homes, one first salutes the holy ikons and then greets one's hosts. When entering a church, one should venerate the ikons before beginning one's own devotions.

In Byzantine areas, small wayside shrines containing ikons often dot the countryside and one is expected to salute them as one passes. Ikons are literally everywhere to remind the Byzantine faithful that they are always surrounded by a "cloud of witnesses," Our Lord, Our Lady, and the saints.

Among our Byzantine Orthodox Brethren, our seven sacraments are known as the "seven holy mysteries," but many are loath to limit sacramentality to those seven alone. There are those who include the instruction of monastics, the consecrations of churches, funerals, and other ecclesiastical rites that can be occasions of grace for the recipients. In the Oriental understanding, sacramental mysteries are events in which God does something to us and for us while we are passive under His efforts. It is God who works in us both to will and to accomplish — in all church ceremonies, it is Christ the Incarnate Wisdom who gives us the power to become the sons and daughters of God.

Corresponding to the Roman Ritual, Byzantines have the *Euchologion/Trebnik* or "*Book of Needs,*" which contains the prayers and ceremonies ranging from the "Blessing of Expectant Mothers" all the way to the "*Prastos/Panicheda*" service for the faithful departed. Thus the Byzantine Christian is encapsulated by the intercessory power of the Church from conception to corruption, thus making him a participant in the kingdom of God and a partaker in the divine nature.

Blessings

Blessing means placing a thing or person under the care of God. A liturgical blessing is one that uses a prescribed formula or ceremony, and it is given by a priest. (Some blessings are reserved to the Pope or to the bishops.) The simplest blessings are made with the Sign of the Cross, and sometimes are accompanied by the sprinkling of holy water. The official blessings of the Church are contained in the Roman Ritual. By the visible signs and the formula of words of blessings, God's benediction is invoked on persons, places, and things.

In the Old Testament, we read of God's blessing our first parents, of Noah blessing his two sons, of Isaac blessing Jacob, and of Jacob blessing his twelve sons. We read of Moses blessing the tribes of Israel. The Jewish priests blessed the people every day. In the New Testament, Our Lord blessed the loaves and fishes, the young children, and the Apostles before the Ascension (cf. Morrow, p. 383).

In the ordination service, the Church, through the bishop, anoints and blesses the hands of the new priest, saying, "May it please you, O Lord, to consecrate and sanctify these hands . . . that whatever they bless may be blessed, and whatever they consecrate may be consecrated in the name of our Lord Jesus Christ." One of the main tasks of the priest is the duty of dispensing blessings. As mediator between God and men, the priest is the dispenser of God's mysteries. For a priest, all else must be kept subordinate to his sacramental ministry. In the first age of the Church, the Apostles began to ordain deacons and assistants to help with their work, but the priest cannot turn over his sacramental powers, including that of bestowing blessings (cf. Weller, p. 385).

The sacramentals, including the blessings, derive their efficacy chiefly from the intercessory power of the Church. The faithful's cooperation has a very large part to play if blessings are to attain their full promise, raising human thoughts and aspirations out of the realm of the profane and up to the realm of the sacred.

From the Church, the sacramentals widen out to embrace the totality of the Christian life. At one time, there were special blessings for all facets of life. To be certain, abuse and superstition eventually crept in, especially in the later Middle Ages. In order to end the misuse, Pope Paul V finally stepped in and, by a Bull of June 16, 1614, published the official Roman Ritual, to which model all diocesan rituals were thenceforth to conform. Unfortunately, in the seventeenth and eighteenth centuries, the abuse was revived, particularly through the religious orders who printed private collections of blessings and especially exorcisms with prayers and formulas of such a nature as to outdo even the superstitions of the late Middle Ages (ibid., p. 391).

The Roman Ritual contains the approved rites of the Catholic Church. Many beautiful blessings are found in this book which, when used fruitfully, may turn all parts of Christian life toward the Creator. Two examples of the variety and beauty of these blessings follow.

Lilies are blessed on the feast of St. Anthony of Padua. As part of the ritual blessing, the priest prays: "You [God] in your great kindness have given them to man, and endowed them with a sweet fragrance to lighten the burden of the sick. Therefore, let them be filled with such power that, whether they are used by the sick, or kept in homes or other places, or devoutly carried on one's person, they may serve to drive out evil spirits, safeguard holy chastity, and turn away illness — all this through the prayers of St. Anthony — and finally impart to your servants grace and peace; through Christ our Lord."

Many things are blessed and designated for ordinary use — items such as bread, cheese and butter, medicine, fire, automobiles, etc. In the solemn blessing for a fishing boat, the priest asks God to "Send your holy angel from on high to watch over it and all on board, to ward off any threat of disaster, and to guide its course through calm waters to the desired port."

Perhaps it is a conscientious fear of reviving superstition that makes us today so hesitant about restoring the sacramentals to their onetime place of honor. Admittedly some of the olden pious customs seem foolish. Yet many of these sacramentals can and should be used to considerable profit even today.

The Book of Blessings which was confirmed by the Apostolic See in 1989 provides a great variety of blessings for persons, places and things which are sacramentals by definition. According to the Bishops' Committee on the Liturgy of the National Conference of Catholic Bishops, there are over forty new blessings for the United States in addition to the ones in the Roman Ritual. Under blessings of persons, we find blessings for families, married couples, children, engaged couples, elderly people confined to their homes, the sick, missionaries, organizations, and travelers, among others. Under the section for blessings related to buildings and various forms of human activity, we find blessings for new building sites, homes, seminaries and religious houses, schools, libraries, hospitals, shops, offices and factories, athletic fields, various means of transportation, technical equipment, tools and other equipment for work, animals, fields and flocks, prayers of thanksgiving for a good harvest as well as the blessings before and after meals. One section contains blessings of objects that are designed for use in churches, in the liturgy, and in popular devotions. There are special blessings of articles meant to foster the devotion of the people and blessings for various other needs and occasions.

Things Designated
for Sacred Purposes

Numerous sacramentals are commonly used inside churches. Each object used has a history and a specific purpose.

The Altar, Sacred Vessels, Altar Linens

The sacrifice of the Mass is offered on a consecrated *altar*. Placing the gift on the altar signifies its handing over to God. In the Christian religion, the altar symbolizes Christ, for He was the altar as well as the priest and the victim of the sacrifice.

In the early centuries, when the threat of persecution was always present, there were few churches and Christians met to worship in private homes where a table was used for an altar. On just such a table, Christ instituted the Mass for the Church on Holy Thursday.

Beginning about the fourth century, Mass was often celebrated over or under the tombs of the martyrs; from this arose the custom of having a saint's *relics* under or in every altar. By the sixth century, Mass was celebrated in churches, and the Holy Sacrifice was offered on altars of stone. In ancient days, the altar was built so that the priest offering Mass faced the people. Later, altars were built in the apse of the church so that the people were behind the priest. In an instruction prepared by a special liturgical commission established by Pope Paul VI for the implementation of the decrees of the Constitution on the Sacred Liturgy of Vatican Council II, the document declared. "It is proper that the main altar be constructed separately from the wall, so that one may go around it with ease and so that celebration may take place facing the people."

Today's altar is consecrated by a bishop with special ceremonies. For the celebration of Mass, a crucifix is placed near the altar, and candles are lit. The Byzantine altar is square and has a wooden top.

Credence tables are small tables or shelves at the side of the sanctuary where the *chalice, ciborium, cruets, basin*, and *towel*, etc., may be placed.

The *tabernacle* is a kind of safe, usually made of metal with a locking door, in which the Blessed Sacrament is reserved. Some early tabernacles took various forms, such as that of a dove, and were sometimes suspended over the altar. In the Old Testament, the tabernacle was the tent which sheltered the Ark of the Covenant. It was a wooden frame covered with cloth and ram skins, and it was portable. The tabernacle for the Holy Eucharist developed over the centuries, and by the sixteenth century its present form was in common use.

A *sanctuary lamp* is kept burning day and night whenever the Blessed Sacrament is in the tabernacle.

The main sacred vessels used for the altar are the *chalice, paten, ciborium*, and *monstrance (ostensorium)*. These vessels, once consecrated, should be handled with reverence.

The most sacred of all the vessels are the chalice, the cup which holds the wine for consecration, and the paten. After consecration, the chalice contains the precious blood of Christ. It represents the chalice in which Our Lord first offered His blood at the Last Supper. It also symbolizes the cup of the Passion, and lastly, it stands for the Heart of Jesus, from which flowed His blood for our redemption. The paten is the small plate on which the Host is laid. In Holy Communion, our hearts become living chalices, our tongues and our handsother patens on which lies Our Lord.

The ciborium resembles the chalice is used to hold the small Hosts distributed for the communion of the faithful. A *pyx* is a small vessel in which the Blessed Sacrament is kept. It is sometimes watch-shaped and is used to carry the Blessed Sacrament to the sick.

The monstrance or ostensorium is the large metal container used for exposition and benediction of the Blessed Sacrament. Often the monstrance is made of gold and other precious metals, and it is sometimes decorated lavishly with jewels. The sacred Host used for Benediction is reserved in a *luna* or *lunette* which is placed in the glassed portion of the monstrance.

The *Missal* is the book which contains the prayers and ceremonies of the Mass.

Cruets are the vessels from which the acolyte or sacristan pours water and wine into the chalice held by the celebrant.

Incense is a perfume burned on certain occasions such as solemn Mass and Benediction. Incense is symbolic of prayer. The incense is scooped from an *incense boat* and burned in a *censer*.

Other sacramentals commonly used in or near the altar are *reliquaries*, a *holy water font* and *sprinkler*, a *missal stand, candlesticks*, and *bells*. An *antependium* or decorated covering, usually of cloth, covers the front of altars which are not richly ornamented or carved in front. Some of these cloths are made elaborate with embroidery or other decorations, and are usually in the color designated for the liturgy.

A number of linen cloths are used for the Holy Sacrifice of the Mass. The *corporal, purificator*, and *pall* have been called "holy cloths." All are made of white linen. A *finger towel* is used by the priest after washing his fingers before the consecration. This towel has no special significance.

The corporal is a square of fine linen with a small cross worked in the

Miscellaneous second- and third-class relics are tiny specks of fabric, metal, or even dust tipped into holy cards, folders, etc., promoting devotion to saints or those considered for sainthood (see "Relics").

center and sometimes bordered with lace. The priest spreads the corporal on the altar, and on it he places the chalice and the Host after consecration. The purificator is an oblong piece of linen, used to wipe the inside of the chalice before putting in the wine, the rim of the cup after reception by the priest and communicants, and after the Ablution. The priest also wipes his mouth with it after the Ablution.

The pall is a small square of linen used to cover the chalice. Originally the corporal was larger and was folded back to cover the chalice. When its size was reduced in about the year 1000, the pall was introduced (cf. Morrow, pp. 292-294). This is no longer, or rarely, used.

Priestly Vestments

In the Old Testament, God Himself gave directions about the vestments of the priests. The main vestments worn by Catholic priests today have come down to us from the time of the Apostles. There are symbolic significances attached to the various vestments, and the prayers said by the priest as he vests — or puts on each piece of attire — show the meaning attached by the Church.

Putting on the *alb*, a white linen tunic which envelops his whole body, the priest prays, "Purify me, O Lord, from all stain and cleanse my heart, that washed in the Blood of the Lamb, I may enjoy eternal delights." The alb is a survival of the long inner tunic worn in Roman times.

Fastening the alb at the waist with the *cincture* (or girdle), he prays, "Gird me, O Lord, with the cincture of purity, and quench in my heart the fire of concupiscence, that the virtue of continence and chastity may remain in me."

The priest formerly prayed "Let me deserve, O Lord, to bear the *maniple* of tears and sorrow, so that one day I may come with joy into the reward of my labors," as he laid a short narrow strip of cloth, the maniple, to hang from his left arm for the "Tridentine" Mass of Pope St. Pius V. Originally the maniple was a handkerchief carried by a Roman official.

The *stole* is the symbol of ordained priesthood. The origin of the stole is not known with certainty, although it is believed to be descended from the official scarf, or *lorum*, of the Roman magistrate.

The outermost vestment worn by the celebrant at Mass is the *chasuble*. It hangs from the shoulders in front and in back, down almost to the knees. As the priest robes in the chasuble, he prays, "O Lord, Who says 'My yoke is sweet and my burden light,' grant that I may carry it so as to obtain Thy grace." The general shape of the chasuble has been the same as those worn in Rome in the seventeenth century. It was originally the ordinary mantle or *paenula* worn by men in the Roman Empire, becoming proper to the

31

clergy in the sixth century. It was reduced in size gradually between the thirteenth and eighteenth centuries.

The chasuble, stole, formerly the maniple, and the veil for the chalice were made as a set of vestments. They are of the same material, color proper to the day, and design.

Outside of Mass, there are a number of other vestments that the priest uses. The *cassock* or soutane is the main vestment used by ecclesiastics. This is a robe reaching down to the feet and buttoned in front. For priests this is black; bishops wear violet, cardinals red, and the Pope wears white. In some countries ecclesiastics go everywhere in their cassocks, and this is also the custom among some religious orders. In the United States in modern times, however, this is more the exception than the rule. Today's priests and bishops generally wear a conservative black suit with a Roman collar.

When a priest is preaching or joins a procession he wears a *surplice*, a short alb. The *cope* is a mantle which is worn at benediction, at processions and for some other occasions. The origin of the cope is the same as that of the chasuble, except that it was worn outside in wet weather. Its Latin name, pluvial, is the quivalent of the English raincoat.

The *humeral veil* is the long silk cloth used by the priest when carrying the Blessed Sacrament and giving benediction. Some of the vestments, such as the amice, alb, surplice, and benediction veil, are always white. The stole for hearing confessions is always purple.

Various liturgical colors are used at Mass according to the season and the event being commemorated. In the early days of the Church, the vestments were all white, although black was used for mourning. Today the priest's vestments are in the prescribed color.

White, symbolic of purity and joy, is worn during Christmastide and Eastertide, and on the feasts of Our Lord, Our Lady, the angels, confessors, and virgins, as well as for funerals.

Red, the color of fire and blood, is used at Pentecost in commemoration of the descent of the Holy Spirit in the form of tongues of fire. Additionally it is used on the feasts of the Apostles and martyrs, feasts commemorating the Passion of Our Lord, and those commemorating the Sacred Relics, on Palm Sunday, and on Good Friday.

Green, a symbol of hope and growth, is used for the greater part of the year. From January 14 to the beginning of Lent, and from Monday after Trinity Sunday till the eve of the First Sunday of Advent, the priest dresses in green except when Masses are offered in honor of saints, martyrs, or for the dead.

Purple vestments are worn during Advent and Lent. (Formerly they were worn on Rogation Days, on Ember days — except those on Pentecost octave — and on the five vigils of the feasts of the Ascension, Assumption, St. John the Baptist, St. Peter and St. Paul, and St. Lawrence.) This color is a penitential color.

Black vestments are rarely used in today's liturgy.

The Pallium

The pallium is a white woolen circular band two inches wide which is ornamented with six small crosses and which has a weighted pendant in the front and in the back. It slips over the head and hangs down in front and back in the shape of a "Y." It is worn during ceremonies by the Pope, metropolitan archbishops, and patriarchs. The pallium is a symbol of the fullness of the episcopal power enjoyed by the Pope and shared in by the archbishops, and of union with the Holy See. Until an archbishop receives a pallium, he may not exercise metropolitan jurisdiction, and if he should be transferred to a new archdiocese, he must ask for a new pallium. The archbishops are buried with their pallia. The investiture of the Pope with the pallium at his coronation is the most solemn part of the ceremony, and it is a symbol older than the wearing of the papal tiara.

The pallia are made by the Oblates of St. Frances of Rome, from the wool of two lambs blessed in the church of St. Agnes on her feast, January 21. Since the fourth century, the lambs have been presented at solemn Mass in the basilica, and they are carefully cared for until the time of shearing. When completed, the pallia are blessed by the Pope on the feast of Sts. Peter and Paul, and they are stored in a casket in the crypt of St. Peter.

Vessels, Vestments, and Other Liturgical Appurtenances of the Byzantine Rite

Just as a pleasant garden has varied and beautiful flowers combining their fragrances for our delight, so too Mother Church blossoms with different rites exhaling the fragrance of their prayers and hymns, virtues and sacrifices, as an incense of perpetual adoration to the Creator.

In many large cities in the United States today there are churches of the Eastern Catholic rites. Members of the Western rite may visit these churches and receive Holy Communion. There the priest with a golden spoon will drop upon their tongue a small piece of bread which has been dipped into the Precious Blood in the chalice. Such a visit will help us to realize in full the meaning of the word "catholic," and help us to realize that the Church is not tied to a single language or a single set of ceremonies and customs.

A number of the sacramentals used in the Mass of the Byzantine rite are described below.

The *antimension* takes the place of the altar stone used in the Western rite. This is a silk or linen cloth laid upon the altar at Mass. The antimension bears the picture of the burial of Christ and the instruments of His Passion. Relics of martyrs are sewn into the center of the front border. Latin-rite military chaplains have used this in time of war.

The *elleton* corresponds to the corporal used in the Western rite. The *poterion* (chalice) is the cup used to hold the Precious Blood. The *diskos*, a shallow plate which is sometimes elevated on a low stand, corresponds to the paten.

The *asteriskos* is placed over the diskos and covered with a veil. This is made of two curved bands of gold or silver which cross each other to form a double arch; a star depends from the junction, which forms a cross. Three veils are used. The smallest of these covers the poterion, the next covers the diskos, and the largest covers both. The *spoon* which is peculiar to the Byzantine rite is used in giving Holy Communion to the faithful. A *lance* is a metal knife used in cutting up the bread which is to be consecrated.

The *sticharion* is a long white garment made of linen with wide sleeves and decorated with embroidery. This was originally used as the vestment for the clerics of minor orders. It signifies the purity of the priest.

The *epitrachelion* is a stole with ends sewn together which has a loop through which the head is passed. The priestly duties are signified by several crosses.

A narrow clasped belt of the same material as the epitrachelion is called a *zone*. This signifies the wisdom of the priest, his strength against the enemies of the Church, and his willingness to fulfill his holy duties.

Ornamental cuffs called *epimanikia* symbolize (right) strength and (left) patience and good will.

The *phelonion* is an ample cape-like vestment which is long at the back and sides and cut away in front. It signifies the higher gifts of the Holy Spirit.

The Holy Bible

The Bible, together with Tradition, constitutes revelation, the supreme rule of faith. Inspired by God and committed once and for all to writing, they impart the word of God himself without change, and make the voice of the Holy Spirit resound in the words of the prophets and Apostles.

The Bible is the guide for all preaching in the Church, and its constant source of nourishment. The first part of the Mass is called the liturgy of the word because here the priest reads, with the people, the word of God, explaining that word to them.

The Bible is the basis for theology in the Church. The sacred Scriptures contain the word of God, and since they are inspired, really are the word of God.

The Bible was written originally in three main languages: Hebrew, Aramaic, and Greek. The earliest Church used the Bible in the Greek translation. When Latin became the common spoken language it was translated into Latin. St. Jerome made one of the better Latin translations, called the Vulgate. Throughout the centuries as Christianity spread, the Church provided translations of the Latin Vulgate into many of the languages of the people. Today, scholars have better facilities to study the ancient languages, and new translations are being made from the original languages. Thus, the translations are closer to what was really written by the inspired authors. Today's Bible scholars use all the scientific means possible to interpret the meaning of the Scriptures. The Church encourages all the people of God to read the Scriptures diligently and to study them carefully.

Since the Council of Ephesus (431) the Gospels have been enthroned at the ecumenical councils. An elaborate stand was put in a prominent place, usually near the altar where Mass was celebrated for the Council Fathers. Enthroned in this manner, the Gospels were to symbolize the presence of Christ Himself at the council.

The Bible is the story of God's revelation in history, written by men under the inspiration of the Holy Spirit and contained in the Old and New Testaments. Depending on the manner in which the sacred books are divided, their number will differ. Catholics have generally divided the Bible into seventy-two books. The books of the Bible were composed by many different writers and were written over a period of approximately thirteen hundred years, from Moses to St. John the Evangelist. The authors of the Bible were free instruments of God and brought their own personalities with them in what they wrote. Therefore, we find various kinds of literary forms, styles of writing, and degrees of grammatical accuracy in their writing.

The Bible is divided into two parts, the Old and the New Testaments. The Old Testament is generally divided by Catholic scholars into 45 books. It contains the story of why man needs salvation and the story of what God did to prepare for the final act of salvation. The New Testament are those books which were written about Jesus Christ and the fullness of revelation brought by Him. The four Gospels (Matthew, Mark, Luke, and John) are the apostolic witness to and interpretation of the words and deeds of Jesus Christ. They were written in the latter part of the first century in order to teach the Christian community what it should know about the Savior. The Acts of the Apostles was written by St. Luke and contains an account of the missionary activity and growth of the early Church. It also contains an account of the missionary journeys of St. Paul. The epistles or letters of St. Paul and others were written to some of the early Christian churches or individuals in response to some particular problem or situation. They give us a good insight into the gradual development of much of the theology of the New Testament. The catholic epistles are called by this name because of their more universal destination, since they were not sent, for the most part, to any particular community or church. The Book of Revelation or Apocalypse of St. John was written to console the early Christians at a time of persecution. It is filled with much symbolism that would have been understood by them. Revelation records the ultimate victory of the kingdom of God.

Relics

Relics, honored in the Catholic Church, are the bodies of the saints, or objects connected with them or with Our Lord. God has often shown His approval of the use of relics as sacramentals by working miracles through them. Relics deserve to be venerated. The bodies of the saints were temples of the Holy Spirit and instruments through which God worked. However, no Catholic is required to believe in miracles (such as that of the *blood of St. Januarius*, which is kept in a vial at Naples and liquefies several times a year for certain periods), any more than one is obliged to believe in private revelations such as those of Lourdes and Fátima. We honor relics by preserving them with reverence, visiting the places were they are enshrined, and praying before them.

The word relic comes from the Latin *reliquiae*, meaning remains. They are classified in three categories. First-class relics are parts of the bodies of saints or instruments of the Passion (like fragments of the true cross). Second-class relics are objects which have been in close contact with the saints, such as articles of clothing or personal items. In the case of a martyr, the instruments of martyrdom are also considered in this category. Third-class relics are objects such as rosaries or cloths which have been touched to the body of the saint or to either first or second class relics.

Veneration of relics is not limited to Catholics, and it has origins that predate Christianity. Relics of Buddha, who died nearly half a century before Christ, are still venerated today throughout the Buddhist world. Those of Confucius have been venerated by the Chinese since 195 B.C. Those of Mohammed (d. A.D. 632) are kept with reverence in Jerusalem in a building called the Dome of the Rock. Other famous leaders whose relics were venerated in early ages were the Persian Zoroaster (Zarathushtra) and the Greek Oedipus. According to Shakespeare, the Romans dipped cloths in the spilled blood of Julius Caesar.

In Victorian times, locks of hair were given to lovers, and family members often treasured the tresses of their departed loved ones. In the United States, hair from family members was made into elaborate floral pictures. The piano virtuoso Pachmann used to hold aloft a couple of pieces of unlaundered clothing just before he began to play. Emotionally, he would sniffle and announce, *"Les chaussettes de Chopin!* [Chopin's socks!]" He would then proceed to reduce the audience to tears with his rendition of the master's works.

In the Old Testament, the miraculous relics of the prophet Elisha are mentioned in 2 Kings 13:20-21. In the New Testament, Acts 19:11-12,

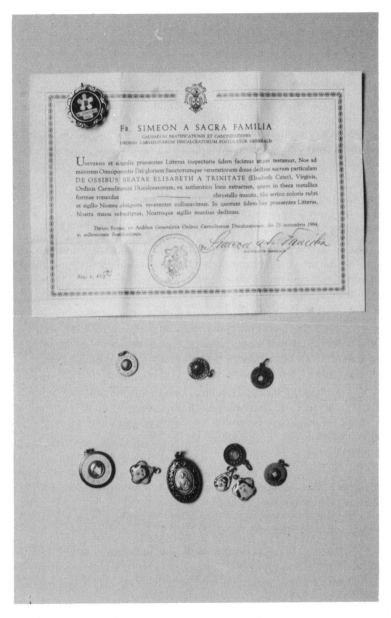

From top: first-class relics, actual fragments from flesh or bone of the saints, are documented; second-class relics were used by saints during life; and third class relics were touched to first-class (see "Relics").

mention is made of second-class relics, cloths being touched to the hands of the Apostle Paul. One of the earliest mentions of honor paid to relics was written by the inhabitants of Smyrna about A.D. 156. These described the death of St. Polycarp, who was burned at the stake. His faithful disciples gathered his ashes and bones and enshrined them. When St. Ignatius, Bishop of Antioch, was thrown to the lions (c. 107), two of his companions came and gathered up his bones for veneration. St. Cyril of Jerusalem (d. 386) wrote that relics of the cross were already distributed throughout the world.

Most prized of all relics are the relics of Christ's passion, particularly of the cross on which He died. Some scoff at the relics of the cross and say that there are too many to be genuine. However, if all known pieces were put together they would make a block smaller than half of a cubic foot. Today the twelve most famous portions of the true Cross range from 6.33 cubic inches to 33 cubic inches. The largest of these are found in Jerusalem, Brussels, Ghent, and Rome. The particles venerated are very small.

The *true cross* was found by St. Helena, mother of the emperor Constantine the Great in the year 326. Her workmen, digging on Mount Calvary in search of the true cross of Christ, found three crosses. Two of the crosses were applied without result to a very sick woman. As soon as the third cross touched her, she was instantly cured. The adoration of the Cross on Good Friday is part of the Holy Week devotions. The Feast of the Exaltation of the Cross is kept on September 14.

The emperor Charlemagne (d.814) instigated a search for relics at Rome, Constantinople, and Jerusalem, and when found shared them with his friends. He hoped to find relics of Our Lord's Passion that had gone undiscovered by St. Helena when she searched for the cross.

After the death of Christ, the persecutions of the Christians resulted in the death of countless martyrs. They were buried in the secrecy of the catacombs, which later became a veritable treasury of relics. The possession of these relics soon began to result in a rivalry, and the remains were divided. Although some shrank from the thought of disturbing the dead, the relics were divided because of acts of veneration, not desecration. As the Christians increased and spread forth throughout the world, they took with them the honored relics.

When the persecutions finally ended in 313 during the reign of Constantine, the graves of the martyrs were turned into magnificent sanctuaries and basilicas. When churches were built apart from the tombs, relics were transferred and enshrined, often within the altars. Even today, relics of saints are enclosed in the altars of modern churches.

No one knows when the practice of venerating minute fragments of the bodies of saints first became popular, but by the fourth century the practice was widespread. The relics were so greatly esteemed by their owners that the cases in which they were preserved were often decorated with priceless jewels and fine work in metal. Pilgrims often traveled great distances to pray and make vows at the shrines of these relics. During the Middle Ages, when the cult of relics was at its pinnacle, many great churches owed their renown simply to the presence of important relics.

It was during the Middle Ages that the possession of relics became so popular that abuses began to creep in. Relics were so eagerly sought that outright theft was often resorted to in order to secure an important relic. Additionally, fraudulent relics began to be distributed. The greatest festivals were the "translations" of the relics of a saint from the tomb to a newly built church or shrine in his or her honor. These were celebrated with great pomp, commemorated annually, and in the earlier centuries amounted to canonization. So great was the popularity of such occasions that often when a body was discovered buried in an ancient church it would be readily assumed to be that of a holy person, and a new shrine would be built for the glory of the saint and the renown of the hometown as a place of pilgrimage. A town without a saint and its own relics was considered a poor town. Rivalries grew up between the larger towns, and this led to the veneration of such historically questionable objects as the crib of Bethlehem and the pillar of Our Lord's scourging. When there was no scandalous money-making at such shrines, the Church seldom questioned the authenticity of relics which had been venerated for centuries so as not to upset genuinely pious people. One problem with many of the oldest relics is that it is nearly impossible to prove their authenticity scientifically. In earlier days, it was as difficult to disprove the authenticity of a relic as it was to substantiate it. Thus the faking of relics, the sale of relics, and other scandalous abuses of the Church doctrine on relics became widespread.

It is reasonable to assume that some of the famous relics such as the nails of the crucifixion are false, but not necessarily deliberate fraud. In the case of the nails, copies which had touched the authentic ones were first venerated as second-class relics from having touched the originals. As time passed and written records were misplaced, eventually many of the copies were regarded as the originals. Even a false relic, however, which has been honored through the centuries does not dishonor God or the saint in question; we venerate the person from whom the relic came, not the piece of bone or cloth called the relic.

St. Augustine, in the fourth century, denounced imposters who wandered about clothed as monks and profited by selling fake relics. St.

Gregory of Tours (d. 593) and St. Gregory the Great (d. 604) mention the trade in fraudulent relics by unscrupulous persons. Church authority did what it could, but the number of relics made the task difficult. The Councils of Lyons in 1245 and 1275 prohibited the veneration of recently found relics unless they were first approved by the Roman Pontiff. The Council of Trent (1545-1563) ordered bishops to take special pains with regard to the distribution of relics, establishing the norm that all relics be subject to the control of the Vatican. It is not known when it became customary for a relic to be accompanied by a document of authentication. Both the Council of Trent and the Code of Canon Law, promulgated in 1918 set penalties for the abuses connected with relics.

There is currently a Relic Office in the Vatican which receives, keeps, and distributes relics of saints and blesseds. Current instructions from the vicar general of the Diocese of Rome read, "Relics should be handled intelligently, without abuses. They are signs which can be useful to spread devotion to holy men and women all over the world. When major relics are requested for private and public veneration they must be accompanied by official papers warranting their validity and authenticity. In no way may they be sold. A contribution may be requested merely to cover expenses such as for the relic case and mailing charges."

The subject of relics is a fascinating one, and Joan Carroll Cruz has written one of the most complete books about relics in print today (*Relics*, Our Sunday Visitor, 1984). The reader who wishes more information than the scope of this text allows is referred to Mrs. Cruz's book for a complete discussion of all the major relics venerated in the Church today.

Because of their very nature, major relics are scarce and difficult to obtain. It is a common custom, however, for the postulators of causes for beatification and for religious orders to distribute second and third class relics, often on cards with prayers for the cause.

Although the Church today neither encourages nor discourages the cult of relics, their use as sacramentals is still popular. While the honor and veneration of relics is commendable, provided superstitious practices do not accompany it, Our Lord himself, in an apparition to St. Gertrude the Great, mentioned a non-materialistic relic that all Christians would do well do consider. The saint had desired to have some relics of the wood of the cross. Our Lord said to her, "If you desire to have some relics which will draw My Heart into yours, read My Passion, and meditate attentively on every word contained therein and it will be to you a true relic which will merit more graces for you than any other . . . thence you may know and be assured that the words which I uttered when on earth are the most precious relics which you can possess."

Crucifixes and Crosses

The *cross* is the most widespread and venerated sacramental of the church. This symbol of mankind's redemption has been used since the early days of the Church, and today it is present in all Catholic and most Christian churches.

During the earliest days of the Church, in the time of the persecutions of the Christians, the cross was often disguised as a part of other symbols. It was often disguised as an anchor or hidden in a monogram. Crosses of various types were found carved on the stone slabs in the oldest sections of the Roman catacombs.

In 326, St. Helena searched for and found the *true cross*. Later it fell into the hands of the Persians, but it was recovered by King Heraclius of Judea in 629. Relics of the cross made their way to many parts of the world, and many of them still exist. A relic of the true cross is the only relic that can be carried under a canopy in procession, and it is the only relic that receives a genuflection when exposed.

Helena's son, Constantine the Great, made a remarkable impact on the history of the world by ending the persecutions of the Christians. During a battle at the Milvian Bridge, an apparition of the cross appeared in the heavens with the words "In this sign, conquer." Constantine had the sign placed on his banner and did, indeed, defeat the enemy.

Until the end of the sixth century, the crosses were shown without the figure of the Redeemer. The usual crucifix today represents Our Lord suffering. This began about the thirteenth century and became most popular during the Counter-Reformation. Traditional crucifixes, particularly those of Spanish influence, depicted Christ as crowned, robed, and reigning from the cross. The crucifix is placed on or above all altars where Mass is offered except in the Nestorian and Coptic churches. In the Eastern Churches, because of the prohibition against rounded representations, the crucifix is usually painted, or a cross with a painted figure is used.

Crosses have been made worldwide and celebrated with artworks in many distinct forms. Crucifixes and crosses adorn vestments and religious habits, other sacramental items, altars, tombs, and buildings. Some sacramental uses of the cross are found below.

Crosses on vestments are a comparatively modern development. The cross on most modern chasubles does not seem to have been originally adopted with any symbolic purpose and was probably used to conceal the seams.

The *papal cross*, which is carried before a pope, is a cross with three transverse bars of varying length, the smallest at the top. The *patriarchal cross*, or *archiepiscopal cross*, is a cross with two crossbars, of which the upper is shorter than the lower. This is usually carried before an archbishop in processions in his own province. A *pectoral cross* is a cross worn on the breast by a bishop. It is suspended from a cord or chain and worn outside the clothing. Usually, this is of gold, ornamented with precious stones, and contains relics. The pectoral cross can be worn by others who are not bishops, such as a prefect apostolic, when they have the privilege of pontificating.

Processional crosses are crucifixes mounted on long shafts of metal or wood and carried aloft at the head of processions. The figure is turned forward, and the processional cross is accompanied on either side by an acolyte with candle.

The *Russian cross* is a three-barred cross used by the Russian Church. The upper bar represents the title of the cross, the second the arms, and the lowest, which is always inclined at an angle, the foot rest. This last is angled because Christ is said to have pushed it down in a moment of extreme pain.

St. Andrew's cross (cross saltire) is a cross shaped like the Greek letter chi (X). This is also known as *crux decussata*, so called from its resemblance to the Greek symbol for the numeral ten. St. Andrew is said to have suffered martyrdom on such a cross, his hands and feet bound to its four arms.

The *altar cross* is the crucifix placed behind or above the tabernacle on the old baroque altars, usually visible to all in the body of the church and with the tabernacle the center of the altar.

It is usually suspended above or behind the table altars recommended by Vatican Council II.

A small cross held in the hand is a sacramental used in giving blessings, both liturgical and nonliturgical. This *hand cross* is commonly employed by priests of the Armenian, Maronite and Syrian rites and by bishops of all Eastern rites.

The crucifix has been the inspiration and comfort of millions. A number of saints have received mystical graces, visions, and communications through the cross of Our Lord. The cross figures prominently in art and literature worldwide.

The making of the *sign of the cross*, professing faith both in the redemption of Christ and in the Trinity, was practiced from the earliest centuries. St. Augustine (d. 430) mentioned and described it many times in his sermons and letters. In those days, Christians made the sign of the cross

(Redemption) with three fingers (Trinity) on their foreheads. The words "In the name of the Father and the Son and the Holy Ghost" were added later. In the third century, Tertullian had already reported this touching and beautiful early Christian practice:

"In all our undertakings — when we enter a place or leave it; before we dress; before we bathe; when we take our meals; when we light the lamps in the evening; before we retire at night; when we sit down to read; before each new task — we trace the sign of the cross on our foreheads" (Weiser, p. 256).

The Stations of the Cross

The stations of the cross are fourteen tableaux which depict fourteen important events in the Passion and death of Our Lord. The stations are the prevailing popular devotion in Lent. Both the Eastern and Western Church practice this touching devotion, which originated in the time of the Crusades when the knights and pilgrims began to follow the route of Christ's way to Calvary in prayerful meditation, according to the ancient practice of pilgrims. The devotion spread throughout Europe and developed into its present form through the zealous efforts of the Franciscan friars in the fourteenth and fifteenth centuries.

Devotion to the Passion actually began with the Crucifixion. It is a constant tradition that the Blessed Mother walked over and over the narrow streets which led from the Praetorium of Pilate to the gate of the Holy City. From time to time along the road sanctified by His suffering and consecrated by His Blood, the Sorrowful Mother knelt and prayed. The Blessed Virgin herself revealed to the mystic St. Bridget of Sweden that she had daily walked the way of Christ's sorrows, and visited the stations of His bitter Passion and death.

Likewise, the Apostles, disciples and friends of Jesus who lived in Jerusalem and the surrounding areas walked this hallowed way of memories, meditating anew on the sufferings of their Master and Redeemer. From as far back as the fifth century, we know by the writings of St. Jerome that pilgrims who came to visit the Holy City always made their pilgrimage along the Way of the Cross.

Therefore, the devotion was in existence from apostolic times, although it did not attain a high form of development until the sixteenth or seventeenth century. Up to that time, the devotion remained a private exercise of piety which sprang spontaneously from faith and love. Only a limited number of faithful were actually able to make the trip to Jerusalem and walk in the footsteps of Christ on the Way of Sorrows from the ruined court of Pilate to the basilica on the hill of Calvary. From the fifth century,

Stations of the Cross were erected in a few places in Europe, but the devotion was not a general practice. These European stations were probably replicas of those along the true Way of the Cross, and their number varied.

The first stations of which there are authentic and documented records were erected in the Church of San Stefano in Bologna in the fifth century and were called "Hierosolyma" (Jerusalem). The Franciscans erected a set of stations in their cemetery in Antwerp sometime during the early years of the fifteenth century.

In the early thirteenth century, St. Francis of Assisi traveled to the Holy Land in an attempt to convert the Saracens and infidels who dwelt there. As he conceived it, his effort was in vain. However, the Franciscans did become the custodians of many of the sacred places in the Holy Land. The friars determined to bring the sacred places of Palestine to the world. In the year 1686, the Franciscans applied to Pope Innocent XI, who granted the same indulgences that pilgrims to the Holy Land obtained to all who made the stations of the cross in any Franciscan church. Then the Franciscans began promoting the devotion worldwide. Franciscan preachers, writers, and workers publicized the spiritual richness of the devotion. In particular, St. Leonard of Port Maurice became the great preacher of this devotion. Soon the Stations of the Cross were erected in every city, town, and hamlet of Europe.

The devotion has been called by various names: Way of the Cross, Via Dolorosa, Stations of the Cross, and Way of Christ's Sorrows. An Englishman named Wey was the first to use the word "stations" to describe the fourteen halts in the procession following along the Way of the Cross. These halts were made for meditation and prayer, and each commemorated some specific incident on the road to Christ's sacrifice. The number of incidents commemorated varied; Bologna had five stations, Antwerp had seven. Andrichomius, in the sixteenth century, enumerated twelve stations in the Way of the Cross in Jerusalem. At Vienne at the beginning of the nineteenth century there were eleven stations, with the first being the agony in the garden.

The stations were originally made in inverse order, beginning at the garden of the tomb and finishing in the judgment hall of the Praetorium. St. Leonard systematized and arranged the stations according to the actual sequence of the occurrence. From this time forward we find there were fourteen stations commemorated.

The Stations of the Cross, when erected in churches, may begin at either side of the church. During Lent or other times when the devotion is public, the priest moves from station to station; when the devotion is being

Above: Pardon Crucifix, from France, is sculpted on both sides (see "Crucifixes, etc."). Below: The Red Cross of St. Camillus de Lellis beat the secular Red Cross by nearly 300 years (see "Scapulars, etc.").

made privately, the person making the devotion goes from one to another while meditating on the Passion of Christ.

Many beautiful meditations have been written for this devotion. There are meditations written using scriptures, those written especially for children, those which reflect modern problems in conjunction with the traditional commemorations. Short meditations have been written for use in the missions and for daily use. Many of today's meditations add a fifteenth station in honor of the Resurrection.

Christ said, "If any man would come after me, let him deny himself and take up his cross daily and follow me" (Lk 9:23). The Franciscan Apostolate of the Way of the Cross promotes worldwide daily devotion to the Way of the Cross. They consider the devotion consoling and comforting to the elderly, the sick, or shut-ins, and helpful for all in search of a practical way of bringing God into their personal lives. This apostolate distributes information on the Way of the Cross and includes a blessed cross as a reminder of the Cross of Our Lord as well as a brief and simple meditation for making the Way of the Cross at home (see appendix).

Your Cross

"The everlasting God has in His wisdom foreseen from eternity the cross that He now presents to you as a gift from His inmost Heart. This cross He now sends you He has considered with His all-knowing eyes, understood with His divine mind, tested with His wise justice, warmed with loving arms, and weighed with His own hands to see that it be not one inch too large and not one ounce too heavy for you. He has blessed it with His holy Name, anointed it with His grace, perfumed it with His consolation, taken one last glance at you and your courage, and then sent it to you from heaven, a special greeting from God to you, an aims of the all-merciful love of God" (St. Francis de Sales).

The Pardon Crucifix

In the early days of this century, there came into being in France a Pious Union of the Pardon Crucifix. The aim of this union was to obtain pardon of God and to inculcate in the wearer of the crucifix the desire to pardon his neighbor. The headquarters for this pious union was in Lyons, France.

The faithful were recommended to carry or wear the crucifix on their person, and to devoutly kiss it with the following intentions: To testify love for Our Lord and the Blessed Virgin; gratitude toward the Holy Father, the Pope; to beg for the remission of our sins; the deliverance of souls in purgatory; the return of the nations to the Faith; forgiveness among Christians; reconciliation among the members of the Catholic Church.

Two invocations which were to be said before the crucifix are: "Our Father who art in heaven, forgive us our trespasses as we forgive those who trespass against us," and "I beg the Blessed Virgin Mary to pray to the Lord our God for me."

The front of the crucifix is ornately chased metal. The obverse is plain and is centered with a design of the Sacred Heart. Along the length are found the words, "Behold this heart which has so loved men." On the crossbar are found the words, "Father, forgive them."

The Crucifix That Spoke to St. Francis

Francis Bernardone, the son of a wealthy cloth merchant, had been sent to Foligno to sell a bolt of velvet. On the way, he passed the little half-ruined church of San Damiano. Something made Francis stop his horse and enter. Inside, among the ruins, it was dark and quiet. Only a single light shone before a Byzantine cross with a painted image of the crucifix. The eyes of the painting seemed to look lovingly at him.

For some time, Francis had been disturbed about his carefree way of life. He had determined to follow God's will for him, but was uncertain how to proceed. In front of this beautiful crucifix, in the little deserted church, Francis prayed, "Great God, and You, my Savior Jesus Christ, dispel the darkness of my soul, give me pure faith, lasting hope, and perfect charity. Let Thy will, O God, be my will; make me and keep me Thine, now and forever."

Suddenly, the lips of the crucifix appeared to move. A silverly voice that Francis seemed to have been hearing in his heart in the past few weeks said, "Francis, my son. Do you not see that my church is failing into ruins? Go quickly and build up its walls." Three times the injunction was repeated.

Francis joyfully raced to the market, sold the cloth, and returned to the church. He attempted to give the money to the resident priest to rebuild the church.

Francis' father, learning of his son's actions, became furious. He appealed to the bishop of Assisi to return the funds. Through the intercession of the bishop, Francis returned his father's money. Peter Bernardone disinherited his son. Francis then embraced "Lady Poverty" and begged for the funds to restore the church.

Thus, Francis of Assisi went out into the world to preach. He had built up the walls of the little chapel of San Damiano; now he started forth to repair his Father's Church — men's faith in God.

Francis banded together with some companions, and they became mendicant friars and the seed of the Franciscan Order. Copies of the crucifix which spoke to St. Francis, like the brothers and sisters of the Franciscan family, have spread throughout the world. The crucifix, an Umbrian twelfth-century egg tempera, is preserved in the Church of St. Clare in Assisi.

The Crucifix of Christ of the Agony of Limpias

In Limpias, a town on the northern coast of Spain, the parish church contains a life-size wooden crucifix known as the "Christ of the Agony." The crucifix is the work of a seventeenth century artist, Pedro de Mena. It was brought from southern Spain and donated to the church by a parishioner about the year 1776.

In the first part of the twentieth century, many of the inhabitants of the small town had moved, and the Limpias church was being visited by only a handful of the faithful, even on Sundays. The parish priest asked two Capuchins, Fathers Jalon and Agatangelo, to conduct a parochial mission, which they did from March 22 to 30, 1919.

On the final Sunday of the mission, while Father Agatangelo was preaching and Father Jalon was hearing confessions, a young girl came up to Father Jalon and excitedly said, "Father Jalon, come and see! Christ has closed his eyes!" The priest, thinking the child was playing a joke, sent her back to her seat, but soon other girls came to him ready to swear that they, too, had witnessed the phenomenon. After the sermon, the two priests went up to the altar, but could see nothing unusual.

Soon, however, the strange phenomenon was seen again by a number of adults. Father Jalon, at the request of the faithful, had a ladder brought. He climbed up and touched the corpus, then noticed that his fingers were covered with what seemed to be perspiration that was running down from the neck and chest of the figure. Not all of the people in the church saw the phenomenon, but all were moved by the faith of the witnesses. The news spread rapidly, and the manifestations continued.

In April of 1919, the eyes of the figure were seen to move, and on Easter Sunday the lips were also seen to move. The manifestations continued for over a year, and some fifteen thousand persons declared to have benefited from these supernatural manifestations. Fifteen hundred persons gave sworn testimonies in the years 1919 and 1920. Different witnesses testified to seeing different things; for some, the eyes appeared to move, for others the expression on the face of the Christ changed. For some, the crucifix appeared to be alive, and suffering in agony.

One doctor who came to ridicule the believers became terrified and ran out of the church after witnessing a metamorphosis of the corpus. First he saw the body turn into a skeleton, then into a mummy, and then it appeared to grow back the flesh. After his experience, his disbelief changed to belief, and he gave a sworn testimony of what he had seen.

The testimony of a Dr. Penamaría was published in a Fonsagrada newspaper in May 1920. He stated that he had not expected nor desired to see a miracle, but that a sense of curiosity rather than piety led him to go to the church and look attentively at the "*Santo Cristo de la Agonía*." Surprisingly, he was an immediate witness of the miracle. First the eyes of the crucifix appeared to open and close. Thinking that it could be due to an optical illusion, the doctor moved to various spots in the sanctuary. The eyes of the Christ, however, followed him and appeared to be looking at him in a way that moved the doctor to state, "The Cristo then looked at me in a way that was so deep, so expressive that it felt as if He wanted to heal me of my disbelief."

Dr. Penamaría, fearing that he was hallucinating, attempted to pray for more proof, upon which he seemed to see the complete agony of the crucifixion. The statue moved and went through the motions of the suffocation and death that, as a medical doctor, Dr. Penamaría was familiar with. For over two hours, Dr. Penamaría witnessed the agony of the miraculous crucifix of Limpias. He concluded his testimony thus: "While the death of a beloved one leaves in one's heart a deep bleeding, incurable wound, the sight of Christ's death leaves way down in one's soul a feeling of bliss, inner peace, deep calm, a feeling of happy release, similar to what one feels when awakening from a nightmare."

The crucifix of Limpias is only one of many representations of Christ which have, throughout the years, been surrounded by supernatural phenomena. In January and February of 1986, a copy of the head of the Limpias crucifix belonging to Mrs. M. Linden of Maasmechelen, Belgium, was seen to shed tears of blood.

The Crucifix of El Cristo Negro de Esquipulas

From the late sixteenth century a beautiful crucifix has been venerated by the faithful in Guatemala under the title "The Black Christ of Esquipulas."

In 1525, the Chorti Indians of the Mayan group were conquered by the Spanish and branded as slaves. Thus began a long period of suffering for the Indians. In 1595, one of the Indians experienced a vision of a giant host with the image of Christ crucified on it. The Indian community then banded together and embraced Christianity. The provisor of the bishop of Guatemala, Fray Cristobal Morales, ordered an image made for the faithful of the town of Esquipulas.

The sculptor, Quirio Catano, was a mystic as well as an artist. Originally from Portugal, he was living in Antigua, Guatemala. Through his art, he was able to project the pain and the compassion of Our Lord dying on the cross.

The expression on the face of the corpus, along with the dark color of the skin, appealed greatly to the Indians. The Chortis were dark and had also suffered. The image seemed to reflect their own race and feelings.

Devotion to the image began from the day of its delivery, March 9, 1595. Bishop Gómez Fernéndez de Córdova led the image in procession from Antigua to Esquipulas. Throughout the journey, people went to meet the procession, and a number of cures of illnesses were reported. The fame of the image began to spread because of the miracles, and soon pilgrimages to Esquipulas began. These pilgrimages still occur today.

The crucifix, carved of orange wood, was first displayed in the parish church, Santiago de Esquipulas. Because of the ever increasing number of pilgrims, a larger church was needed. In 1737, Archbishop Pedro Pardo de Figueroa, miraculously cured through prayers before the crucifix, ordered the building of a new shrine in gratitude.

By 1953, devotion to the black Christ of Esquipulas had spread throughout Central America. A copy of the crucifix was blessed before the original and taken to the cathedral in Guatemala City. In 1957, a prelature of Esquipulas was created and a bishop named for it. In 1961, the shrine was elevated to the status of a minor basilica.

Today, Esquipulas is considered one of the holiest places of Central America. Thousands of miracles have been claimed. Crutches, retablos, and other thanksgiving offerings testify to the gratitude of the petitioners of *"Señor Cristo Negro."* In 1984, a group of one thousand went on foot from Tiquisate to Esquipulas, asking for peace for Central America and for Guatemala. The journey took seventeen days. When the Central American presidents met to work out a peace plan, they were lodged at the Benedictine convent that is charged with the pastoral care of the basilica.

In 1988, another replica of the Black Christ of Esquipulas was blessed and was brought to San Antonio, Texas, to San Fernando cathedral.

The Miraculous Crucifix of Buga

In Buga, Colombia, there is a miraculous crucifix which has inspired love and devotion for nearly four hundred years. The story of this crucifix contains both pious legend and historical fact. Since 1937, the church containing the Lord of Miracles has been designated a minor basilica which is in the care of the Redemptorist fathers. Pilgrims come from all over the world to pay homage to Our Lord here under the title of Christ of Miracles.

The crucifix itself is by no means a work of art, as it suffers from a lack of proper proportion. The corpus, if extended, would be approximately one and a half meters in length. It is made of wood and depicts Our Lord in death. Disregarding its lack of artistic value, the crucifix inspires a tender devotion, and records testify to numerous miracles obtained by its devotees.

The legend of the origin of the devotion was written in the chronicles of the convent of the Redemptorist Fathers, who arrived in Buga to be in charge of the devotion in 1884. In these chronicles, the writer states that the source and origin of the sacred image is not found in authentic documents but rather in ancient tradition.

About 1580, there was a small village in the dense jungle with only a few houses, a parochial church, and a town hall. The Buga River then ran where the Church of the Hermitage is today. On the left bank of the river was a small hut that belonged to an old Indian washerwoman. This woman was very faithful, and for a long time she had been saving her money to purchase a small image of Christ to keep in her home. Eventually, she had saved about seventy reales (coins), which would be enough to buy a small crucifix.

On the day she was going to travel to Quito to make her purchase, an old friend of hers passed by her house crying. When she asked him what was wrong, the man, father of a family, told her that he was going to be sent to jail because of debt. He owed precisely seventy reales.

Moved by the plight of her neighbor, the woman gave him the money she had saved. With much gratitude, the man blessed her. The woman determined to begin again to save in order to buy an image of Christ.

Some days later, as the old woman was washing clothes in the river, a wooden crucifix floated up and landed by her feet. As no one lived upriver, the happy woman, with a clear conscience, took the image home. She set up a little altar and put the crucifix in a small wooden box for safekeeping.

One night, the woman heard a knocking sound from the area where she kept the crucifix. When she went to see what was there, the crucifix had grown in size. At first she thought she was imagining it, but several days later she realized that the crucifix had grown to the size of a small child.

Surprised by this miracle, the old woman contacted the parish priest. Along with other town notables, they visited her home to see the image. All agreed that the old woman had no resources or money to obtain such a large crucifix. Its existence could not be explained, and it was considered a miracle. Her home became a place of worship, and a number of other miracles occurred. The crucifix became famous, and was known as the Lord of Miracles.

After the old woman's death, the people wanted to erect a temple to the honored image. They discussed whether to build it where her hut was or in the main plaza of the town. While they were undecided about the location of where to build the church, a great flood occurred and the river moved to the south, about three blocks from where the crucifix had appeared. Accepting this as the will of God, and as another miracle, the people erected a chapel where the crucifix first appeared. The chapel was called the Hermitage, for that was what the old woman's home had been called.

From historical records, more information is given about the history of the devotion to the Lord of Miracles of Buga. Between the years of 1573 and 1576, a small hermitage was constructed in Buga on land donated by Rodrigo Diez de Fuenmayor. An image of Christ was honored here. With the passing of the years, the chapel began to deteriorate. In the first years of the seventeenth century, an ecclesiastical visitor from Popayán ordered the chapel burned. The flames did not destroy the crucifix; instead, it began to sweat abundantly, and the townspeople saved the sweat with cotton. Historical records in the church in Buga contain a description of this phenomenon, which was witnessed by a number of persons that were present. In 1665, Doña Luisa de la Espada gave testimony before a notary. She testified that the image sweated for two days, and the community took cotton and wiped it off. From that time a great devotion began.

In 1783, Dr. D. José Matias García, rector of the college-seminary of Popayán and chaplain of Christ the Miraculous of Buga, wrote to the Holy See to obtain indulgences and privileges in favor of the hermitage and the pilgrims of Buga. His request was approved by the Bishop of Popayán. He wrote, "Through the image, the Almighty works stupendous miracles, not only to the faithful of Buga but to those in America and Europe. These miracles have been repeated for more than two centuries — blind are able to see, mutes can again speak, lame and lepers have gotten well immediately. There is no illness that hasn't been cured, even when the doctors had abandoned the case and the persons were close to death."

In 1884, when the Redemptorists arrived to take charge of the devotion, they realized that the temple had to be enlarged. In 1891, with the approval of the Bishop of Popayán, the task was begun. Construction was not completed until 1907. The church was named a minor basilica by Pius XI in 1937.

The Crucifix That Spoke to St. Francis,
a 12th-century Umbrian cross painted
in egg tempera, is now preserved in the
Church of St. Clare in Assisi, Italy (see
"Crucifixes and Crosses").

Water

Our pre-Christian ancestors knew nothing of chemistry or physics, but from constant observation they knew the effects of rain, or the lack of it, on vegetation and life. To them, *water* assumed a magical property which produced fertility and new growth. This became the basis for many pre-Christian water rites.

The Church, acknowledging the life-giving properties of water and its significance in Christian history, provided a Christian version of the ancient water rites, thus elevating the pre-Christian symbolism of nature into a Christian sacramental.

Water is used in many ways liturgically. The mingling of a few drops of water with the wine to be consecrated at Mass was observed from the beginning, possibly by Our Lord Himself, for the Jews took water with their wine. It symbolizes the union of two natures in Christ, the unity of Christ and His people, and the water that came out with blood from His side. Water is used in the sacrament of baptism, blessing of bells, consecrating a church, and in the blessings and all the other uses for holy water.

The ceremony of blessing originated in the eighth century in the Carolinian Empire, as did most of the other liturgical blessings. The words of St. Paul that through baptism we rise with Christ into the newness of life (Rom 6:4-6) point to a special relation between the weekly memorial of the Resurrection and our own baptism. In the ninth century this thought seems to have prompted some bishops of the Frankish realm to introduce the custom of sprinkling holy water upon the faithful before Mass, to remind them of the grace of baptism. A century later, the same practice was prescribed at Verona, Italy, and soon afterward it was accepted by Rome. Thus, the rite of the Asperges became a part of the solemn service on Sunday. In many places during the Middle Ages a procession around the church was held, and holy water was sprinkled upon the graves of the faithful (cf. Weiser, 1958, p.15).

Holy water is ordinary water sanctified by the blessing of the Church. The blessing once consisted of exorcisms of water and salt; the salt was added to the water in the form of a cross to signify that this water is now preserved from corruption. The practice of putting salt into the water came from the incident of the miraculous cure of the poisoned water, when the prophet Elisha used salt to purify the water of the spring (2 Kings 2:19-22).

In the Roman ritual, the priest prays, "May this creature of yours, when used in your mysteries and endowed with your grace, serve to cast out demons and to banish disease. May everything that this water sprinkles in the homes and gatherings of the faithful be delivered from all that is unclean and hurtful; let no breath of contagion hover there, no taint of corruption; let all the wiles of the lurking enemy come to nothing. By the sprinkling of this water may everything opposed to the safety and peace of the occupants of these homes be banished, so that in calling on your holy name they may know the well-being they desire, and be protected from every peril; through Christ our Lord. Amen."

Christ's faithful are permitted to take holy water home with them to sprinkle the sick, their homes, fields, etc. It is recommended that they put it in fonts in the rooms of their homes and use it to bless themselves daily and frequently.

Water blessed during the Easter Vigil is known as *Easter Water*. It is customary for millions the world over to obtain for their homes this Easter water which has been blessed on Easter Saturday.

A special blessing of water on the Eve of the Epiphany was approved for the Roman ritual in 1890. This blessing comes from the Orient, where the church has long emphasized the mystery of our Lord's baptism in her celebration of Epiphany. Years before the Latin Rite officially adopted the blessing of *Epiphany water*, diocesan rituals in lower Italy had contained such a blessing.

Water is specially blessed and is a part of the cultus of a number of the saints. A papal brief of 1628 authorizes the blessing of water for the sick in honor of the Blessed *Virgin Mary and St. Torellus*. This water is drunk by the sick. Water is blessed in the name of *St. Peter the Martyr*, asking through his intercession that all who drink it or are sprinkled with it may be delivered from evil spirits, illness, and suffering of both body and spirit. The blessing for the water in honor of *St. Vincent Ferrer* asks that in the name of God the Father and of St. Vincent, the water may "heal the sick, strengthen the infirm, cheer the downcast, purify the unclean and give full well-being to those who seek it." This water is blessed with a relic or image of the saint. The blessing for water in the name of *St. Raymond Nonnatus* asks that "all who suffer from fever may be delivered from every infirmity of body and soul when they bathe in this water, or drink it, or are sprinkled with it, and so deserve to be restored unharmed to your church where they will always offer their prayers of gratitude." This water is then sprinkled with holy water.

In the blessing of the water in honor of *St. Albert, Confessor*, the exposed relics of the saint are immersed in the water. The prayer for this blessing asks that through the prayers of Blessed Albert, the faithful who reverently drink this water may regain health of body and soul and so persevere in God's holy service. The same is true of water blessed in honor of *St. Ignatius, Confessor*, and *St. Vincent de Paul*, except the relics are left in the reliquary and a medal may be substituted for the actual relics. In some churches, the people bring water, wine, bread, and fruit to church on St. Blaise's feast day to be blessed. The blessing of these items, which are sprinkled with holy water, asks that all those "who eat and drink these gifts be fully healed of all ailments of the throat and of all maladies of body and soul, through the merits of St. Blaise, bishop and martyr."

Lourdes Water

In 1858, Bernadette Soubirous, a young, poor, uneducated French girl, was favored with a number of visions of Our Lady. Messages given to the world by Our Lady through this humble seer called for penance and confirmed the dogma of the Immaculate Conception recently proclaimed by Pope Pius IX.

At first, people thought the visions were the foolish dreams of a sickly child. Because she looked so beautiful while in ecstasy, more and more people came to see for themselves. At the ninth apparition on February 25, 1858, the crowd, who could not see the beautiful lady Bernadette spoke of, nor hear her words, noticed Bernadette do a strange thing. She was praying at the grotto called Massabielle when she turned from the grotto and started toward the nearby river. Then she turned back toward the grotto and appeared to be digging in the earth. A muddy ooze began to seep from the hole she had scraped out and Bernadette attempted to drink it, and she put it on her face. The crowd had not heard the directions to Bernadette to drink from and wash with the water from the spring where Our Lady indicated Bernadette would find one. The crowd simply thought that Bernadette had gone crazy.

Soon, however, clear water began to trickle from this spot toward the river. Water today flows from this spring at the rate of over 30,000 gallons a day. People began to imitate Bernadette, and drink and wash with the water. The sick got well; the injured were cured. The people began to call the water miraculous. Although by 1981 only sixty-five of the cases examined at Lourdes had been declared to be miraculous by the competent Church authorities, millions of people worldwide claim that they were cured or helped by the water of this spring, or through the intercession of Our Lady of Lourdes.

Today, Lourdes is a popular place of pilgrimage. Water from the spring has been piped to taps and to baths at the grotto. This water is shipped all over the world.

Lourdes water is not holy water; it is water that comes from the miraculous spring at Lourdes, France, and has received no special blessing. It may be drunk or used externally. The Lourdes Center in Boston, Mass., founded by the Archbishop of Boston and the Bishop of Lourdes, was entrusted to the Marist Fathers to promote devotion to Our Lady of Lourdes in America, to distribute Lourdes Water, to organize pilgrimages to Lourdes, and to serve as a center of information on Lourdes. Lourdes water is free, but a donation to cover the cost of shipping and mailing is requested.

St. Odilia Water

Authentic particulars about the life of St. Odilia are almost wholly lacking, although she is widely venerated in Europe and in America. Popular tradition has her the daughter of a nobleman, born blind, and hated by her father on that account. At length she recovered her sight, and he was reconciled with her. Later, she and a group of virgins, of which she was abbess, were martyred at Cologne.

In 1287, she appeared to John Novelan, a lay brother of the Crosier Order in Paris, and told him she had been appointed to be patroness of his order. She begged him to obtain permission to travel to Cologne to get her relics, and told him where they were to be found in an orchard near the city. After a third apparition, he was given leave to go with a priest of the order to search for the relics. The two had little trouble finding the relics, and they joyfully informed the archbishop, who came personally to witness the discovery. The relics were taken from Cologne to the motherhouse of the Order at Huy, Belgium, and on the way a number of miraculous cures took place.

During the French Revolution, the monastery at Huy was destroyed. Although the relics were saved, they were lost to the Order for over a century and a half.

At last, in 1949, the relics were returned to the Crosier Order, and in 1952 a major relic of the saint was brought to the seminary in Onamia, Minnesota, where a shrine in her honor was established.

St. Odilia is a patroness of the blind and of those afflicted with eye disease. For centuries it has been the practice in the Crosier Order to bless water in honor of St. Odilia, dipping her relic in it and asking God to give it a "power against all diseases and bodily infirmities." Many cures, especially of diseases of the eyes, are credited to her intercession.

Fátima Water

In 1917, when Our Lady appeared at Fátima, the nature of the soil at the Cova da Iria was so porous that there was no pocket of water. As this greatly inconvenienced the pilgrims, the Bishop of Leiria decided to build a concrete cistern to hold rain water for the use of the pilgrims. As ground was broken for this event in 1921, a pure spring of drinking water bubbled up in a crystaline stream. The water flows by the monument of the Sacred Heart in the Sanctuary of Fátima at the very spot where Our Lady deigned to appear to the three seers.

Father Cacella, the American "Apostle of Fátima," obtained a supply of this water by contacting the Bishop of Fátima. Monthly, ten to fifteen five-gallon demijohns of the water arrived in New York. Each was tightly sealed in wax, and each seal bore the imprint "SF" — Sanctuary of Fátima.

In America, the water was transferred to sterilized vials and packed in boxes for distribution. Many miracles have been claimed as a result of the use of this water.

Christmas Sacramentals

No other season of the year is celebrated as festively as Christmas, the birthday of Our Lord. Throughout the centuries, worldwide, beautiful customs and sacramentals have increased the devotion of the season. Unfortunately, in our own times, the commercial value of Christmas has often been emphasized to the point where the religious significance of the holiday seems overlooked. Few seem to realize that nearly all of the popular Christmas customs have a religious background.

The variety of customs worldwide has brought forward a number of sacramentals unique to the area where they originated. The most popular, such as the Christmas tree, have found their way to other countries.

The celebration of Christ's nativity as a special feast on December 25 was introduced in Rome about the middle of the fourth century. In the Roman Empire it was a custom to celebrate the birthdays of rulers and other important persons. Often the celebrations continued after the death of the individual. Soon after the end of the last great persecution about the year 330, the Church in Rome definitely assigned December 25 for the celebration of the birth of Christ. The date varied in the Eastern Churches, but by the end of the fourth century the Roman custom became universal. The most probable reason for the choice of the date is that the Romans from the time of Emperor Aurelian in 275 had celebrated the feast of the sun god on that day, and it was called the "Birthday of the Sun". Thus, it was natural for the Christians to celebrate the birth of Him who was "The Light of the world" and the "Sun of Justice".

By the fifth century, Christmas had become a feast of such importance that it marked the beginning of the ecclesiastical year. After the tenth century, the season of Advent had become an integral part of the Christmas cycle and the ecclesiastical year began on the first Sunday of Advent. In 529, Emperor Justinian prohibited work and public business on Christmas and declared the day a civic holiday. The Council of Agde (506) urged Christians to receive Holy Communion on the feast. The Council of Tours (567) established a sacred and festive season over the *twelve days* from Christmas to Epiphany.

As the great missionaries brought Christianity to the pagan tribes of Europe, they brought the celebration of Christmas with them. Most of these missionaries were the first bishops of the countries they converted, and thus they established and regulated the feast. By 1100, all the nations of Europe had accepted Christianity, and Christmas was celebrated everywhere with great devotion and joy. This was a time of colorful and inspiring religious services; Christmas music and plays were written, and this was the time that most of the delightful Christmas customs of each country began. Some of these customs have died out; some, because of improper and scandalous actions, were suppressed, and many have survived to our day.

In the sixteenth century, with the Reformation, there came a sharp change in the Christmas celebrations for many countries in Europe. The Mass was suppressed, and in many countries all that remained was a sermon and a prayer service on Christmas Day. In England, the Puritans condemned even the reduced religious celebration held in the Anglican Church after the separation from Rome, becoming determined to abolish Christmas altogether. They contended that no feast of human institution should ever outrank the Sabbath. In Scotland the celebration of Christmas was forbidden in 1583, and persons observing it were to be punished. When the Puritans finally came to political power in England, they promptly proceeded to outlaw Christmas, and in 1647 Parliament set punishments for anyone observing Christmas and other holidays. Each year, town criers went through the streets a few days before Christmas reminding the citizens that "Christmas day and all other superstitious festivals" should not be observed. During the year 1647 popular riots broke out in various places against the suppression laws, and the government had to break up Christmas celebrations by force of arms. With the restoration of the monarchy in 1660, Christmas celebrations were restored, but the religious aspect of the feast was left mostly to the ministers in the church service on Christmas day, and the celebrations at home were mere nonreligious amusements and general reveling. A spirit of goodwill to all and of charity to the poor did remain a part of the celebration.

Christmas came to America with the missionaries and settlers from the various European countries. Thus where the Spaniards and French settled, the feast was celebrated with liturgical solemnity and traditional customs. In the New England colonies, however, the Puritans' zeal against Christmas persisted into the middle of the nineteenth century. It was when immigrants from Ireland and continental Europe arrived in large numbers toward the middle of the last century that Christmas in America began to flourish.

The Christmas Crib

Various representations of the Christmas story, including the Child in the manger, have been used in church services from the first centuries. The oldest known picture is the Nativity scene dating from about 380 that

61

*"Christ of St. John of the Cross" by
Salvador Dali, the highly publicized
Spanish surrealist, shows Christ on the
Cross over a seascape with fishing
boats (reproduced from the collection
of the Glasgow Art Gallery and
Museum, Scotland; see "Images").*

served as a wall decoration in a Christian family's burial chamber, discovered in the Roman catacombs of St. Sebastian in 1877.

The use of the crib in its present form and its use outside the church is credited to St. Francis of Assisi. The saint, three years before his death, went to his friend Giovanni Velitta, a native of Greccio, and told him to "prepare what I tell you, for I want to enact the memory of the Infant who was born at Bethlehem, and how He was deprived of all the comforts babies enjoy; how He was bedded in the manger on hay between an ass and an ox. For once I want to see all this with my own eyes." Thus, that good man on Christmas Eve 1223 prepared in the place that Francis had requested all the saint had told him.

The Franciscan friars were called from many communities. The people of the neighborhood prepared torches to light the night. Finally the saint arrived, and the crib was made ready. Greccio became a new Bethlehem. The crowds rejoiced in the novelty of the celebration, and they sang in praise of God. A solemn Mass was sung at the crib. St. Francis sang the Gospel and preached a delightful sermon about the Nativity of the poor King and the humble town of Bethlehem.

Since the time of St. Francis, the Christmas crib has become a familiar sight in churches and homes all over the world. In Central Europe, the beautiful family cribs are sometimes made up of hundreds of figures and fill an entire room of the house. The Moravian Germans were among the sects that kept the tradition of the Christmas crib even after the Reformation, and it was they who brought the custom to the United States. They called it *Putz*, from the German word for decorate, and their scenes include not only the figures of the Nativity but dozens of figures, fanciful landscaping, waterfalls, houses, villages, etc.

The Christmas Candle

It has been a religious practice to represent Christ the Lord by a burning candle since the early centuries of Christianity. This symbolism of the liturgy was adopted by the faithful in the early centuries. At Christmas, a large candle symbolizing the Lord used to be set up in homes on Christmas Eve and kept burning through Holy Night. The candle was lit every night during the holy season.

Different countries have different customs regarding the Christmas candle. In the Slavic nations, the candle is put on the table after being blessed by the priest in Church. The Ukrainians stick their Christmas candle in a loaf of bread. In parts of South America the candle is put in a paper lantern with symbols and pictures of the Nativity on its sides. In France and England, the candle was often made of three candles twisted together in honor of the Holy Trinity. In Germany, the candle was put on top of a wooden pole decorated with evergreens (*Lichtstock*) or many small candles were distributed on the shelves of a wooden structure made in the form of a pyramid, adorned with fir twigs or laurel and draped with tinsel. This pyramid was gradually replaced with the Christmas tree, although the Christmas pyramid has remained a traditional custom in some parts of Germany. In Ireland, a large holly-bedecked candle is lit on Christmas Eve, and the entire family prays for all its dear ones, living and dead. The Irish also placed candles in the windows (Weiser, p. 96).

The Christmas Tree

The use of Christmas trees is a fairly recent custom in all countries outside of Germany, and even there it attained its immense popularity as recently as the end of the last century. The tree has its origin in a combination of two medieval religious symbols, the *Paradise tree* and the Christmas light or candle.

Beginning in the eleventh century, religious plays used to be performed in or near churches. One of the most popular of these "*mystery plays*" was the Paradise play. The play told the story of the creation and of the expulsion of Adam and Eve from Paradise after their sin. The ending of the play was a consoling promise of the coming Savior. This play was a favorite at Advent.

To indicate the Garden of Eden, a fir tree was hung with apples. This "Paradise tree" was the only prop on the stage, and attracted much attention, especially on the part of the children.

The mystery plays were gradually forbidden in the fifteenth century because of abuses that had crept in. The people were so fond of their Paradise tree that when they could no longer see it in church, they began putting it up in their homes in honor of the feast day of Adam and Eve, December 24. Although the Latin Church has never officially celebrated Adam and Eve as saints, the Eastern Churches do so, and thus the custom of keeping their feast spread into Europe. In medieval religious "mystery" pictures, the Paradise tree stood for the Tree of Life as well as the Tree of Sin. In addition to the red apples, the fruit of sin, the trees bore wafers representing the Holy Eucharist, the fruit of life. Later, the wafers were replaced by candy and pastry representing the sweet fruit of Christ's redemption.

The people in western Germany, during the sixteenth century, began to combine the two symbols they had in their homes on December 24 — the *Paradise tree* and the *Christmas pyramid*. They began to transfer the decorations from the Christmas pyramid (see entry "Christmas Candle") to the tree. The Paradise tree already bore apples and sweets. The Germans added glass balls, tinsel, and topped the tree with the Star of Bethlehem. During the seventeenth century, the lights were also transferred to the tree.

The first mention of the tree as it is now known dates from 1521 in German Alsace. Another description is found in a manuscript from Strasbourg in 1605. The tree slowly became popular, first in southern Germany and then throughout Europe. The tree was introduced into France in 1837 when Princess Helen brought it to Paris after her marriage to the Duke of Orléans. Prince Albert of Saxony, the husband of Queen Victoria, had a tree set up at Windsor Castle in 1841.

The Christmas tree arrived in America with the first wave of German immigrants about 1700. The second wave of German immigration began about 1830. Through them the Christmas tree was brought to the attention of their neighbors and soon became a much admired and familiar sight. In 1850, Charles Dickens called the Christmas tree "a new German toy." The custom of setting up lighted Christmas trees in public places began in Boston in 1912. This custom spread rapidly over the United States and found its way to Europe shortly before World War II.

There are a number of legends regarding the origin of the Christmas tree, but all merely give a fictional explanation for the origin of an already-existing custom. The origin of the tree in legend has been ascribed variously to the Christ Child Himself, to St. Boniface, to St. Ansgar, and to Martin Luther.

Christmas Plants and Flowers

The custom of decorating homes at festive times is worldwide and ancient. After the time of the persecutions, the Church soon approved the custom of decorating both church and home with plants and flowers at the Christmas season. Pope St. Gregory I (604) in a letter to St. Augustine of Canterbury advised him to permit and even encourage harmless popular customs which in themselves were not pagan and which could be given Christian interpretations.

Most of the plants traditionally used at Christmas are *evergreens* for two reasons: 1) they were usually the only ones available in winter and 2) from ancient times evergreens have been symbolic of eternal life.

Mistletoe was a sacred plant in the pagan religion of the Druids of Britain. The Druids believed it has all sorts of miraculous qualities. It was considered so sacred that even enemies who met beneath mistletoe in the forest would lay down their arms and keep a truce until the following day. From this practice came the modern practice of suspending mistletoe over a doorway as a token of goodwill and peace. A kiss under mistletoe was interpreted as a pledge of love and a promise of marriage, an omen of happiness and good fortune to the lovers who sealed their engagement by a kiss beneath the sacred plant.

After Britain was converted to Christianity, the bishops did not allow mistletoe to be used in churches because it had been the main symbol of a pagan religion. To this day, it is rarely used as a decoration for altars. However, the Cathedral of York was an exception, and at a period before the Reformation a large bundle of mistletoe was annually brought into the sanctuary at Christmas and solemnly placed on the altar by the priest. The plant that the Druids had called "All heal" was used as a symbol of the Divine Healer of nations, Christ.

Later, the English adopted the mistletoe as a decoration for their homes, and the pagan meaning was soon forgotten. It simply became a token of goodwill and friendship, and the kissing lost its solemn meaning.

Holly was a symbol, to early Christians of northern Europe, of the burning thorn bush of Moses and the flaming love of God that filled Mary's heart. The prickly points and red berries resembling blood also reminded them that the Divine Child would wear a crown of thorns. The appearance of holly in the homes of old England opened the season of feasting and good cheer. Today its green leaves and red berries have become a symbol of Christmas, decorating not only homes and churches but also cards, wrapping paper, and other Christmas items.

In the medieval age, superstition endowed holly with power against witchcraft, and unmarried women were advised to fasten holly to their beds at Christmas to guard them from being turned into witches by the Evil One. In Germany, branches of holly which had been used in church were brought home as a protection against lightning. Holly was supposed to be lucky for men, as ivy was to women.

Ivy, in pagan Rome, was the badge of the wine god Bacchus, displayed to symbolize drinking and feasting. Later, for this reason, it was banished from Christian homes. In England, it was banned from the inside of homes and only allowed to grow on the outside. Thus, its use as a Christmas decoration was not common during medieval times. The symbolism of human weakness clinging to divine strength was frequently ascribed to ivy, and some poets in old England defended its use as a decoration. Later, the delicate ground ivy became a favorite plant of the English home, and it traveled to the New World with the pioneer settlers.

The *bay laurel* is an ancient symbol of triumph and has been used for Christmas decorations to proclaim the victory over death and sin that the birth of Christ signifies. It was probably the first plant used as a Christmas decoration, being used by the early Christians at Rome to adorn their homes at the Nativity. The *wreath* was a Roman symbol of victory, and it is from Rome that the modern custom derives of hanging laurel wreaths on the outside of doors as a friendly greeting to our fellowmen. It was introduced to the United States by immigrants from England and Ireland, gradually becoming part of American culture. Today, evergreen wreaths are as common, if not more so, than laurel wreaths.

According to an old legend, the delicate *rosemary* was honored by God in reward for its humble service to Mary and her Child on the flight into Egypt. On the way, Mary washed the tiny garments of the Christ Child and spread them over a rosemary bush to dry. In other medieval legends, this plant is pictured as a great protection and help against evil spirits, especially if it has been used in church on Christmas Day.

It is a custom in some parts of central Europe to break off a branch of the *cherry tree* on St. Barbara's Day (December 4), place it in a pot of water in the kitchen, and wait for the twig to blossom at Christmastime. Such cherry branches flowering at Christmas were considered omens of good luck.

A native of Central America, the *Poinsettia* is widely used in churches and homes at Christmas because the flaming star of its red bracts resembles the star of Bethlehem. Dr. Joel Roberts Poinsett (1851), the U.S. ambassador to Mexico, brought this flower with him back to his home in South Carolina. In Mexico, the flower is called the "flower of Holy Night." Its origin is explained by a charming Mexican legend. A poor little boy went to church on Christmas Eve in sadness because he had no gift to bring to the Holy Child. He knelt humbly outside the church and prayed fervently in tears, assuring Our Lord how much he wished to offer Him a lovely present, telling Him that he was poor and afraid to approach with empty hands. When the child rose from his knees, he saw a green plant with gorgeous blooms spring up at his feet. The Poinsettia is a prolific bloomer and has spread throughout the United States (Weiser, pp. 104-107).

Advent Wreaths, Calendars, and Plays

The *Advent wreath* is a Lutheran custom which originated in eastern Germany a few hundred years ago. It probably was suggested by one of the light symbols used in folklore at the end of November and beginning of December. Our pre-Christian forefathers celebrated the month of Yule, December, with the burning of fires. Medieval Christians kept many of the light and fire symbols alive as popular customs, and in the sixteenth century these lights became a religious symbol of Advent in the homes of Christians.

The Advent wreath is made of evergreens which may be suspended from the ceiling or placed on a table, usually in front of a family shrine. Four candles are fastened to the wreath to represent the four weeks of Advent.

Daily at a certain time the family gathers for a short religious observance. Each Sunday another candle is lit until all four candles announce the approaching birthday of the Lord. The traditional symbolism of the wreath reminds the faithful of the Old Testament when humanity was in darkness awaiting the Light of the Redeemer. The wreath, an ancient symbol of victory, symbolizes the fulfillment of time in the coming of Christ and the glory of His birth.

Advent calendars originated in Germany and have recently spread worldwide. A colored scene printed on cardboard is put up at the beginning of December. Every day a "window" is opened by the children, revealing a picture or symbol that points to the coming feast of Christmas. On December 24, the door is opened, showing the Nativity scene.

An *Advent play* called *Herbergsuchen* originated in Germany. The play, whose name means "search for an inn," is a dramatic rendition of the Holy Family's fruitless efforts to find an inn in Bethlehem. A similar custom is the Spanish *Posadas*, traditional in Latin American countries, especially Mexico. A procession led by actors portraying Mary and Joseph wends its way through the *ciudad* (town), stopping and knocking at the doors of homes along the way. Shelter for the holy family is requested, and refused by the homeowners until at last the procession arrives at a pre-designated home where they are welcomed. In this home, a traditional crib is set up with an empty manger. After prayers and blessing by the priest, a gay party is held for adults and children alike. The children are especially entertained with the *piñata*, a papier-mâché figure hung from the ceiling. Blindfolded, the children attempt to hit the swinging piñata with a stick, breaking it so the contents, candy and sweetmeats, will shower on all (cf. Weiser, pp. 56-59).

Christmas Carols

The word carol comes from the Greek word *choraulein* and originally referred to a dance accompanied by the playing of flutes. Such dancing, usually done in a circle, was very popular in ancient Greece and Rome. The Romans took the custom and the name to Britain.

In medieval England, caroling referred to a ring or circle dance accompanied by singing. Gradually, the meaning of the word changed and was applied to a song.

The first Christmas hymns were written in the fifth century. These hymns, written in Latin, increased in number as time passed. The early Latin hymns from about 400 to about 1200 were profound and solemn. The birthplace of the modern Christmas carol was Italy. There, St. Francis and the early Franciscans introduced the joyful spirit which soon spread throughout Europe. St. Francis himself wrote a beautiful Christmas hymn called *Psalmus in Nativitate*. From Italy the carol spread quickly to other parts of Europe, and a large number of popular Christmas carols were written in Germany in the fourteenth century under the inspiration of the Dominicans.

The earliest known English Christmas carol was written about the beginning of the fifteenth century. After the Reformation, most of the old hymns and carols were no longer sung and were forgotten in many countries until their revival in the nineteenth century. Carols in general were discouraged by the Calvinists and suppressed altogether by the Puritans. After the restoration of Christmas in England, there were numerous festive songs, but few were religious carols. The Methodist revival in the eighteenth century inspired a number of modern hymns, first used only in Methodist churches but gradually welcomed by all English-speaking people. The best-known of these is "Hark, the Herald Angels Sing" written by Charles Wesley. The Lutherans wrote new hymns for their own use, and some of those written by Martin Luther are treasured in many churches today.

The first American carol was written by the Jesuit missionary to the Huron Indians, St. John de Brébeuf. He adapted a sixteenth-century French folk song and wrote the Christmas hymn *Jesous Ahatonnia* ("Jesus Is Born") in the Huron language.

A great number of beautiful American carols have been introduced since the widespread revival of Christmas customs in America. A number of these were inspired by the Methodist revival, but carols have come from most of the religious sects in America. Those American carols differed from the average English Christmas songs of the past centuries because they reflected a religious spirit, whereas the English songs praised the external pleasures of feasting, reveling, and general goodwill without direct reference to the Nativity (cf. Weiser, pp. 72-82).

One English Christmas carol well-known worldwide today is, however, more than a repetitious tune with pretty phrases and strange gifts. *"The Twelve Days of Christmas"* is a song with different levels of meaning.

From 1558 to 1829, the Catholics in England were not permitted to

Pantokrater, Jesus Ruler of heaven and earth: Byzantine ikon
based on a Greek monastery mosaic (see "Images").

practice their faith openly. During this period, "The Twelve Days of Christmas" was written in England as a catechism song for young Catholics. The hidden meanings of the song's gifts were intended to help the children remember lessons of their faith. Instead of referring to an earthly suitor, the "true love" mentioned in the song refers to God Himself. The "me" who receives the presents is symbolic of every baptized person. The partridge in a pear tree is Jesus Christ. In the song, Christ is symbolically presented as a mother partridge which feigns injury to decoy predators from her helpless nestlings. The meaning of the other symbols are:

Two turtle doves — the Old and New Testaments;

Three French hens — Faith, Hope and Charity;

Four calling birds — the four Gospels;

Five golden rings — the first five books of the Old Testament, which give the history of man's fall from grace;

Six geese a-laying — the six days of creation;

Seven swans a-swimming — seven gifts of the Holy Spirit;

Eight maids a-milking — the eight Beatitudes;

Nine ladies dancing — nine choirs of angels;

Ten lords a-leaping — the Ten Commandments;

Eleven pipers piping — the eleven faithful Apostles;

Twelve drummers drumming — the twelve points of belief in the Apostles' Creed (cf. Newsletter of the Catholic Medical Mission Board, December 1988).

Lent and Easter Sacramentals

In the liturgy of the Church, Lent is the season of penitential and prayerful preparation for the great feast of Easter. Penance was practiced from earliest times by fasting, additional prayer services, and other exercises for public sinners and in which the faithful joined in token of humble, voluntary penance (cf. Weiser, p. 168).

From Ash Wednesday to Easter, solemn weddings and other joyous celebrations are prohibited in church. In the ancient Church, Lent was also the season of preparation for baptism.

From the time of the Apostles, Sunday, which replaced the ancient Sabbath as the new "Day of the Lord," and Friday, in memory of His death, have been singled out for special observation in honor of Christ's Resurrection. Eventually a longer period of fasting was observed.

The first day of Lent is called *Ash Wednesday* from the ceremony of imposing *blessed ashes* in the form of a cross on the foreheads of all the faithful while the priest pronounces the words, "Remember, man, that you are dust, and to dust you shall return" (Gen 3:19). The name of the day itself was officially introduced in 1099 by Pope Urban II; previously it was called "Beginning of the Fast."

The ashes used are made from burning the *blessed palms* of the previous Palm Sunday. They are given a special blessing before being distributed on Ash Wednesday, and the prayers in the Roman Missal for this ceremony date back to the eighth century.

Ashes have been used as a token of penance and sorrow from the time of the Old Testament. The Church accepted the custom from Jewish tradition and kept its original meaning. Originally, the imposition of ashes applied only to public sinners. By the end of the eleventh century, many devout people voluntarily submitted to it, and it has become a general practice worldwide. In medieval times, the Popes walked barefoot on Ash Wednesday, accompanied by their cardinals, to the church of Santa Sabina, where the Pope received the ashes from the oldest cardinal-bishop and distributed them to all the cardinals.

The imposition of ashes was discontinued in most Protestant churches after the Reformation, but was kept alive for a time in the Church of England. In recent times, some Protestant churches have returned to this ancient practice. Ash Wednesday is not observed in the Oriental Churches. Their Lent begins on the Monday before Ash Wednesday, which they call "Clean Monday" because the faithful cleanse their souls in penance and also wash and scrub all cooking utensils to remove all traces of meat and fat for the penitential season.

The fourth Sunday in Lent, formerly called Laetare Sunday, is a day of joy within the mourning season. The altars may be decorated with flowers, and rose-colored vestments may be worn instead of purple ones. The historical background for this sudden joyful note in the middle of the penitential season comes from the ancient practice of the *traditio symboli*, or handing over of the Apostolic Creed to the catechumens. After their period of trial, this was the last and decisive step toward baptism for those who had successfully stood the test, and Mother Church exulted over the approaching increase of her children through baptism. Hence, the liturgical expression of joy. In later centuries, when the practice of the *traditio* in Mid-Lent was discontinued and combined with the baptismal ceremony, the reason for the Sunday's liturgical joy was forgotten, and in 1216 Pope Innocent III mentioned in one of his sermons that the day marked "a measure of consoling relaxation . . . so that the faithful may not break down under the severe strain of Lenten fast but may continue to bear the restrictions with a refreshed and easier heart" (ibid., p. 178).

As a symbol of joy on Laetare Sunday, the Pope used to carry a *golden rose* in his right hand when returning from the celebration of Mass. This was originally a natural rose until the eleventh century, when it became customary to use one made of gold. Since the fifteenth century, this golden rose consists of a cluster or branch of roses made of pure gold and set with precious stones. The Popes bless the branch annually and sometimes confer it on churches, shrines, cities, or distinguished persons as a token of esteem and paternal affection. If the rose is bestowed, a new rose is made during the next year. In the prayer of blessing, the symbolism is expressed. The rose represents Christ in the shining splendor of His majesty, the "flower sprung from the root of Jesse."

The fifth Sunday in Lent, before Vatican II reforms, was called Passion Sunday and from the ninth century occurred two weeks before Easter and inaugurated Passiontide, the final and particularly solemn preparation for the great feast. Formerly, thus, the last fourteen days of Lent were devoted entirely to the meditation of Christ's Passion. On the eve of Passion Sunday, the crucifixes, statues and pictures in the churches were draped in purple cloth as a sign of mourning. This custom originated in Rome in ancient times with the shrouding of the images in the papal chapel in the Vatican. Since Vatican II, Passion Sunday and Palm Sunday (see below) are combined.

The prevailing popular devotion of Lent in both the Western and Eastern churches is the Stations of the Cross (see separate entry).

An interesting survival of early Christian Lenten fare is familiar today. The Christians in the Roman Empire made a special dough with flour, salt, and water only, as fat, eggs, and milk were forbidden. This was shaped in the form of two arms crossed in prayer. The little breads were called "little arms." The Latin word was changed by the Germans to the term brezel or prezel, which became in English the word *pretzel*. The oldest known picture of a pretzel is found in a fifth-century manuscript. From medieval times to the present, these breads remained an item of Lenten food in many parts of Europe, and in some cities were distributed to the poor during Lent (ibid., p. 183).

From the very beginning of Christianity, Holy Week has been devoted to special commemoration of Christ's Passion and death. After the time of the persecutions, Christian emperors of both the East and West issued various decrees forbidding amusements and games and directed that the sacred days were to be spent free from worldly occupations and entirely devoted to religious exercises. Pardons were granted to those in prison, and many charges in court were dropped in honor of Christ's Passion. In medieval times, all secular business was prohibited, and the time was spent in recollection and prayer. Kings and rulers often secluded themselves in a monastery. During the Middle Ages, the Sacred Triduum of Holy Week — Thursday, Friday, and Saturday - was a time of obligation. No servile work was done and the faithful were present at all of the impressive ceremonies of those days. In 1642, Pope Urban VIII, due to the changed conditions of social life, rescinded this obligation.

By the fourth century, the faithful in Jerusalem began to reenact the solemn entry of Christ into their city on the Sunday before Easter, holding a procession in which they carried branches and sang the "Hosanna." In the early Latin Church, the faithful held aloft twigs of olives during Mass. The rite of the *blessing of the palms* seems to have originated in the Frankish kingdom, and an early mention of the ceremony is found in the Sacramentary of the Abbey of Bobbio in northern Italy, which dates from the eighth century. The rite was soon incorporated into the liturgy and celebrated in Rome. A Mass was held outside the walls of the city at some church where the palms were blessed. Then the faithful walked in solemn procession into the city to the basilica of St. John Lateran or to St. Peter's, where the Pope said a second Mass. The first Mass was later discontinued, and only the ceremony of blessing was performed. During medieval times, a procession composed of the clergy and laity carrying palms moved from a chapel or shrine outside the town, where the palms were blessed, to the cathedral or main church. Christ was represented by the Blessed Sacrament or by a crucifix adorned with flowers and carried by the celebrant. Later in the Middle Ages, a wooden statue of Christ sitting on a donkey, the whole image on wheels, was drawn in the center of the procession. These statues known as *Palmesel, Palm Donkeys*, may still be seen in a number of museums in European cities. Today's blessing of palms and the procession are usually held within the churches, and the blessing is short and simple compared to the former elaborate ritual (ibid., p. 188).

In most countries, real palms are unattainable, so a variety of other branches are used. Centuries ago, not only branches but flowers were blessed, and in some countries the day is called "Flower Sunday". The term *Pascua Florida*, which in Spain originally meant just Palm Sunday, was later applied to the entire festive season of Easter Week. Thus the state of Florida received its name when Ponce de León first sighted the land on Easter Sunday 1513 and named it in honor of the great feast.

In central Europe large clusters of plants interwoven with ribbons and flowers are fastened to a top of a wooden stick, and are called *palm bouquets*. The main plant used, however, is the *pussy willow* bearing their catkin blossoms. In the Latin countries and the United States, palm leaves are often braided or shaped into little *crosses* or other symbolic designs. The faithful reverently keep these in their homes during the year.

In the early Christian centuries the bishop celebrated three Masses on Maundy (Holy) Thursday. The first, the Mass of Remission, was for the reconciliation of public sinners. The second was the Mass of the Chrism for the blessing of holy oils, and the third commemorated the Last Supper of Christ and the institution of the Eucharist. Today the Mass of the Chrism is still celebrated in every cathedral. During this Mass the bishop blesses the *holy oils* — oils of the sick, holy chrism, and oil of the catechumens. In the evening the Mass of the Lord's Supper is celebrated in all churches as one of the most solemn and impressive ceremonies of the year. The altar is decorated, and white, the liturgical color of joy, is used. After Mass, the Blessed Sacrament is carried in solemn procession to a decorated side altar, where it is kept in the tabernacle until the Good Friday service.

After the Mass the altars are stripped, and decorations except those at the repository shrine are removed in symbolic representation of the body of Christ, which was stripped of its garments.

Finally there is the ancient rite of the washing of the feet, *Mandatum*. From ancient times all religious superiors and the Popes performed the Maundy; the rite was prescribed as early as 694 by the Synod of Toledo. In medieval times and in some countries up to today, Christian emperors, kings, and lords washed the feet of old and poor men, to whom they afterward served a meal and distributed alms.

Good Friday was celebrated from the earliest centuries as a day of sadness, mourning, fasting and prayer. The first part of the Good Friday service is the only example of the ancient Roman Synaxis, or prayer meeting without Mass, that has survived to the present. After the synaxis, one of the most moving ceremonies of the year takes place, the *Veneration of the Cross*. The priest unveils the crucifix in three stages, and it is placed on a pillow in front of the altar. The priest and his assistants approach it, genuflecting three times, and devoutly kiss the feet of the image. The lay people follow performing a similar humble act of homage.

The Veneration of the Cross was adopted by the Roman Church from Jerusalem, where the true Cross of Christ was venerated every year on Good Friday from the fourth century. After the Muslims conquered Jerusalem in 1187, the relics were taken away and no trace of them was ever found.

After the solemn veneration of the cross, the Blessed Sacrament is carried in procession from the repository shrine to the main altar and the Communion service is celebrated. After the solemn ceremonies of Good Friday are concluded, the altar is stripped again, the tabernacle (if one remains) is left open, no lights burn in the sanctuary, and only the crucifix takes the place of honor on the naked altar or in front of the empty tabernacle.

The faithful practice various extraliturgical devotions in most countries of the world which are today celebrated with solemn piety. The faithful of some countries have a ceremony and *vigil of the Holy Sepulcher*. In Spanish-speaking countries a representation of Calvary is erected, and the priest detaches the body of Christ from the Cross and places it in the shrine of the Sepulcher. The faithful visit the shrine, praying all through the evening and on Holy Saturday. In the Byzantine Church, the elders of the parish carry a cloth containing a picture of Our Lord's body resting in death and walk in procession to the shrine of the Sepulcher, where the cloth is placed on a table to be venerated by the people. This ceremony is called *Platsenitsia* by the Ukrainians and other Slavs of the Oriental Church. From the second century it was a widespread custom for people to fast day and night for forty hours from Good Friday afternoon until Easter Sunday morning. To this fast was added a forty hours' prayer at the Holy Sepulcher shrine. This custom remained through the Middle Ages, and later in other places. Liturgically speaking, however, only the fasting is provided in the Roman Rite, and the Eastern Rites have a "burial" service in their Good Friday ritual. The *Forty Hours' Devotion*, which grew out of the ancient forty hours' "wake," was separated from its original place and officially established as a liturgical devotion at various other times of the year. Devotions connected with the seven last words of

Christ, processions, Passion plays and other para-liturgical ceremonies have developed in many countries (ibid., p. 197).

Holy Saturday commemorates Christ's rest in the tomb, and there is no service during daylight hours. As Christ rested in the grave, the faithful wait in prayer and fasting until the evening star announces the Easter Vigil. In the early centuries the catechumens would assemble in the church during the afternoon, and the rites which are still practiced in baptism were performed. This day is traditionally spent around the home in preparing the home and food for the Easter celebration.

From the beginning of Christianity, the feast of the Resurrection of Christ was celebrated as the most important and festive day of the whole year. For Christians, every Sunday is a "little Easter," consecrated to the memory of the risen Christ.

The word Easter originally meant the celebration of the spring sun, which had its birth in the East and brought new life to the earth. This symbolism was transferred to the supernatural meaning of our Easter — the new life of the risen Christ, Who is the eternal and uncrated Light. The Jewish Passover and the Christian Easter are significantly linked because Christ died on Passover Day. The lamb that had to be sacrificed for the deliverance of Israel is considered by the Church as prophetic of Him Who is the "Lamb of God, who takes away the sin of the world" (John 1:29).

In the early centuries, the faithful embraced with the words "*Surrexit Dominus vere*" (Christ is truly risen), to which the reply was "*Deo gratias*" (Thanks be to God). From the fourth century on, the mood of Christians turned into radiant joy at the sight of the first stars in the evening of Holy Saturday. The churches began to blaze with the light of lamps and candles, and the homes of the people shone with light. Multitudes crowded into the churches, joining in prayer. In later centuries, the vigil service began with the lighting of the *paschal candle*, a sacred symbol of Christ's Person. After the blessing of the candle, a prayer service was held, Bible passages were read, and the priests and people recited psalms, antiphons, and orations. The faithful spent the entire night in church.

Near midnight, the bishop and clergy went in procession to the baptismal font, usually found in a structure outside the church. There the baptismal water was consecrated with the same prayers used today. The catechumens were baptized, anointed, and given garments of white linen which they wore at all services until the end of Easter week. The vigil was concluded about dawn of Easter Sunday with the celebration of the Holy Sacrifice. During later centuries, some other rites, such as the blessing of the *Easter fire*, were added. This blessing was incorporated into the Roman

Our Mother of Perpetual Help, painting in the Redemptorist Church of St. Alphonsus in Rome, stolen and transported to Rome from Crete in the 15th century and similar to an original work in Constantinople attributed to St. Luke, is the object of ancient and worldwide devotion and novenas (see "Images").

liturgy during the latter part of the ninth century, and the blessing of the fire became the opening rite of the ceremonies on the Vigil of Easter.

The solemn words of the official calendar of the Western Church announce the celebration of Easter Sunday: "This is the day the Lord has made, the Feast of Feasts, and our Pasch — the Resurrection of our Savior Jesus Christ according to the flesh." Although there are no special ceremonies other than the Mass itself, the Latin church celebrates Mass in all churches with festive splendor and great solemnity on Easter Sunday.

The Easter Lamb

The lamb is the most significant symbol of Easter. The lamb, representing Christ, is usually shown with a flag of victory.

Prayers for the blessing of lambs date back to the seventh century. From the ninth century, the main feature of the Pope's Easter dinner was roast lamb. The ancient tradition of the Paschal lamb inspired the use of lamb as a popular Easter food among all the faithful. In Europe, small figures of a lamb made from butter, pastry, and sugar are popular.

Easter Eggs

The custom of Easter eggs developed among the nations of northern Europe and Christian Asia soon after their conversion to Christianity. Their history stems from the fertility lore of the Indo-European races. It was a startling event to see a living creature emerge from a seemingly dead object, and to our pre-Christian ancestors the egg became a symbol of spring and fertility. Converts to Christianity gave the egg a religious interpretation, seeing it as a symbol of the rock tomb out of which Christ emerged to new life. Additionally, since eggs were forbidden during the fast of Lent, they became a special sign of Easter joy, and the faithful painted them in gay colors. They were blessed and then eaten or presented as gifts to friends.

A special blessing in the Roman Ritual read thus: "We beseech Thee, O Lord, to bestow Thy benign blessing upon these eggs to make them a wholesome food for thy faithful, who gratefully partake of them in honor of the Resurrection of our Lord Jesus Christ."

In medieval times eggs were traditionally given at Easter to all servants, and to the children, along with other gifts. In most countries the eggs are stained in plain vegetable-dye colors. Among the Chaldeans, Syrians, and Greeks, the eggs were dyed crimson in honor of the blood of Christ. In Poland and Ukraine, simple designs are found on eggs called *krasanki*, and a number of eggs are made each year in a very distinctive design. These latter are masterpieces of patient labor and exquisite workmanship. These, called *pysanki*, are unique and are saved from year to year as heirlooms.

In Central Europe, eggs used for cooking Easter food are pierced with a small needle and the contents blown out. The shell is reserved and given to the children for use in egg games. The Armenians decorate these empty eggs with religious pictures as gifts, and in parts of Germany the eggs are decorated and hung from shrubs and trees much like a Christmas tree. The custom of hiding the eggs is universal.

The Easter Bunny

The rabbit was the most fertile animal our pre-Christian ancestors knew, serving as a symbol of abundant new life in the spring season. The Easter bunny has never had a religious symbolism, although the white meat is sometimes said to suggest purity and innocence. The Church has never had a special blessing for rabbits, and there is no link with the spiritual meaning of the sacred season. Throughout history, however, the Easter bunny has acquired a cherished role as the provider of Easter eggs for children in many countries.

The first mention of the Easter bunny and his eggs seems to be from a German book of 1572. In many sections of Germany, the children believed that the Easter bunny laid red eggs on Maundy Thursday and multicolored eggs the night before Easter Sunday. The first Easter bunnies of sugar and pastry were popular in southern Germany at the beginning of the last century (ibid., p. 236).

Easter Lily

Lilies have traditionally been symbols of beauty, perfection and goodness. Both in the Old and New Testaments, the Scriptures often make use of this symbolism. Our Lord Himself pointed the lily out to His Apostles, saying that "even Solomon in all his glory was not arrayed like one of these" (Mt 6:28).

The Easter lily did not directly originate from religious symbolism; it has, instead, acquired religious symbolism. This large white lily was introduced in Bermuda from Japan at the middle of the last century. The florist W.K. Harris brought it to the United States in 1882 and spread its use here. In America, it flowers first around Easter time, and soon came to be called the "Easter lily." The American public quickly made it a symbolic feature of the Easter celebration. Churches began using it as a decoration for Easter Day, and people made it a favorite in their homes for the Easter season (ibid., p. 236).

Images

One of the major criticisms of the Catholic church by uninformed fundamentalist Christians deals with the Catholic veneration of images. Catholics, according to them, are idolaters.

Catholic doctrine is quite clear on this point. We are not guilty of idolatry because the pictures and statues in the Church are honored, not adored. Just as people cherish photographs of their family and friends as reminders of them, so too we cherish our sacred images as reminders of Our Lord, the Blessed Virgin, and the saints. We honor our national flag not because of the cloth out of which it is made, but because of what it represents. It is this type of honor and respect that belongs to sacred images.

By the veneration of sacred images, effective and sometimes supernatural graces are obtained. There have been instances of miraculous pictures, statues and, crucifixes. Sacred images help us avoid distractions while praying by fixing our attention. They serve as a silent admonition which encourages us to imitation. Finally, they are a good means for instructing the faithful in religion. The greatest artists in the world have been Catholic artists, and their greatest masterpieces treat of religious subjects. Even an illiterate can understand a picture.

We honor Christ and the saints when we pray before crucifixes, relics, and sacred images. We honor them because it is the persons they represent that we are honoring; we adore Christ and we venerate the saints. Holy images have a holy purpose. We venerate the saints for God's sake and to increase in ourselves the wish to imitate their virtues. We venerate these images by praying before them, adorning them with flowers or precious objects, burning lights before them, and kissing them with reverence. We make visits to the tombs or shrines of the saints just as on civil holidays we honor our heroes by placing wreaths on their graves.

Of all sacred representations, the crucifix deserves our highest veneration because it is the sign of our redemption. It was on the cross that Our Lord died to save us sinners from the consequences of sin. The Church pays such honor to the crucifix that sacraments are administered, Mass is celebrated, and all acts of worship are performed in the presence of a crucifix. The crucifix is placed in the hands of the dying.

Catholics do not pray to the crucifix or to the sacred images, but to the persons they represent. Disrespect to a sacred image is disrespect to the one represented. Catholics do not believe that any divine power resides in any sacred image, and it is not the image that works any miracles. The numerous miracles worked through the use of relics and images are a result of God acting through them. Even today, relics and images continue to play a part in the working of miracles and the suspension of the natural law, but always and only as mere instruments of Almighty God.

There are literally hundreds of thousands of famous or well-known sacred images. Although paintings and statues are more common in the Western church, and icons (*ikons*) more prevalent in the Eastern churches, there is no form of artistic expression which has not been used in the creation of sacred images. The history of art itself cannot be separated from religion, for man has always given of his best artistic talents to his God. Just as with the case of relics, Christianity is not alone the custodian of sacred images.

Each painting, statue, or icon has its own unique history in the church. In this section, only a few representative images are included.

The Infant Jesus of Prague

Devotion to the Child Jesus under the title "Infant Jesus of Prague" is over three and a half centuries old. The devotion originated in Spain, spread to what is now Czechoslovakia, and from there to all parts of the globe. Replicas of the original statue dressed in royal priestly vestments are to be found in thousands of churches and private homes. In the United States, there is a national shrine in honor of the Christ Child under this title in Prague, Oklahoma.

In 1556, Maria Manriquez de Lara brought a precious family heirloom, a statue of the child Jesus, with her to Bohemia when she married the Czech nobleman Vratislav of Pernstyn. The statue of the child is eighteen inches tall, carved of wood, and thinly coated with wax. The left foot is barely visible under a long white tunic. The statue stands on a broad pedestal, and there is a waist-high silver case which holds it upright. The left hand holds a miniature globe surmounted by a cross, signifying the worldwide kingship of Christ. The right hand is extended in blessing in a form usually used by the Supreme Pontiff; the first two fingers are upraised to symbolize the two natures in Christ, while the folded thumb and last two fingers touch each other to represent the mystery of the Holy Trinity.

Since 1788, there have been two jeweled rings on the fingers of the statue. These were gifts of a noble family in thanks for the miraculous cure of their daughter. The head of the image has a wig of blond human hair. Old carvings and pictures indicate that at one time the wig may have been white. In 1655, the statue was solemnly crowned in a special coronation ceremony. The crown was presented by the supreme burgrave of the Czech kingdom. The original garments worn by the statue when it arrived in

Bohemia are still preserved. Since the great cholera epidemic of 1713, however, the garments of the statue have been changed with the liturgical season. The wardrobe of the Infant of Prague resembles liturgical vestments.

There are a number of sets of vestments belonging to the statue which are of artistic and historic importance, including sets presented in thanksgiving by Empress Maria Theresa and Emperor Ferdinand. Today, the nuns from St. Joseph's Church in the Mala Strana quarter of Prague enjoy the privilege of clothing the Infant in keeping with the ancient custom. At the time the change of vestments is made, numerous devotional objects such as medals, pictures and rosaries are touched to the statue to be distributed to all parts of the world.

Princess Polyxena Lobkowitz inherited the statue of the infant from her mother. She had a great devotion to it, honoring it highly in her own home. On the death of her husband in 1623, she determined to spend the rest of her life in works of charity and piety. She was particularly generous to the Discalced Carmelites of Prague. Their monastery had been founded by Emperor Ferdinand II. After the emperor moved to Vienna, the monastery, having lost its wealthy founder and patron, fell on hard times, often not even having enough to eat. (At that time, cloistered monasteries depended heavily on donations for their daily needs.)

In 1628, Princess Polyxena presented her beloved statue to the friars, telling them, prophetically, that as long as they honored the Child Jesus as king, venerating His image, they would not want. Her prediction was verified, and as long as the Divine Infant's image was honored the community prospered, spiritually and temporally. However, when the devotions relaxed, it seemed as if God's blessing departed from the house.

The statue was set up in the oratory of the monastery, and twice daily special devotions were performed before it. The novices were particularly devoted to the Holy Infant. One of them, Cyrillus of the Mother of God, was suffering interior trials. After prayers to the Child Jesus, he found a sudden relief from his worries and became the greatest apostle of the Holy image.

During the Thirty Years' War, the novitiate was moved to Munich, Germany in 1630. In 1631, King Gustavus Adolphus of Sweden, an inveterate foe of Catholicism, invaded, and many inhabitants of Prague fled, including all of the Carmelites except two who remained to protect the monastery. The enemy took possession of the monastery in November of 1631, and the house was plundered. The image of the Infant was thrown in a heap of rubbish behind the high altar, where it lay forgotten for seven years.

In 1637, Father Cyrillus returned to Prague. The monastery had suffered many reverses in recent years, and the city was again overrun with hostile troops. The prior of the community called the monks together to offer prayers. Father Cyrillus remembered the favors formerly received through the intercession of the Infant, and he asked permission to search the monastery in hopes that the statue might have been left behind when the monastery was plundered. At last the statue was found, and Father Cyrillus placed the dusty little image on an altar in the oratory, where the long-forgotten devotions were renewed with vigor.

One day, after the other monks had left the oratory, Father Cyrillus remained kneeling in front of the statue for hours, meditating on the divine goodness. In a mystical ecstasy, he heard the statue speak these words: "Have pity on me, and I will have pity on you. Give me my hands, and I will give you peace. The more you honor me, the more I will bless you!" Startled, the priest looked and noticed for the first time that the statues hands had been broken off. He went immediately to the prior to beg him to have the statue restored. The prior, not having the same devotion or understanding as Father Cyrillus, excused himself by saying that the monastery was too poor.

Shortly thereafter, a wealthy and pious man came to Prague and fell ill. Father Cyrillus was called to the dying man, who offered financial help to repair the statue. The prior, however, used the donated money to buy an entirely new statue instead of having the old one repaired. On its very first day, the new statue was shattered by a falling candlestick. To Father Cyrillus, this was an indication that the wishes of the Infant must be fulfilled literally.

The sorrowing priest took the damaged statue to his cell, where he prayed through the intercession of the Blessed Virgin for the money to repair the statue. No sooner had he finished his prayer than he was called to the church, where he found a noble lady waiting for him. She handed him a considerable amount of money and then disappeared.

Happily, Father Cyrillus took the money to the prior and again requested the repair of the statue. At last, the prior agreed, provided the repairs did not exceed a certain amount. Unfortunately, the estimates were too high, so again the statue was not repaired. Interiorly, the priest heard a voice telling him to place the statue at the entrance of the sacristy. He did so, and soon a stranger came and noticed the broken hands of the statue. The stranger offered to have the statue repaired at his own expense, an offer that was joyously accepted.

At last the repaired statue was placed in the church. A pestilence was raging in Prague at the time, and the prior himself nearly died. He vowed to spread the devotion of the Infant if he were cured. Shortly thereafter, he ordered a general devotion to the Infant, in which all the friars took part. At last the Infant had won the hearts of the Carmel of Prague and become a cornerstone of their devotion.

In 1641, a generous benefactress donated money to the monastery for the erection of an altar to the Blessed Trinity with a magnificently gilded tabernacle as the resting place for the miraculous statue, which was then exposed for public veneration. In 1642, a baroness financed the erection of a handsome chapel for the Infant which was blessed in 1644 on the feast of the Most Holy Name of Jesus, which has remained the principal feast day of the miraculous Infant ever since. In 1648, the Archbishop of Prague gave the first ecclesiastical approval of the devotion when he consecrated the chapel and gave permission to priests to say Mass at the chapel altar. In 1651 the Carmelite general made a canonical visitation to the monastery to examine matters regarding the devotion. The statue was solemnly crowned in 1655.

In 1741, the statue was moved to its final magnificent shrine on the epistle side of the church of Our Lady of Victory. It became one of the most famous and popular shrines in the world. In 1739 the Carmelites of the Austrian Province made the spread of the devotion a part of their apostolate. The popularity of the little King of Prague spread to other countries in the eighteenth century. Pope Leo XIII confirmed the Sodality of the Infant of Prague in 1896 and granted many indulgences to the devotion. Pope St. Pius X unified an organizing membership into a confraternity under the guidance of the Carmelites which increased the spread of the devotion in our own century. Church authorities have canonically established a U.S. national shrine to the Infant Jesus of Prague at Prague, Oklahoma.

Santo Niño de Atocha

Portrayed as a small boy, the image of the child Jesus known as *Santo Niño de Atocha* (Holy Child of Atocha) is usually dressed in a long gown with a cape that has a wide lace collar and frilled cuffs. On the cape is a cockleshell, a Spanish symbol for a pilgrim. Seated on a small chair, the Infant holds a basket of food, and a water gourd is suspended from a staff in his hand. The statues show the child wearing buckled sandals, often made of metal. He wears a large, floppy hat with a feather.

The story of *Santo Niño de Atocha* is a story rich in both history and pious devotion. Although the Holy Child is the miracle worker, the devotion is a Marian one too. As is proper, before a child is asked to do something, first the petitioner asks permission from his mother. Thus, the

Medals, from left: top, two of the Holy Face and St. Christopher; middle, St. Joseph; bottom, St. Maria Goretti (and Our Lady of Confidence) and the Miraculous Medal (see listings in "Medals").

novena to the Infant of Atocha begins with a prayer to Mary, Our Lady of Atocha.

Tradition says devotion to Our Lady of Atocha and her wonderworking child originated in Antioch, and that St. Luke the Evangelist was the sculptor of the first mother-and-child image. Thus Atocha could be a corruption of Antiochia. The devotion spread rapidly, and by 1162 it had reached Spain. The statue was in Toledo in the Church of St. Leocadia. In 1523, Charles V of Spain paid for an enormous temple and placed the statue under the care of the Dominicans. The image of the Divine Child was detachable, and devout families would borrow the image of the infant when a woman was about to give birth to her child.

The story of the miraculous nature of the statue begins in Spain during the dark years of the Moorish invaders. The Spanish were persecuted for their faith. In Atocha, a suburb of Madrid, many Spanish men were thrown into Moorish dungeons. As the Moors did not feed their prisoners, food was taken to them by their families. During one persecution, an order went out from the caliph in Atocha that no one except children twelve years old and younger would be permitted to bring food to the prisoners. Those with young children would manage to keep their relatives alive, but what of the others?

The women of the town went to the parish church, where there was a statue of Our Lady of Atocha with the Child Jesus that had been venerated for many years. They begged Our Lady to help them find a way to feed their husbands, sons, and brothers. Soon the children came home from the prison with a strange story. Those prisoners who had no young children to feed them were being visited and fed by a young boy. None of the children knew who he was, but the little water gourd he carried was never empty, and there was always plenty of bread in his basket to feed all the hapless prisoners without children to bring them their food. He always came at night, slipping past the sleeping guards or smiling politely at those who were alert. Those who had asked the Virgin of Atocha for a miracle began to suspect the identify of the little boy. As if in confirmation of the miracle they had prayed for, the shoes on the statue of the child Jesus were worn down. When they replaced the shoes with new ones, those too were worn out.

After Ferdinand and Isabella drove the Moors from Spain in 1492, the people continued to invoke the aid of Our Lady and her Holy Child. They especially asked help for those who were in jail and those who were "imprisoned" in the mines.

When the Spaniards came to the New World, they brought along the devotions of their native regions. Those from Madrid naturally brought their devotion to Our Lady and her miracle-working pilgrim Infant. In 1540, silver mines were found in Mexico, and mineworkers migrated here. In Plateros, a tiny village near the mines of Fresnillo, a church was built in honor of *El Niño de Santa Maria de Atocha*. Here the Holy Child continued his miracle-working for those who appealed to him, through his mother, for help. Soon the shrine became a major place of pilgrimage. The original statue in the shrine there was donated by a rich mine owner. It was made as a duplicate of the one in Spain. It too had a removable Infant which could be borrowed. The Infant at one time was lost, and then a replacement was carved to size to be affixed to the original statue; the new Babe had Indian features. Those whose prayers were answered left *retablos* in thanksgiving. These are pictures painted on wood or on tin in which folk artists show the story of a miracle. There are few words, but the pictures tell the story. There are *retablos* there dating from the 1500s to our own times. In Mexico, a land of many churches, only the shrine of Our Lady of Guadalupe has more of these thanksgiving plaques. Through a century of revolution, Mexico has provided many prisoners for the Holy Child to aid. Annually, other miraculous cures are reported here.

The original statue of Our Lady of Atocha in the shrine holds the Holy Child in her left arm. The detachable infant is often taken in procession, and sometimes taken on "visits" to other churches in other cities.

In the 1800s, a man from New Mexico made a pilgrimage to Fresnillo and took back with him a small statue of the Holy Child. This statue was enshrined in Chimayo, near Santa Fe. There, the devotion grew as it had when it came to the New World.

Some of the first American troops to see action in World War II were from the New Mexico National Guard. They fought bravely on Corregidor, with its underground tunnels and defenses. The Catholics remembered that the *Santo Niño de Atocha* had long been considered a patron of all who were trapped or imprisoned. Many of them made a vow that if they survived the war they would make a pilgrimage from Santa Fe to Chimayo in Thanksgiving. At the end of the war two thousand pilgrims, veterans of Corregidor, the Bataan death march, and Japanese prison camps, together with their families, walked the long and rough road from Santa Fe to Chimayo. Some walked barefoot to the little adobe shrine.

The prayers and novenas to the miracle-working little Child Jesus all begin with prayers to Our Lady of Atocha. As Jesus is shown as a small child, first His clients have to ask His mother's permission for him to go to their aid. Then the miracle working child Jesus hastens to assist those who need His help — He visits the hearts of all with His tender love.

The Holy Child of Aracoeli

A crowned, jeweled, life-size figure of the child Jesus is venerated in a special chapel at the Basilica of Santa Maria in the Aracoeli quarter of Rome. The statue is world-famous, and pilgrims flock to venerate it because of many reported miracles, favors, and answered prayers.

The statue of the Holy *Bambino* dates back to the end of the fifteenth century. It was carved from the wood of an olive tree from the Mount of Olives near Gethsemane by a pious Franciscan friar. A quaint tradition tells that the friar did not have the necessary paints to complete his work, and that the statue was miraculously finished by an angel. As the friar returned to Rome, a severe storm at sea caused him to throw the small case containing the statue overboard. The case floated to the port of Livorno by itself in the wake of the ship.

In the Eternal City, the statue soon became famous for reported miracles and was treated with special honor. One day during the Christmas season, a noble Roman matron stole the statue and hid it carefully in her home. She became severely ill, and her confessor ordered her to return the statue. The legend continues having the statue leave her house by itself during the night and return to its place in the church as the bells of the basilica rang in joy at the miracle.

Rich gifts of gold and precious stones give witness to the gratitude of the faithful for the innumerable graces received. A number of times attempts have been made to sacrilegiously despoil the statue. In 1798, Serafin Petrarca, a Roman citizen, paid a huge ransom to save the statue from being burned by Napoleon's troops.

Pregnant women often visit the Holy Bambino to receive a special blessing, and many return bringing their infants to be consecrated to the Divine Child. Often the statue has been divested of its golden trappings and carried to the bedside of the sick faithful.

Pope Leo XIII and the Vatican Chapter ordered its coronation, which took place with a solemn ritual in 1897.

At Christmas, a special crèche is set up in the church. Sometimes the Infant is placed in the lap of a statue of the Virgin. Other times he is placed in a crib. Throughout the season, the children of Rome come to sing, recite poems, and perform playlets for the Infant King. At dusk on the Feast of the Epiphany, in a special ceremony, a blessing is given to the pilgrims gathered on the Capitoline Hill.

Christ of the Andes

In Uspallata Pass, on the border line between Argentina and Chile is the most famous statue in South America. It is the Christ of the Andes.

There were a number of disputes between Chile and Argentina over the boundary line between the two countries. Finally war seemed certain. Then the two countries wisely decided to divide the disputed land between them. A friendship grew between the two countries. The people wanted to erect a monument to remind future generations that peace is better than war.

A famous sculptor was commissioned to make a figure of Christ out of the melted cannon of the two countries. Then came the problem of how to move the tremendously heavy statue up the steep mountain trails. Mules were used for part of the distance, but finally even they were unable to complete the chore. Thousands of soldiers and sailors of the two countries hitched themselves to the ropes and dragged the statue to the place where it now stands, twelve thousand feet above the sea. At the base of the statue is an inscription which reads: "Sooner shall these mountains crumble into dust than the Argentines and Chileans break the peace sworn at the feet of Christ the Redeemer."

Christ of St. John of the Cross

One of the most moving and beautiful modern religious paintings is Salvador Dali's "Christ of St. John of the Cross." Replicas of the painting are found worldwide, although people often do not connect this deeply religious picture to the flamboyant, often outrageous master of surrealism Salvador Dali.

After Dali's famous painting "The Persistence of Memory," easily recognizable by any school-age art student because of its limp watches and bleak landscape, Dali's style became increasingly photographic in its realism. In the mid-'30s, he began to make visits to Italy, and the classical art style of the Renaissance stimulated a new interest in both his realism and his fantasies. This classical ambition combined with religious conversion to inspire a continuing series of monumental mythological and religious subjects. "Christ of St. John of the Cross" was painted in 1951. The monumental oil, 80 3/4 by 45 5/8 inches, is Dali's challenge to the Renaissance masters of anatomy and perspective. The figure is strongly foreshortened like a crucifix inclined toward a worshiper as he kisses it. Christ on the Cross is suspended over a port landscape with fishermen and boats. It is considered one of Dali's most dramatic and popular pictures. The picture is in the Glasgow Art Gallery and Museum.

The Pantokrator

The Pantokrator is the name given in Eastern Rites to an image of Our Lord as the Ruler of Heaven and Earth. It is derived from the Greek word meaning "almighty" and corresponds to the title "Christ the King" in the

Roman rite. This picture of Christ is the major one used in the Eastern Rites. The picture is generally located on one of the central domes of the church.

Our Lady of Guadalupe

In the beginning of the sixteenth century in Mexico, an idolatrous worship of Quetzalcoatl and other gods flourished. Although Mexico had been conquered for Spain by Cortez, the Indians still held to their ancient religion, which emphasized human sacrifice. In the Aztec nation alone, twenty thousand human lives were sacrificed annually to their gods.

Our Lady appeared to Juan Diego, a Christian convert, on the hill of Tepayac on December 9, 1531. She requested that he go to the Bishop of Mexico, in Mexico City, and ask that a church be built on the spot. The hill held special significance in the pagan religion of the Indians. At first, the bishop refused the appeal, thinking that Juan was merely imagining things. The next day, Our Lady appeared again and repeated her request. This time, Juan was so sincere in his petition that the bishop was more inclined to listen and told Juan to ask the lady for some sort of a sign as proof of the apparition. At a third meeting, Juan mentioned the bishop's request, and the lady promised to give the sign the following morning. The morning of December 12, Juan awoke to discover that his aged uncle was very ill, and he left hurriedly to bring a priest from the city to administer the last rites. As he neared the hill, he remembered the request of the lady and, thinking that she would delay him, hurried around the bottom of the hill to avoid her. There she was, however, and when she asked him where he was going, he explained about his sick relative.

Our Lady assured Juan that his uncle would recover, and then sent him to the top of the hill to fetch some flowers for her. Juan knew that nothing grew there except some cactus, so he was greatly surprised to find many flowers in bloom. He picked a large bouquet, and so as not to drop them, he put them in his *tilma*, a cloak woven of vegetable fiber.

When Juan reached the lady again, she tied the ends of the *tilma* at his neck and charged him not to show the flowers to anyone until he was in the presence of the bishop.

On reaching the bishop's palace again, and after a lengthy wait, Juan was at last admitted to the bishop's presence. Only then did he unfold his tilma. Castillian roses cascaded to the floor. Immediately, all those in the room fell to their knees. A beautiful image of the Blessed Virgin was imprinted on the tilma.

Juan rushed home to tell his uncle, but his uncle was coming to meet him with the news that he too had seen the beautiful lady. She had spoken in his native language and told him that the image was to be known by the name of the "Entirely Perfect Virgin, Holy Mary," and that the image would be the means to crush or stamp out the religion of the stone serpent. That Our Lady's mission was successful is shown by the fact that within seven years, eight million Indians had come voluntarily to the Franciscans and other missionaries and requested instructions and baptism.

Juan and his uncle spoke to the Spanish bishop through the use of interpreters, and when they were telling about Mary's words to Juan's uncle, or so most modern scholars believe, the words they spoke were not translated correctly. To the Spanish ears of the translator, their words seemed to say that the image was to be known by the name "Virgin of Guadalupe", which was the name of a popular shrine in Spain dedicated to the Virgin.

Is the image really miraculous, or only a painting? It has been studied from time to time by various experts from all fields, and all are in agreement that no artistic process currently known on earth was used to make the picture. The gold on the picture is a precious gold powder which is not held on by any fixative or glue. The fine black lines which outline the picture were drawn on by human hands at a later date, as was a crown which was not originally on the image. It is interesting to note that the crown, although of real gold, has tarnished and almost disappeared, whereas the other gold on the image is still in good condition.

The image is sixty-six by forty-one inches, and the figure is four feet eight inches tall. This makes the image lifesize. The colors have stayed fresh.

In 1921, during the revolution and the persecution of Catholics in Mexico, a stick of dynamite hidden in a bouquet of flowers was placed on the altar to destroy the image. It exploded, causing a great deal of damage. It broke all of the windows in the church, tore out marble blocks from the altar, and knocked a heavy bronze crucifix standing under the image to the floor, leaving it bent and twisted. Nothing, however, happened to the image. The glass which covers it was not even cracked. The preservation of the image in this case is miraculous in itself.

In 1976, work on a new basilica was completed and the shrine re-dedicated. Study and research on the image continues, and annually thousands flock to the site to pay homage to Mary under the title Our Lady of Guadalupe.

Twenty popes have issued decrees concerning the image. Our Lady of Guadalupe is the patroness of all the Americas.

Our Mother of Perpetual Help

One of the best-loved and most widely known images of Our Lady is that of Our Mother of Perpetual Help. From 1865 when Pope Pius IX gave custody of the image to the Redemptorist Order, the members of this congregation have followed his command to "make Our Mother of Perpetual Help known throughout the world." Today, copies of the original Byzantine Madonna are found worldwide, and devotion is strong for this mother who always stands ready to help her children. The Redemptorist Fathers are most willing to foster devotion to Our Mother of Perpetual Help, and will help bishops, priests, parish councils, religious organizations and individuals to learn of her (see appendix).

The picture of Perpetual Help is similar in many ways to the Byzantine Madonna known as the Hodegetria, which tradition holds St. Luke painted from life. However, the theme of the Perpetual Help image is a portrayal of sorrow and thus falls into the "Passion type" of Byzantine Madonnas. Mary's head is tilted maternally toward her Child. Her hand loosely clasps the tiny hand of her Son. The Christ Child has a look of fright and sorrow as he gazes into the future and sees the vision of His Passion and death awaiting him. Hastily He has run to find refuge in the arms of His Mother. So swiftly has he run to her that his little sandal has come loose. The background of the picture is a simple, unadorned field of gold. This symbolizes divinity. The Greek letters identify the persons portrayed in the picture. They are the Mother of God, Jesus Christ, and the Archangels Michael and Gabriel, who hold the symbols of the Passion.

The Mother of God is the central figure of this picture. Her eyes are gazing toward those who are looking at the picture. With sorrow and love she invites all to place their confidence in her. With her left arm she supports her Child so closely that the lines of his body blend into hers. On Mary's forehead is a simple eight-pointed star of gold and a four-pointed ornamental cross which may have been added to the original picture by a later artist. Around her head is a plain golden halo, while the halo of the Child is decorated with a cross to show his dignity and office. Her tunic, visible at the neck and sleeves is red and fringed with golden stripes. A green inner veil holds back her hair. A cloak of rich blue covers her head and drapes over her shoulders. In typical Byzantine artistic style, shadows are omitted, so the folds of her clothing are indicated by thin gold lines.

The image of Christ seems to gaze with wide-open eyes into space. His face shows serious contemplation. Christ foresaw His crucifixion, and when the realization of the anguish and suffering He was to undergo seemed to overwhelm Him, He knew he could find refuge in the loving embrace of His Mother. The Child's fingers hold His Mother's right hand,

*Miscellaneous commemorative medals not specified in the text,
including medals from Lourdes, Guadalupe, etc. (see "Medals").*

although they rest loosely. Though Mary is the Mother, He is her God and to Him she owes all her graces. The features of the Child closely resemble those of the Mother. His head is covered with curly auburn hair and is surrounded with an embellished halo, a sign of His divinity. He is clothed in a full-sleeved green tunic, held in at the waist with a reddish sash. A yellowish-brown mantle is draped over His right shoulder and covers most of His body. To the left of the picture is the Archangel Michael. The Archangel Gabriel is on the right. Both are clothed in purple tunics and their wings are green, streaked with gold. In order to show great reverence to the instruments of the Passion, the angels are carrying them in veiled hands. Michael holds the urn which contains the gall mixed with myrrh offered to Our Lord by the soldiers. In the urn are the lance and a reed topped by a sponge. Gabriel carries the cross and holds the nails.

Inscriptions in Latin are found on some of the copies of this ancient picture. On a few copies are found these words: "Behold Thy Son! Behold Thy Mother!" Other copies carry a longer inscription which gives the full significance of the picture: "He who first brought to the Most Pure Lady the news of joy now shows beforehand the signs of the Passion; but Christ, clothed in mortal flesh and featuring death, is frightened at this vision."

The first known part of the story of the image of Our Mother of Perpetual Help was written on a large piece of parchment affixed to a wooden tablet which hung, along with the picture, for many years in St. Matthew's Church in Rome. Later the parchment was fastened to the picture itself. Written in both Latin and Italian, the document gives a history of the picture's arrival in Rome in 1499 and its enthronement in the Augustinian church of St. Matthew. Copies of this parchment are in the Vatican Library.

A condensed translation of the document tells that a merchant, native to Crete, stole the picture of the Virgin which had been the instrument of many miracles on the island. He boarded a ship, and at sea a storm arose. Although the sailors knew nothing of their precious cargo, their fervent prayers to the Mother of God were heard and they were saved from the storm. The merchant came to Rome and was stricken with a fatal disease. He asked a Roman friend to care for him, and he was taken into his friend's home and nursed tenderly. Before his death, the merchant begged his friend to fulfill a last request. He told him about the theft of the famous picture and asked his friend to put the picture in a church where it could be properly venerated.

After the merchant's death, the picture was found among his belongings, but the Roman's wife fancied it and hung it in her bedroom. The Blessed Virgin, in a number of visions, told the Roman to put the picture in a more honorable place, but he ignored her requests. Finally, the Virgin appeared to the Roman's six-year-old daughter, telling her to warn her mother and her grandfather to take the picture out of the house. After further delays, she appeared to the child again and commanded her to have her mother place her picture between St. Mary Major and St. John Lateran in the church dedicated to St. Matthew. At last, the mother obeyed the heavenly injunction and called the Augustinian fathers who were in charge of that church. Thus the picture was enshrined in the church of St. Matthew in March 1499. Here the image of the Mother of Perpetual Help reigned from her own chosen place for three centuries until the destruction of the church by the French invaders in 1798. During these centuries, the Church of St. Matthew was one of the most important pilgrimage sites in Rome, and pilgrims came from all corners of the world to worship at the shrine of Our Mother of Perpetual Help.

In 1798, the French military governor of Rome ordered that thirty churches be destroyed and the land put to better use. The Church of St. Matthew was one of those to be destroyed. The Augustinians hastily removed some of the artworks and the church furnishings, taking some items to St. John Lateran and some, including the miraculous image, to St. Eusebio's. Our Mother of Perpetual Help was sent into exile and oblivion.

The picture remained at St. Eusebio's until 1819, when the Augustinians were transferred to the small church and monastery of Santa Maria in Posterula on the other side of the city. Here there was already a picture of Our Lady in the church, so the image of Perpetual Help was put in the monastery chapel, where it remained until 1865. One of the Italian lay brothers was transferred to this monastery in 1840. He recognized the picture and remembered his devotion to the picture when it was in St. Matthew's. Brother Augustine told the story of the picture to his favorite altar boy, Michael Marchi.

The Congregation of the Most Holy Redeemer, also known as the Redemptorists, was founded by St. Alphonsus Mary Liguori in 1732 to minister to the most abandoned. The congregation grew rapidly, and in 1853 the Pope commanded the vicar general of the order to establish a house in Rome to serve as their worldwide headquarters. The property they bought was on the Esquiline Hill and was shaped like a triangle. The estate lay along the base of the hill, and at the tip of the triangle were the ruins of the old St. Matthew's church. As the Redemptorists built, they also began to research the history of their property. In 1859, their historian discovered some documents telling of a famous image of Our Lady which used to be enshrined in the church of St. Matthew. Father Michael Marchi, the former altar boy, told his Redemptorists brothers that he knew about the famous image and where its current location was.

During 1862-63, a Jesuit preacher named Father Francis Blosi delivered a series of sermons on some of the famous pictures of Our Lady that hung in the churches of Rome. One picture that he spoke about was the image of Perpetual Help. In his sermon he spoke of the previous fame of the picture and asked if any of his hearers knew where the picture was. He expressed the wish that the picture, if it could be located, be returned to Mary's chosen place on the Esquiline Hill so that all the faithful might come and pray before it.

When the Redemptorists heard of Father Blosi's sermon and realized that Our Lady had designated a spot for her shrine, they became excited. Again Father Michael Marchi was called on to tell his story of the picture and of its hidden repose in the chapel of the Augustinian monastery. The community brought the news to the highest superior of the Redemptorists, Father Nicholas Mauron. Father Blosi was contacted and sent a copy of his sermon for the consideration of the superior. Instead of hastening to claim the picture, Most Reverend Father Mauron directed the men at St. Alphonsus to pray for the guidance of the Holy Spirit in this matter. They complied with his directive and prayed for almost three years until December 1865, at which time Father Mauron obtained an audience with the Holy Father Pope Pius IX. To him Father Mauron unfolded the detailed story of the picture of Our Mother of Perpetual Help. After reading the sworn statement of Father Marchi, the Holy Father, a great devotee of our Blessed Mother, took the paper and on the reverse wrote directions that the image of Perpetual Help be given into the care of the Redemptorists at the church of St. Alphonsus, with the provision that the Redemptorist superior substitute a suitable picture to the Augustinians. The Augustinians chose a careful copy of the image, and rejoiced that the picture would receive the honor she deserved at the site which she herself had chosen almost four centuries before.

The image was brought to St. Alphonsus on January 19, 1866. Although the picture was more than four centuries old, and possibly four times that age, the colors were still bright and fresh. Only a small section of one of the sleeves had faded. The picture, painted on wood, had suffered some small damage on the reverse from worms. There were a number of nail holes left in the picture, but no irreparable damages. A skillful Polish artist was chosen and entrusted with restoring the picture. His work was done, and a solemn procession was held April 26, 1866. During the course of the procession, a number of striking miraculous events were reported.

When the picture reached the Church of St. Alphonsus, it was placed on the high altar. The image of Mary had at last come home and remains there to this day.

The wealthy Italian nobleman Alexander Sfirzo had left in his will a large sum of money for the purpose of crowning certain images as directed by the Pope. Images crowned must meet three conditions: (1) the devotion to the image must be approved by the bishop of the area, (2) the devotion must have a long history and (3) the picture or statue must have a reputation for being divinely chosen and with a reputation as an instrument of miracles. The Image of Perpetual Help fit all three of the requirements, and on June 23, 1867, the image was solemnly crowned.

Our Lady of Czestochowa

In the town of Czestochowa, Poland, is a church containing a painting of Our Lady which is regarded by many as an actual portrait of the Madonna, painted during her life time by St. Luke the Evangelist on the top of a cypress-wood table.

An ancient legend tells how the painting was brought to Poland. Nothing is known of the first years of the picture's history. In 326, when St. Helen went to Jerusalem to search for the true cross, she also found the picture of Our Lady. She gave the picture to her son, Constantine, who had a shrine built for it in Constantinople. There it was credited with saving the city from attacking Saracens when it was displayed from the city's walls during battle.

Years later, the Emperor Charlemagne visited Constantinople, and when he was offered his choice of any of the treasures in the city, he chose only the portrait of our lady. Charlemagne presented the painting to Prince Leo of Ruthenia.

For hundreds of years, the picture remained at the royal palace. Then enemy troops invaded the country. Urgently the king prayed to Our Lady to aid his tiny army. Through the intercession of Our Lady, a heavy darkness fell on the enemy, and in the confusion they began destroying their own troops. Later, the Ruthenian king had a dream in which the Blessed Mother requested him to take her picture to the Mount of Light (*Jasna Gora*) in Poland. He took the picture at once and left it with a group of Paulite fathers.

The monks built a shrine for the painting at Czestochowa, and a number of miraculous events occurred there. Soon it became the most famous shrine in Poland.

An attempted theft resulted in a slashmark on the face of the virgin. Later, vandals set fire to the shrine and only the picture remained unburned. The smoke (or centuries of vigil lights) darkened the picture which resulted in its popular name, "The Black Madonna."

In 1655, in gratitude for a military victory, the King of Poland placed the country under the protection of Blessed Mother and named Our Lady of Czestochowa the queen of the crown of Poland.

Today, Poland is no longer a monarchy. The Black Madonna remains, however, queen in the hearts of Polish Catholics everywhere.

Our Lady of the Rosary of Pompeii

Blessed Bartolo Longo, while visiting the valley of Pompeii on business in 1872, was shocked and filled with great pity at the ignorance, poverty, and lack of religion of the inhabitants of the area. His generous heart was moved, and he promised Our Lady to do all in his power to promote devotion to the rosary among the people of the area.

In order to encourage the people, he determined to purchase a picture of Our Lady with her rosary to be exposed for veneration. Dominican sister offered him a large painting which had been bought at a junk shop for three francs. Seeing his hesitation, as the picture was in poor condition and rather ugly, she told him not to hesitate about taking the picture and predicted that it would work miracles. Bartolo accepted the picture and made arrangements for a wagoner to transport it to Pompeii.

Blessed Bartolo himself described the picture, which was dilapidated, wrinkled, soiled, and torn —"Not only was it worm-eaten, but the face of the Madonna was that of a course, rough countrywoman . . . a piece of canvas was missing just above her head . . . her mantle was cracked. Nothing can be said of the hideousness of the other figures. St. Dominic looked like a street idiot. To Our Lady's left was St. Rose. This latter I had changed later into a St. Catherine of Siena. . . . I hesitated whether to refuse the gift or to accept."

The wagoner arrived at the chapel door with the large painting wrapped in a sheet on top of a load of manure which he was delivering to a nearby field! Thus did Our Lady of Pompeii arrive in the valley which would become one of the major places of pilgrimage in honor of Our Lady.

At first, everyone who saw the picture was disappointed. An artist refurbished the unsightly canvas and ornamented it with diamonds donated by the faithful. A crown was placed on the head of the Madonna, and the painting was solemnly mounted on a throne of marble imported from Lourdes.

Bartolo later commented, "There is something about that picture which impresses the soul not by its artistic perfection but by a mysterious charm which impels one to kneel and pray with tears."

Immediately on its exposition, the picture became a veritable fountain of miracles.

First, a young epileptic girl in Naples was restored to health on the very day that the picture was re-exposed for veneration. Her aunt had heard of the plans to form a rosary confraternity in Pompeii and vowed to assist in the building of the church if the child got well. Next, a young woman dying in agony was completely recovered, immediately after her relatives had made similar promises to Our Lady of Pompeii. A Jesuit priest who had been persuaded by the Countess di Fusco to put his faith in the Virgin of Pompeii was cured of terminal disease immediately, and the following Feast of the Holy Rosary he sang the Mass and acknowledged his cure from the pulpit at Pompeii. In less than ten years, over 940 cures here reported at the shrine.

Today, the picture is framed in gold and encrusted with diamonds and precious gems which hide all but the faces of the saints and the Holy Child. Daily, pilgrims plead with Our Lady for her graces and favors. In this valley where once a pagan religion thrived, Our Lady reigns over her subjects whom she calls to adoration of her son.

Our Lady of Prompt Succor

The Ursuline monastery of New Orleans was founded under the auspices of Louis XV of France by a band of French Ursulines in 1727. Other sisters came from France, and in 1763, when Louisiana became a Spanish possession, Spanish sisters helped to carry on the work. In 1800 when Louisiana again became French territory, the Spanish sisters left for Cuba, fearing that the horrors of the recent French revolution would be repeated in the colonies. Thus by 1803 only seven Ursulines remained to carry on the boarding school, day school, orphanage, courses of instruction for the Indians and Negroes, and the nursing of the sick. The superior appealed to a cousin of hers in France, Mother St. Michel, for aid and personnel.

Mother St. Michel had been driven from her convent by the Reign of Terror, and as soon as the first indication of religious tolerance appeared, she had, with another young woman, opened a boarding school for young girls which was beginning to realize all the hopes the bishop of her diocese had for it. Her bishop was happy to have such a zealous worker among his flock and did not want to lose her. On receiving the appeal from her cousin, Mother St. Michel asked her spiritual director for his advice. He demurred. On direct appeal to the bishop, the answer came, "Only the Pope can give you authorization." This reply amounted almost to a definite "no," as the Pope was in Rome, a virtual prisoner of Napoleon, and his jailers were under strict injunction not to allow him to correspond with anyone. Additionally, there was no reliable way of sending messages. Nonetheless,

Mother St. Michel wrote her request, concluding, "Most Holy Father, I appeal to your apostolic tribunal. I am ready to submit to your decision. Speak. Faith teaches me that you are the voice of the Lord. I await your orders. 'Go' or 'Stay', from Your Holiness will be the same to me."

The letter had been written for three months, but no opportunity had presented itself to send it. One day, as she was praying before a statue of Mary, Mother felt inspired to call on the Queen of Heaven with these words, "O Most Holy Virgin Mary, if you obtain a prompt and favorable answer to my letter, I promise to have you honored in New Orleans under the title of Our Lady of Prompt Succor."

That Mother St. Michel's trustful prayer was pleasing to Our Lady, and that she wished to be honored in the New World under this title are shown by the prompt and favorable reply she received. The letter was dispatched on March 19, 1809, and the reply is dated in Rome on April 28.

That the reply directed Mother to place herself at the head of religious aspirants and go to Louisiana is miraculous in itself. The Pope was well aware of the need for workers such as Mother in France. Many would be needed to regenerate what the Revolution had torn down. Nonetheless, he gave his approval of her voyage, and her bishop acknowledged that his hopes to keep her in France were defeated. He requested the privilege of blessing the statue of Our Lady which Mother St. Michel had commissioned according to her promise.

On the arrival of the pious missionaries in New Orleans in December of 1810, this precious statue was solemnly installed in the convent chapel, and from that time the veneration to Mary under the title of Our Lady of Prompt Succor has been constantly growing and spreading all across the United States.

Prayers before this statue are credited with saving the Ursuline convent from fire in 1812. The victory of Andrew Jackson's American forces over the British in the battle of New Orleans in 1815 is another favor attributed to the all-powerful intercession of Our Lady of Prompt Succor. The chronicles of the Ursuline monastery record numerous favors, both spiritual and temporal, wrought through the intercession of Our Lady of Prompt Succor. By papal decree in 1851, Pius IX authorized the celebration of the feast of Our Lady of Prompt Succor. The statue was solemnly crowned by the papal delegate in 1895. This was the first ceremony of this type in the United States. In 1928, a new shrine in Our Lady's honor was consecrated, and by a decree of the Sacred Congregation of Rites the Holy See approved and confirmed the choice of Our Lady of Prompt Succor as the principal patroness of the City of New Orleans and the State of Louisiana.

BLESSED
LOUIS ORIONE
1872 - 1940

Founder of the
Sons of Divine Providence
(Don Orione Fathers)
Little Missionary Sisters
of Charity

BEATIFIED
October 26, 1980

DON LOUIS ORIONE

DON LUIGI ORIONE

SAINT ANNE

PRAYER TO ST. ANNE
With my heart full of the
most sincere veneration, I
Prostrate myself before thee,
O glorious St. Anne. Thou
art that creature of privilege
and predilection, who by the
extraordinary virtues and holiness did merit from God
the high favor of giving life
to her who si the Treasury
of all graces, blessed among

*Medals commemorating various saints and beati (blessed); St.
Odilia Medal (right, center) is a third-class relic, touched
to a first-class relic at the saint's shrine (see "Medals").*

Our Lady of Grace

Our Lady of Grace is the title of a picture of the madonna found in 1610 by Venerable Dominic of Jesus and Mary, a Spanish Discalced Carmelite. In 1610, Ven. Dominic bought an old dilapidated building to convert into a convent. On a rubbish heap he found a bust painting of Our Lady in bad condition. He cleaned it, repaired it, and began to venerate it. Legend has it that one night while he prayed before the picture the face became animated, and Our Lady spoke to Dominic. She promised to answer favors and especially hearken to prayers for those in Purgatory.

The portrait shows the Madonna wearing a full veil, a blue mantle decorated on the right shoulder with a rosette-backed star, and a red gown. A jeweled crown and a necklace were added later. The head is slightly inclined to the left, and the image is sometimes called "Our Lady of the Bowed Head."

A number of miracles were associated with the picture. It was moved several times, and finally enshrined in the Carmelite Church in the District of Dobling in Vienna. In 1931, on the occasion of the third centenary of its appearance in Vienna, the revered picture was given a papal crown, presented by a legate of Pope Pius XI.

Our Lady of Providence

The original picture of Our Lady of Providence was painted about the year 1580 by Scipione Pulzoni, a native of Gaeto, Italy. In 1664, this painting was placed in the Church of San Carlo ai Catinari in Rome. Placed in the keeping of the Barnabite Fathers, the picture was enshrined in a monastery corridor and given the title *Mater Divinae Providentiae.* Many people who visited the shrine reported remarkable favors received through the intercession of Our Lady of Providence.

The Icon of Our Lady of Good Counsel
Our Lady of Shkodra

Shut behind a corroding iron curtain, deep in the hearts of the faithful Albanian Catholics, lies a deep devotion to Our Lady under the title of Our Lady of Shkodra. The miraculous image is in Genazzano, Italy, venerated throughout the Western Church under the title Our Lady of Good Counsel. In spite of Communist persecution, however, the Catholics in Albania even today love and honor *Zoja e Bekueme* (The Blessed Lady) and ask Our Lady of Shkodra for her help and protection in their struggles and sufferings.

The holy legend of the ancient icon has been told from generation to generation and has even been recorded by Church commissions.

Albanians have always cherished a particular love for *Zoja e Bekueme.*

Churches and chapels in her honor covered the countryside. One of these, beneath the old Illyrian fortress of Shkodra, was a center of special devotion because of its beautiful icon of Our Lady. The painting hung over the main altar, and its fame abounded with stories of miracles and protection.

The church became a source of consolation and encouragement during the time of the invasion the Ottoman Turks. As the Turks overran Albania, the last stronghold of Albanian resistance was Shkodra. Throughout the land, the Turkish invaders had desecrated and destroyed churches and had massacred the "infidel Christians." One day during the siege of Shkodra, two escaping Albanians stopped at the church to pray for their safe journey. While fervently praying, they noticed the painting moving slowly away from the wall. They followed it outside and suddenly the icon began to glow as brightly as a star. The two Albanians, Gjorgji and DeSclavis, kept their eyes fixed on the bright icon as it began to lead them across plains and mountains, then over the Adriatic Sea. They followed it to Rome, where the painting disappeared. Questioning everyone they met, they finally heard of a miraculous image which had appeared in Genazzano. Here they found the icon, and thus they settled down and made the city their home.

Numerous miracles and favors were reported by those who prayed before the icon. According to testimony given by several pilgrims from Albania before a papal investigatory commission appointed by Pope Paul II in 1470, the painting had originally been venerated at a church in Shkodra, Albania, and had been miraculously transported to the church in Genazzano. The commission decreed that this Madonna was none other than the *Zoja e Bukueme* venerated for many centuries in Albania.

Urban VIII made the first papal visit to the shrine in 1630, petitioning an end to the pestilence raging in Rome and throughout Italy. In 1864, Pius IX came on pilgrimage to Genazzano, declaring his own devotion to the Mother of God under the title of Our Lady of Good Counsel. Leo XIII was born near the church and had a great devotion to Our Lady under this title. He inserted the title into the Litany of Loreto. Pius XII dedicated his pontificate to her, and Pope John XXIII made a pilgrimage to the sanctuary to ask her aid for the Church before Vatican Council II.

At the beginning of this century, a magnificent sanctuary was constructed in Albania, and annually on her feast thousands of pilgrims walked barefoot to the sanctuary while praying the rosary. The bishops of Albania officially declared the Madonna of Shkodra the patroness of Albania in 1895. Sadly, with the advent of communism, public displays of Marian devotion were brutally suppressed, along with all other religious activity. The Communists attempted to prevent private devotion, although they admit themselves that they have had little success in this regard. Soon after a reconsecration of the country in 1946, the sanctuary was confiscated by communist authorities and turned into a dance hall. It was razed in 1967.

Albanian Christians continued to visit and pray at the ruins in devout simplicity. In 1987 they were forbidden to enter the ruins, but the ban was lifted on the day before the feast of Our Lady of Good Counsel.

Our Lady, Queen of Peace

The miraculous statue of Our Lady, Queen of Peace, is venerated in the chapel of the Religious of the Sacred Hearts of Jesus and Mary in Paris, France. The statue is eleven inches high and is carved of chestnut-brown wood. The Virgin is represented holding her Divine Son on her left arm, while in her right hand she holds the symbol of peace, an olive branch. The Christ Child holds a cross, representing the price paid for the gift of peace to mankind.

Documents trace the statue to the possession of a noble French family of the sixteenth century. The family members who showed the greatest devotion to Our Lady was charged with custody of the statue. While praying before this statue, one of the family members, the Duc de Joyeuse, was inspired with a call to the religious life. He had a chapel built in her honor in the Capuchin house in Paris, later opened to the faithful, and it became a place of prayer and veneration of the Queen of Peace.

For about sixty years, the image was placed in a niche outside the door of the monastery. There for several years a clear light seemed to miraculously illuminate it during the night. Later, in 1651, the people heard the *Salve Regina* being chanted by unseen singers. A number of miraculous occurrences brought much attention to the image and made it famous.

The sacred image was moved to the place where the former duke, Father Ange, was buried; miracles kept multiplying, and a new chapel had to be built to contain the crowds who came to venerate her. At the beginning of the Revolution, the Capuchins were forced to abandon the monastery, and gave the image into the keeping of a pious lady named Madame Pepin. The statue then passed through a number of hands until it was given to a certain Madame Riolet, who gave it to Father Coudrin, the founder of the Congregation of the Sacred Hearts of Jesus and Mary. The statue was placed in the chapel of the Religious in the Rue de Piepus, Paris, in 1806. Since that day, favors have been constantly granted through her intercession, and numerous gifts are left at the shrine in testimony. The statue was crowned in 1906 in the name of Pope St. Pius X.

Girdles, Cinctures, and Cords

The liturgical girdle, or *cincture*, is a long rope of linen or hemp, tasselled at the end, with which the alb is confined at the waist. It may be the color of the other vestments, but is usually white. Its practical use is to control the loose alb, but symbolically it refers to sacerdotal purity. The cincture has been recognized as a part of liturgical attire since the ninth century, but may date back as far as the seventh century, and from early times prayers were recited in putting it on. In earlier times, the cincture was not always the simple cord it is now; surviving examples are made of silk and other precious cloths, sometimes richly embroidered, or interwoven with gold and silver thread.

Some form of cincture is included in many religious or ecclesiastical costumes. In certain religious orders it receives a special blessing and is sometimes sanctioned or indulgenced by the Church as a sign of allegiance or affiliation to a particular institute.

In the early Church, virgins wore a cincture as a sign of purity. Wearing a cord or cincture in honor of a saint is of ancient origin, and an early mention of this practice is found in the life of St. Monica. During the Middle Ages, cinctures were often worn by the faithful in honor of saints, and a cincture in honor of *St. Michael* was general throughout France. Later on, ecclesiastical authority set special blessings for cinctures in honor of *Our Lady*, the *Most Precious Blood, St. Francis of Paola, St. Francis of Assisi, St. Thomas Aquinas*, and *St. Joseph*, among others. The blessing of a cincture in honor of the Blessed Virgin Mary was originally reserved to the Hermits of St. Augustine; that of the cord in honor of St. Francis of Assisi was originally reserved to the Order of Friars Minor Conventual. The Order of Minims blessed and invested wearers with a wool cincture in honor of St. Francis of Paula; the Dominicans blessed and distributed cinctures in honor of St. Thomas Aquinas for the preservation of chastity. The Roman Ritual contains blessings for cinctures to be worn in honor of Our Lord, Our Lady, or a canonized saint.

The Cord of St. Thomas Aquinas

St. Thomas Aquinas, the great medieval doctor of the church, was born near Aquino, one of many children of a nobleman of Lombardic descent. After receiving a good education, he decided to join the Dominicans. His wish to be a mendicant friar shocked his noble relatives, so his brothers kidnapped him and attempted to change his mind.

The devotion known as the Angelic Warfare, or the Cord of St.

Thomas, stems from an event that occurred during this period of family imprisonment. While Thomas was held in the castle Montesangiovanni, his brothers attempted to destroy his holy purity, thereby discrediting his vocation. Thomas repulsed the advances of a woman sent by his brothers, forcing her out of his room by threatening her with a firebrand. He then burned a cross on the door of his room, and prayed in thanksgiving for the preservation of his virtue. That night in a dream, two angels came to him from heaven and girded his loins.

Although this episode was romanticized by early historians, his mystical experience is recorded in the acts of his canonization process and by his earliest biographers. Serious historians see in the account of the girdle of chastity not a material cord but a spiritual "cord of fire." One account in the canonization process states that Thomas nevermore experienced the "movements of sensuality," and indicates that he was never again to suffer any temptation against chastity. The account of the angel's speech seems more realistic: "On God's behalf we gird you with the girdle of chastity, a girdle which no attack will ever destroy."

Although it is difficult to determine how soon after his death the practice of wearing the cord or girdle in memory of St. Thomas's chastity began, it was probably a fairly common devotion before the first local confraternities of the fifteenth and sixteenth centuries were founded in Spain and Italy. The Dominican Francis Duerwerdes is considered the founder of the Angelic Warfare Confraternity. This union was instituted at the University of Louvain in 1649 and was constituted as an apostolic confraternity in 1727 under Pope Benedict XIII. Pope Pius XI and seven other popes recommended the confraternity to youth, and he granted permission to wear a medal in place of the cord.

The object of this devotion includes the young St. Thomas, the excellence of his chastity, and the benefits of a religious vocation. The confraternity venerates the Angelic Doctor and directs its members to imitate not only his chastity but all his virtues.

The cord is white and sometimes made of linen. It is worn around the waist to remind the wearer that he is a temple of the Holy Spirit. There are fifteen knots on the cord as reminders of the mysteries of the rosary. Each knot has three twists, a reminder of the Holy Trinity and the three theological virtues. A loop is made at one end of the cord, and its two strands represent the natural and supernatural life in each man. The circular loop serves as a reminder that the supernatural life leads us to God.

The confraternity medal has on one side an image of St. Thomas being girded by angels, and on the other side Our Lady, Queen of the Holy Rosary. In the mid-'60s, a new confraternity medal was designed by an American

Dominican nun, Sister Mary of the Compassion, a well known religious artist from Union City, New Jersey. One side has an image of St. Thomas with the two angels as bearers of God's help. The border is made up of the design of the cord itself. On the other side, Our Lady is symbolized by the moon, and the sun of justice symbolizes Our Lord. The sun is held in the moon as a symbol of the Incarnation of God through Mary. This side has a border whose design is a reminder of the fifteen mysteries of the rosary.

One part of the enrollment ceremony in the confraternity is the beautiful prayer of St. Thomas for purity: "Dear Jesus, I know that every perfect gift and especially that of chastity depends on the power of your Providence. Without you, a mere creature can do nothing. Therefore, I beg you to defend by your grace the chastity and purity of my body and soul. And if I have ever sensed anything that can stain my chastity and purity, blot it out, Supreme Lord of my powers, that I may advance with a pure heart in your love and service, offering myself on the most pure altar of your divinity all the days of my life. Amen."

St. Joseph's Cord

In 1657, in Antwerp Belgium, an Augustinian nun, Sister Elizabeth, was dying. Her physicians had given up hope and expected her death within a few days. Sister Elizabeth, a devotee of St. Joseph, prayed to him. Then she asked for a cord to be made and blessed in his honor. The dying sister's wish was granted.

Sister Elizabeth put on the cord and implored the intercession of St. Joseph for the recovery of her health. While praying, she felt her strength return and rose from her sickbed, instantly cured.

In 1858, the cord of St. Joseph was approved by the Sacred Congregation of Rites, and indulgenced by Pope Pius IX. The cord is made from simple cotton twine. Seven knots at one end of the cord remind the wearer of the seven joys and the seven sorrows of St. Joseph.

Father John Drumgoole, a New York priest who founded the Mission of the Immaculate Virgin for the care of needy children, placed his life and his work under the protection of St. Joseph. He established St. Joseph's Union to further the work of the mission. This union today is in charge of the Cord of St. Joseph in the United States.

Medals

The custom of wearing medals is an ancient one, traced back as far as the time of the catacombs. Religious medals are flat metal disks, usually in the form of a coin, which are struck or cast for a commemorative purpose. Religious medals are enormously varied and are used to commemorate persons (Christ, the Blessed Mother, the saints), places such as famous shrines, past historical events (dogmatic definitions, miracles, dedications), or personal graces such as First Communion, ordination, etc. Medals are often concerned with ideas, such as the mysteries of our faith, and some serve as badges of pious associations.

Medals are worn around the neck or on the person and serve as a reminder as does a photograph or other relic of a loved one. Medals should be regarded in the same way as any other image; they are merely signs of the prototype inscribed thereon and in themselves have no efficacy. To consider them otherwise would be superstition. The medal is to be used as a reminder to honor the subject displayed on the medal, and a reminder of the need to advance in Christian perfection. The benefit of the medal used as a sacramental is the blessing called down from God on the wearer. Indulgences have sometimes been attached to various types of the innumerable medals struck.

The use of amulets in pagan antiquity was widespread. These were talismans worn about the neck. It is possible that the early Church tolerated an analogous practice.

Christians sometimes wore *phylacteries* containing relics or other devotional objects, and in Africa ancient molds for crosses have been found. The wearing of these phylacteries and *encolpia*, or *pectoral crosses*, soon lent itself to abuses when magical formula began to join the Christian symbols. Thus we find record of protests from many of the Church fathers from the fourth century on. There are some early medals which have been found in the catacombs. Sometimes, regular coins were overprinted with a Christian symbol and holes were drilled so the medals might be hung around the neck. There is no way of telling, however, how popular the custom was prior to the Middle Ages. By the twelfth century there was a custom at well-known places of pilgrimage of casting tokens of lead and sometimes other metals, which served the pilgrims as souvenirs, objects of piety, and a proof that a pilgrim had reached his destination. These *signacula*, or pilgrim's signs, were cast in a variety of forms and worn prominently on the hat or breast. By the sixteenth century, these had begun to be replaced by medals cast in bronze or silver with more artistic work on

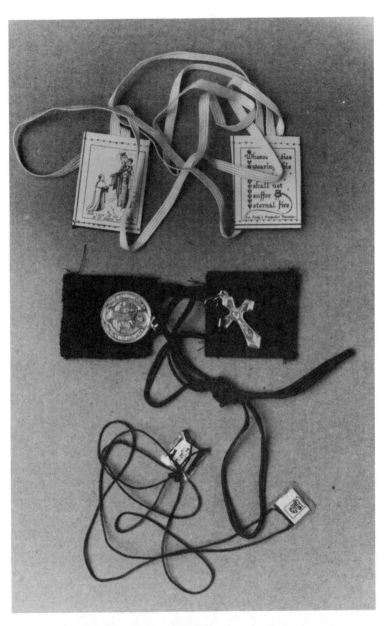

From top: Brown Scapular of Our Lady of Mount Carmel in two versions, one with a medal of St. Benedict (see "Scapulars, etc."); Scapular of Atocha not mentioned in text (see "Images").

them. Beginning in the thirteenth century, *jetons*, or counters, began to be used for religious purposes. These were flat pieces of metal, generally a form of brass but later more precious metals, used as vouchers for attendance at ecclesiastical functions, or given as souvenirs.

Commemorative medals began in the last years of the fourteenth century. The first ones were elaborate works of art, and therefore restricted to the wealthy. *Papal Jubilee medals* began as early as 1417.

During the sixteenth century, the custom began of giving papal blessings to medals. One of the first of these was a medal worn by the Spaniards during the revolt of the Gueux in Flanders in 1566. This medal bore an image of Our Lord on one side and an image of Our Lady of Hal on the other. Pope Pius V granted an indulgence to those who wore this medal on their hats. This vogue soon spread throughout Catholic Europe, and soon each city had craftsmen of its own.

Medals became so popular, and were struck for so many reasons and in so many designs, that it seems almost impossible to even classify them. Only a few are outlined here.

Plague medals were struck and blessed as a protection against pestilence. Popular subjects for these are St. Sebastian, St. Roch, and shrines of the Virgin, sometimes with a view of a particular city on them. These medals often carried letters as abbreviations for prayers or mottoes.

Eucharistic miracles were often commemorated with medals, especially on jubilees or centenaries. These were issued in the different places where the miracles were believed to have happened, and some carry picture stories of the miraculous events.

There is a large class of private medals which were struck to commemorate incidents in the life of individuals and were distributed to friends. *Baptism medals* often contained precise details of the date of birth so that a child's horoscope could be calculated.

The *cross of St. Ulrich* of Augsburg is an example of medals commemorative of special legends. Supposedly an angel brought a cross to St. Ulrich so that he might carry it into battle against the Huns in 955. More than 180 examples of this one commemoration have been found.

Papal medals, especially in conjunction with the opening and closing of the Holy Door during jubilee years, have been struck since 1417. Almost all major events of the reigns of the popes since that time have been commemorated in medals. Other semi-devotional medals have been struck by religious associations such as the Knights of Malta, and by abbeys in commemoration of their abbots.

St. Christopher Medal

Practically nothing is known about St. Christopher other than his name and the fact of his martyrdom, probably about the third century. Although his veneration was widespread in both the Eastern and Western Church from the earliest centuries, early legends supplied with abundant fantasy what history could not provide; all manner of startling details were told of him. In 1969, Christopher's feast was dropped from the liturgical calendar, and his cultus is no longer promoted by the Church.

A pious and the most popular legendary biography of him is found in the thirteenth-century *Golden Legend*. This legend tells of a heathen king who, through the prayers of his wife to the Blessed Virgin, had a son whom he named Offerus. This young man grew to great size and strength. The boy decided to serve only the strongest lord in the world and began in the service of an emperor. Discovering the emperor was frightened of the Devil, Offerus then served the Devil for a while until he saw how the Devil trembled at the sight of a crucifix. Thus the young giant determined to serve Christ, and asking advice from a hermit, he was instructed to make a home by a deep and treacherous river and carry Christian pilgrims across.

One night a little boy asked to be carried, so Offerus placed the child on his shoulders and entered the churning water. As he forded the river, the child became heavier and heavier until Offerus thought he would fail. When he reached the other side, he asked with surprise why the child was so heavy. The child replied that he had carried not only the whole world but Him who made it. The child identified Himself as Christ, then took Offerus into the water and baptized him, giving him the name of Christopher, or Christ-bearer. He instructed the saint to jam his staff into the ground; it immediately burst forth into leaves and blossoms, and the Christ child disappeared. Christopher later went joyfully to persecution and death for his beloved Lord. One account of his martyrdom has him being shot with arrows for twelve hours and finally beheaded.

The legends inspired many devotions. St. Christopher was venerated as a patron against sudden and unexpected death, especially during the times of epidemics and plagues. The faithful believed that if they prayed before his picture in the morning, no harm would come to them that day. The custom began of hanging his picture over the door of the house, or painting it on the walls outside so that others could also venerate the saint. He is the patron of ferryboats, pilgrims, travelers, gardeners, and freight ships. He is also known as a patron of skiing.

Churches and monasteries were dedicated to St. Christopher as early as 532. A breviary from the early seventh century has a special office in his honor. In 1386, a brotherhood was founded under his patronage in Tyrol and Vorarlberg to guide travelers over the Arlberg. Temperance societies were established in his name as early as 1517.

Although coins with his image are from a much earlier period, use of the medals and plaques which people now carry on keychains or in their cars began in the sixteenth century. Their original purpose was to serve as a picture of the saint for travelers to gaze on in the morning and to protect them from sudden death that day. Although the original custom has long died out, the medals remain as a token of St. Christopher's help and protection in modern traffic. Today many Christians, not just Catholics, keep these medals which honor the saint as patron of travelers.

Medal of the Holy Face

Twelve-year-old Giuseppina de Micheli was praying in her parish church, St. Peter in Sala (Milan), on Good Friday. Quite distinctly, she heard a voice tell her, "Nobody gives me a kiss of love in my face to make amends for the kiss of Judas." As she believed all in the church had heard the voice, she was pained to observe that the pious members of the congregation passed by the statue of Jesus, kissing devoutly the wounds, yet not the face. To herself she thought, "Have patience, dear Jesus, I will give You a kiss of love." In turn, this young soul already filled with a spirit of reparation, kissed the countenance of the replica of Him who would become her Divine Spouse.

In 1916, Giuseppina joined the Daughters of the Immaculate Conception, taking the name of Sister Maria Pierina. From the earliest days of her postulancy, Sister Pierina began to experience mystical meetings with Our Lord, who taught her the devotion of reparation to the Holy Face. In 1936, Our Lord told her, "I wish that my face, which reflects the deep pains of my soul, the sorrow and love of my heart, be better honored; who contemplates me consoles me." Later he told her, "Every time my face is contemplated, I will pour out my love into the heart of those persons and by means of my holy face the salvation of many souls will be obtained."

In 1940, under Sister Pierina's direction, a medal of the Holy Face was cast and approved by the Curia of Milan. The design for this medal had been given to her during one of the manifestations she had experienced from Our Lady.

The front of the medal has the Latin words for "May, O Lord, the light of Thy countenance shine upon us" (cf. Ps 66:10). The words encircle a picture of the face of Christ. On the reverse of the medal is a radiant host with the words "Stay with us, O Lord." This medal is to be worn in a spirit of reparation for the outrages committed against the Holy Face of Our Lord during His Passion, and for those committed against Him every day in the

Sacrament of His divine love. If possible, the wearer should make a visit to the Blessed Sacrament each Tuesday.

The Queen of All Hearts Medal

"Mary is Queen of heaven and earth by grace, as Jesus is King of them by nature and by conquest. It is principally in the hearts that she is more glorified with her Son. And so we may call her, as the saints do, the Queen of All Hearts" (St. Louis de Montfort).

The Queen of All Hearts Medal is worn by the members of the Confraternity of Mary, Queen of All Hearts, a pious union of the faithful established in 1899. Pope Pius X erected the confraternity as an archconfraternity in 1913.

The purpose of this confraternity is to help the members live and publicize the Marian Way of Life as explained in the writings of St. Louis de Montfort, as a way to sanctify themselves and to restore the reign of Christ through Mary. The confraternity promotes consecration to Mary, Queen of All Hearts, and its members share in all the good works and prayers of the members of the Company of Mary and the Daughters of Wisdom.

The medal is heart-shaped. On the front is a design of the Queen of All Hearts statuary group found in the Regina dei Cuori Chapel in Rome. Mary is seated, holding the child Jesus. Kneeling at her feet are St. Louis de Montfort and an angel. The book *True Devotion to Mary* is pictured under the group. On the obverse of the medal is a shield with a monogram of Mary surmounted by a crown. The shield is circled with a rosary entwined with a lily, symbolizing Mary's purity.

The Medal of St. Benedict

The medal of St. Benedict is one of the oldest and most highly honored medals used by the Church. Because of the extraordinary number of miraculous occurrences, both physical and spiritual, attributed to this medal, it became popularly known as the "devil-chasing medal."

On the face of the medal is an image of St. Benedict standing before an altar. He holds the cross in one hand and the Benedictine rule in the other. On either side of the altar are an eagle and the traditional chalice. Inscribed in small letters beside two columns are the words *Crux E. Patris Benedicti* ("Cross of our Father Benedict"). Written in larger letters in a circular margin of the medal are the words *Ejus in obitu nostro praesentia muniamur* ("May we be protected in our death by his presence"). St. Benedict is considered one of the patrons of the dying because of the circumstances of his own happy death. He breathed his last while standing

114

in prayer before the Most Blessed Sacrament. Below the figure of the saint is the year the medal was struck — 1880. This is known as the Jubilee medal as it was struck to commemorate the fourteenth centenary of the birth of the saint. Near this is the inscription of Monte Casino, the abbey where the medal was struck.

The back of the medal has a cross of St. Benedict surmounted by the word *Pax* (Peace), the Benedictine motto, and a circular margin which bears the inscription VRSNSMVSMQLIVB. This inscription stands for *Vade Retro Satana* ("Get thee behind me, Satan"), *Nunquam Suade Mihi Vana* ("Persuade me not to vanity"), *Sunt Mala Quae Libas* ("The cup you offer is evil"), and *Ipse Venena Bibas* ("Drink the poison yourself"). On the upright bar of the cross are found the letters C.S.S.M.L., which stand for *Crux Sacra Sit Mihi Lux* ("May the sacred cross be my light") and on the horizontal bar of the cross N.D.S.M.D., *Non Draco Sit Mihi Dux* ("Let not the devil be my guide"). The four large letters around the arms of the cross stand for *Crux Sancti Patris Benedicti* ("Cross of the Holy Father Benedict"). The older version of the medal-cross carried the letters U.I.O.G.D., which stand for *Ut In Omnes Gloriam Deum* ("That in all things God be glorified").

Much of the origin and early history of this medal is hidden in the twilight of antiquity. St. Benedict, the founder of the Benedictine Order, was born at Nursia, Italy, in 480 and died at Monte Cassino in 548. This saint had a profound veneration for the Holy Cross and performed many miracles by its means. He taught his followers to have great reverence for the cross, the sign of our redemption, and to rely on its use in combating the world, the flesh, and the devil.

To a large extent, European culture spread from the medieval monasteries of the Benedictines. St. Benedict has even been called the Father of Europe. His name came to be associated with the cross of Christ, and in the course of time a medal was struck in his honor.

Shortly after the year 1000, a saintly youth named Bruno was miraculously cured of a deadly snakebite by the Cross of St. Benedict. In 1048, this young Benedictine became Pope Leo IX. His reign marked the end of a deplorable period in the history of the papacy. As Pope, St. Leo IX carried out vigorous reforms of the clergy and prepared the way for the future popes to be elected by the cardinals of the Roman church alone. He did much to spread the devotion to the Holy Cross and to St. Benedict. He enriched the medal of St. Benedict, which replaced the Cross of St. Benedict, with many blessings and indulgences. A later Pope, Benedict XIV, gave the solemn approval of the Church to the use of this medal and urgently recommended it to all the faithful.

The life of St. Benedict was characterized by a powerful and all-embracing love for God, a serene dedication to a life based on prayer, and absolute trust in the providence of God. The medal of this saint acts as a reminder to the wearer of those virtues that the saint practiced during his life, and serves as an outward and concrete sign of the person's interior commitment to a life marked by a constant prayerful disposition, trust in God, and practice of charity.

The wearing of the medal is in itself an unspoken prayer, a plea for heavenly protection, and a loving token of our attachment to God.

The medal of St. Benedict may be worn or carried. No special prayers are prescribed, but the wearer should cherish a special devotion to Christ Crucified, and have great confidence in St. Benedict.

The Miraculous Medal

"Catherine, Catherine, wake up. Come to the chapel; the Blessed Virgin is waiting for you."

Sleepily, Sister Catherine Labouré, a novice of the Sisters of Charity at the motherhouse on the rue du Bac in Paris, France, opened her eyes.

"About half past eleven [July 18, 1830], I heard myself called by my name. I looked in the direction of the voice and I drew the curtain. I saw a child of four or five years old dressed in white [who told me to come to the chapel]. Immediately the thought came to me: 'But I shall be heard.' The child replied: 'Be calm . . . everyone is asleep; come, I am waiting for you.'

"I hurriedly dressed and went to the side of the child. I followed him wherever he went. The lights were lit everywhere. When we reached the chapel, the door opened as soon as the child touched it with the tip of his finger. The candles were burning as at midnight Mass. However I did not see the Blessed Virgin. The child led me to the sanctuary and I knelt down there. Toward midnight, the child said: 'Here is the Blessed Virgin!' I heard a noise like the rustle of a silk dress . . . a very beautiful lady sat down in Father Director's chair. The child repeated in a strong voice: 'Here is the Blessed Virgin.' Then I flung myself at her feet on the steps of the altar and put my hands on her knees.

"I do not know how long I remained there; it seemed but a moment, the sweetest of my life.

"The Holy Virgin told me how I should act toward my director and confided several things to me. . . ."

On hearing these words, the young novice's spiritual director, Father Aladel, a young Lazarist, cannot be blamed for thinking that Sister Catherine was possibly the victim of an overactive imagination.

Later, Catherine wrote of the things the Virgin confided to her that night: "The good God, my child, wishes to entrust you with a mission. It will be the cause of much suffering to you, but you will overcome this, knowing that what you do is for the glory of God. You will be contradicted, but you will have the grace to bear it; do not fear. You will see certain things; give an account of them. You will be inspired in your prayers."

Catherine's mission was revealed to her on November 27, 1830. While at community prayer, Catherine again saw the Blessed Virgin. She was standing dressed in a robe of white silk with her feet resting on a globe. In her hands she held a smaller globe, and her eyes were raised toward heaven.

"Then suddenly, I saw rings on her fingers, covered with jewels . . . from which came beautiful rays. . . . At this moment, she lowered her eyes and looked at me, and an interior voice spoke to me: 'This globe which you see represents the entire world, particularly France, and each person in particular. This is a symbol of the graces which I shed on those who ask me.'

"At this moment, where I was or was not I do not know, an oval shape formed around the Blessed Virgin, and on it were written these words in letters of gold: 'O Mary conceived without sin, pray for us who have recourse to thee.'

"Then a voice was heard to say: 'Have a medal struck after this model. Those who wear it will receive great graces; abundant graces will be given to those who have confidence.' Some of the precious stones gave forth no ray of light. 'Those jewels which are in shadow represent the graces which people forget to ask me for.'

"Suddenly, the oval seemed to turn. I saw the reverse of the medal: the letter M surmounted by a cross, and below it, two hearts, one crowned with a crown of thorns and the other pierced by a sword. I seemed to hear a voice which said to me: 'The M and the two hearts say enough.' "

After this last account, Father Aladel still had his doubts, but he requested an interview with the Archbishop of Paris. The Archbishop could find nothing against the faith in the idea, and authorized the medal to be struck. In May of 1832, the first medals were distributed, and soon there was a flood of reported cures and conversions. So many, in fact, that the people soon began calling it the "Miraculous Medal."

On July 27, 1947, Pope Pius XII canonized Saint Catherine Labouré, calling her the "Saint of Silence."

The Miraculous Medal became a sign for a renewal of devotion to Our Lady and an evangelical revival. Millions of Catholics worldwide wear the Miraculous Medal as a reminder of the blessings Our Lady is waiting for them to request.

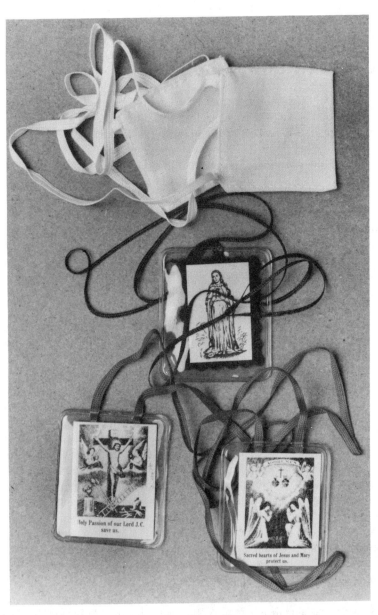

From top, Dominican Scapular, Green Scapular of the Immaculate Conception, Red Scapular of the Passion (see "Scapulars, etc.").

The St. Joseph Medal

Mrs. Martin was nearly hysterical. Her baby was dying. Her mother's heart was breaking, for she well knew the agony a mother feels at the death of an infant. Three other babies she had held only briefly before they were gone. Then she recalled the words of the great saint of Ávila. St. Teresa had said, "I know from experience that this glorious saint [Joseph] helps in each and every need. Our Lord would have us understand that, since on earth He was subject to this man who was called His father, whom as His guardian He had to obey, so now in heaven He still does all that Joseph asks."

Mrs. Martin threw herself at the feet of a statue of St. Joseph and begged for her child's life. The child, Thérèse, lived. Not only did she live, but she lived in such a way that today she is known as one of the greatest of our modern saints — St. Thérèse of the Child Jesus, the "Little Flower."

In 1871, Pope Pius IX, declared St. Joseph the patron of the Universal Church. Just as Joseph was the guardian and protector for the Holy Family, he also is guardian and protector for all the family of God . . . the Church. In 1971, the St. Joseph medal was struck to commemorate the centennial of this declaration. This medal summarizes some of the salient points of the devotion to St. Joseph.

"A medal can be anything from an object of superstition or mere ornament to a valuable means of grace. It can be a silent encouragement in times of stress and trial, a call to virtue in temptation, a bond of union with a great personality, a symbol of loyalty and dedication" (Father Christopher Rengers, O.F.M. Cap., originator of the St. Joseph Medal). Father Rengers expressed the hope that people would wear the St. Joseph medal intelligently and fruitfully, to encourage devotion to the saint, to encourage unity in the family and in the Church, and to encourage loyalty to the Pope. This medal, as are all approved medals, is meant to be a means of grace, an aid against temptation, and a bond of union with God and St. Joseph.

The design for the medal was carved from dense pine, using fine chisels, by Norbert Schrader. Then the plaque was sent to Germany, where the medal was struck. The medal is enameled with the colors purple and white to symbolize Joseph's purity, justice, and humility. A touch of red symbolizes the Holy Spirit and the redeeming love of Christ. The medal is rectangular in shape to preserve the memory of the St. Joseph Scapular which was approved by Pope Leo XIII in 1893 and given to the Capuchin Order to promote.

On the face of the medal, St. Joseph is shown in a protective stance, with his arms about the child Jesus and Our Lady. The Child rests his head against the heart of the saint. The circular position of the family conveys unity. Joseph's short-sleeved garment and the chair on which Our Lady is seated remind us of the fact that Joseph was a carpenter, a worker. The petition inscribed on the face of the medal reads: "That all may be one: St. Joseph Our Protector Pray for Us." The letters GIJM stand for Joseph's fidelity to grace in his interior life and his love for Jesus and Mary.

The obverse of the medal has the words: "Feed my lambs, feed my sheep. The spirit of the Lord his guide." It depicts sheep underneath the shepherd's staff and crossed keys, a symbol of the papacy; the whole is surmounted by a dove symbolizing the Holy Spirit. This side of the medal reminds us to invoke St. Joseph as protector of the Church on behalf of the Holy Father.

Thus the St. Joseph medal honors St. Joseph as patron of the Church, fosters family and Church unity, and encourages loyalty to the Holy Father.

The Scapular Medal

In 1910, Pope St. Pius X introduced a scapular medal which may be substituted in most cases for any of the various scapulars. Valid enrollment in the scapulars must, however, be made before the substitution.

The decree, in translation, reads thus:

"For the future all the faithful already inscribed or who shall be inscribed in one or other of the real Scapulars approved by the Holy See (excepting those which are proper to the Third Orders) by what is known as regular enrollment may, instead of the cloth scapulars, one or several, wear on their persons, either round the neck or otherwise, provided it be in a becoming manner, a single medal of metal, through which, by the observance of laws laid down for each scapular, they shall be enabled to share in and gain all the spiritual favors (not excepting what is known as the Sabbatine Privilege of the Scapular of Our Lady of Mount Carmel), and all the privileges attached to each.

"The right side of this medal must show the image of Our Most Holy Redeemer, Jesus Christ, showing His Sacred Heart, and the obverse that of the Most Blessed Virgin Mary. It must be blessed with a separate blessing for each of the scapulars in which the person has been enrolled and for which the wearer wishes it to suffice. Finally, these separate blessings may be given by a single sign of the cross (*unico crucis signo*), whether in the act of enrollment or later at the convenience of those enrolled, it matters not how long after the enrollment or in what order they may have taken place; the blessing may be given by a priest other than the one who made the enrollment, as long as he possesses the faculty, ordinary, or delegated, of blessing the different scapulars — the limitations, clauses, and conditions attached to the faculty he uses still holding their force. All things to the contrary, even those calling for special mention, notwithstanding" (Holy Office, Rome, December 16, 1910).

Medal of Maria Goretti and Our Mother of Confidence

In 1950, a little Italian peasant girl, Maria Goretti, was canonized as a martyr — not for the Christian faith, but for the Christian life. At the age of twelve, Maria was attacked and stabbed by a young man who wanted to seduce her. She heroically resisted, in defense of her purity, and died twenty-four hours later after having forgiven her murderer. After eight years in prison, unrepentant, her murderer had a change of heart after experiencing a vision of Maria and, when released from prison in 1937, received Communion at the side of Maria's widowed mother.

Maria's canonization stands as one of the fastest modern canonizations on record; she was raised to the honors of the altar only forty-eight years after her death (only St. Maximilian Kolbe's was faster — forty-one years). A medal in her honor was struck about the time of the canonization.

The obverse of this medal displays a picture of Our Lady of Confidence which is surrounded by the aspiration "My Mother, My Confidence." The picture of Mary under this title has been venerated in Italy for centuries. Sister Clare Isabella Fornari, a Poor Clare of Tadi, Italy, whose beatification process has begun, stated that Our Lady promised to grant a particular tenderness and devotion towards herself to everyone who venerates her image under the title of Our Lady of Confidence.

Medal of Our Lady of Fátima

A young Portuguese priest, Father Joseph Cacella, was driven out of his native country when the radical party came to official power. This same government, eight years later, suppressed all writings on the apparitions at Fátima.

After spending five years as a missionary in the Amazon, Father Cacella came to America in 1914 to die. He had contracted jungle fever while on the mission, and his doctors had given him a mere six months to live. In America, he found residence with the Friars at Graymoor in Garrison, New York. Instead of dying, he lived to become the great apostle of Fátima.

While at Graymoor, Father Cacella received letters from his mother in Portugal telling of the apparitions to the three shepherd children of Fátima. Her letters were intimate and full of details, as she knew and had spoken with the parents of the children and with the children themselves. She was convinced the children were speaking nothing but the truth.

A classmate of Father Cacella at the seminary in Portugal, a Msgr. Formigao, visited the children and questioned them. He was the first representative of the Church to question the children and he missed no detail. He began to write inspiring accounts of the apparitions, although he prudently published them under a pen name. The radical communist government tracked down the identity of this priest. Eventually he was suspended, silenced, and imprisoned for months. Msgr. Formigao appealed to Father Cacella's mother to send information to her son. America, with its freedom of the press, would be the herald of the news of Fátima. Father Cacella joyfully took up the task of making Fátima known worldwide.

As the message of Fátima spread, so did the demand for pictures, statues, and medals of Our Lady. Father Cacella went to the religious-goods houses that made medals and statues, but they were not interested in his proposition. They did not want to produce a medal that might be a risk on their hands. The Fátima movement at that time was still in an unknown stage to them. As a last resort, Father Cacella went to an old friend, Vincent Hirten, the head of a company, who agreed to turn out the medals if Father would furnish the die. Unfortunately, with no medals, there were no dies.

Actually, Father Cacella had one medal of Fátima that his mother had sent him from Portugal in 1920. This was probably the only medal of Fátima in the United States. He finally decided to allow it to serve as the design for a medal. Since that day millions upon millions of medals have been struck — from the design of the one medal that Father Cacella had received from his own earthly mother.

Medal of St. Dymphna

One of the most serious problems facing our nation today is presented by nervous and mental diseases. On the grounds of the Massillon State Hospital in Massillon, Ohio, is the National Shrine of St. Dymphna, the patroness of those afflicted with nervous and emotional illness. St. Dymphna has been honored and loved for centuries, and thousands have been helped through her intercession.

St. Dymphna was born in the seventh century in Ireland, the daughter of the king or chieftain of Oriel. Although her father was a pagan, Dymphna's mother was Christian, remarkable both for her piety and her beauty. She had Dymphna instructed in the Catholic faith.

When Dymphna was about fifteen, her mother died. Through grief and bereavement, Dymphna's father slowly lost his sanity. His advisors advised him to marry again, and he sent messengers throughout the countryside looking for a replacement for his wife of her same quality. No new bride could be found to suit him, and eventually he decided that his daughter was the only one in the kingdom who would make a suitable wife.

Dymphna and her confessor fled to Gheel in Belgium to escape the incestuous advances of the chieftain. After a lengthy search, Dymphna's father tracked down the escapees, beheading both the priest and his own daughter. The people of Gheel first buried the martyrs in a cave. Later, according to the legend, when workers excavated the cave in the thirteenth century to rebury the remains more fittingly, they found the relics in two white marble coffins. A red tile identified the relics of the teenage girl saint.

When the bodies were removed to a small church, a woman suffering from nervous disorder touched the tomb and was instantly cured. People began to flock to Gheel, and when St. Dymphna's relic was touched to those suffering mental and emotional disorders, the number of cures defied belief.

Through the centuries, the fame of Gheel grew, and caring for the emotionally disturbed became the major occupation of the inhabitants. The people loved their little princess, and she showered graces on those who, like her once-beloved father, suffered from an illness no scientist could lay under a microscope and examine.

The town whose people first befriended the refugees continued to befriend those who came to honor her. Rather than institutionalize those who came, the townspeople took them into their own homes to care for them.

The shrine in Ohio is the first church in American to be built in honor of St. Dymphna. It was dedicated in 1938, and since then has served as a storehouse of grace for those suffering from depression, anxiety, and all other mental disorders. Medals, as well as statues and information about the Irish martyr, are distributed from this national shrine. The shrine is the home of the League of St. Dymphna, a group of members throughout the country whose intentions are remembered at the shrine. She who died at the hands of her insane father intercedes graciously and willingly for those who suffer and for their families.

Scapulars and Badges

The scapular began in the early middle ages as a long narrow piece of cloth about the width of the shoulders with an opening in the center so that it could be slipped over the head and hang in equal lengths. It was worn over the tunic and sometimes under a belt. Some, such as those worn by the early Benedictines, had a hood attached. Originally, the scapular was a work garment, meant to protect the tunic; through the years it became considered as a part of the habit. A number of the scapulars worn by the religious orders had great religious significance stemming from the way the scapular was received by the order.

Later, an abbreviated form of the scapular came into proper use and was given to the laity in order to give the wearer a share in the merits and good works of the particular group of which it served as a badge. These scapulars are connected to third orders and confraternities. The wearer is invested in the scapular by religious authority, and the scapular is worn according to specific directions. These abbreviated scapulars are generally formed from two pieces of cloth about three inches long and two inches wide, and are connected with strings so that it may be worn front and back. The scapulars generally have embroidered or stamped representations on them. There are nearly a score of scapulars which have received approval for use in the Universal Church, although several of these are little known in America. Just as with many other sacramentals, care must be taken that the wearers understand fully the devotion connected with the scapular and that they must guard against superstition.

In 1910, Pope St. Pius X authorized the wearing of a blessed medal as a substitute, under certain conditions, for wearing one of the small scapulars. This medal, commonly called the "scapular medal," shows a representation of the Sacred Heart on one side and a representation of the Blessed Virgin on the other. Investing in any scapular cannot be done with the medal; the actual scapular must be used. The priest who blesses the medal must also have the faculties to invest in the scapular it represents.

In addition to the scapulars, cloth badges will be treated in this section.

The Brown Scapular of Our Lady of Mount Carmel

Along with the rosary. the brown scapular is one of the most ancient and best-loved of the sacramentals. Its Carmelite tradition of Marian devotion extends back to 1251, when Our Lady herself presented the first one to St. Simon Stock, or as he is sometimes called, St. Simon of England. This scapular carries a unique promise from Our Lady regarding the hour of death of the pious wearer. It has received approbations from more than fifteen popes.

According to the annals of the Carmelite Order, Our Lady presented the scapular to St. Simon on the night of July 15, 1251. In that year, he was the prior general of the Carmelite Order, which was in danger of extinction due to persecutions both from within and outside. Devoutly, the prior prayed to Our Lady. Suddenly he experienced a vision where he seemed to see angelic choirs, at the center of which stood the Blessed Virgin Mary. In the vision, the Blessed Mother spoke to him, saying "Receive, my beloved son, this habit of thy Order. This shall be to thee and to all Carmelites a privilege, that whosoever dies clothed in this shall never suffer eternal fire."

After the vision, St. Simon was left with the brown scapular in his hands. Two priests were sent to Rome and returned with the blessing of the Pope. The dissension in the Order began to wane. Gradually persecutions ceased, and the Holy Father took Simon's monks of Mary under the special protection of the Holy See. For the next three hundred years, the devotion spread rapidly, and later more slowly, throughout the world. Four centuries later, the devotion culminated with the declaration in the Universal Church of a feast day, July 16.

Seventy-one years after Mary gave the brown scapular to St. Simon Stock, she came to the Supreme Pontiff of the Universal Church. Pope John XXII published the message she gave to him in the papal bull of March 3, 1322. "So that with hastened step they shall pass over Purgatory, I, the Mother of Grace, shall descend into Purgatory on the Saturday after their death, and whomsoever I shall find I shall free, so that I may lead them unto the holy mountain of life everlasting."

It would be foolish indeed to expect that the mere wearing of a piece of cloth would gain for the wearer the guarantee of eternal life. Mary's promises to St. Simon and to Pope John appear so startling that they have often been misconstrued or made the basis for a superstitious belief in the efficacy of the sacramental itself.

The sacraments of the church were instituted by Christ, and give their grace "*ex opere operato*," which is to say that they give grace of themselves when fruitfully received. The sacramentals were instituted and approved by the Church and are productive of grace "*ex opere operantis*," by virtue of their ecclesiastical approval and the dispositions with which they are used. The sacramentals have grown in number through the centuries and in accordance with certain needs. Many of them are Marian in character and have some claim to private revelation in their nature.

The first scapular promise, "Whoever dies piously wearing this scapular shall not suffer eternal flames," has been interpreted by Catholic

Above, Black Scapular of the Seven Dolors; below, Sacred Hearts Badge (left) and Precious Blood Badge (see "Scapulars, Badges").

theologians and authorities to mean that anyone wearing the scapular at the hour of death will receive from her the favor of dying in the state of grace. Popes and saints have warned against the folly of abusing Mary's promise. Pope Pius XI said, "I learned to love the Scapular Virgin in the arms of my mother." He also warned the faithful, "Although it is very true that the Blessed Virgin loves all who love her, nevertheless those who wish to have the Blessed Mother as a helper at the hour of death must in life merit such a signal favor by abstaining from sin and laboring in her honor."

The wearing of the brown scapular, therefore, is a sign that the wearer is in the livery of Our Lady and dedicated in a special way to her. Any priest with diocesan faculties, the Carmelite priests, and laymen who have special faculties from the Carmelite Order may invest persons in the scapular.

The *Sabbatine Privilege*, based on the bull said to have been issued by Pope John XXII, is frequently understood to mean that those who wear the Scapular and fulfill other conditions, made by the Blessed Virgin in an apparition to Pope John before he became Pope, will be freed from Purgatory on the first Saturday after death. However, all that the Church has ever said officially in explanation of this is that those who fulfill the conditions will be released from Purgatory through the intercession of Our Lady soon after death, and especially on Saturday.

At a time when the origin and the nature of the Sabbatine Privilege were both under serious question, Pope Paul V in an official document said, "It is permitted to preach that the Blessed Virgin will aid the souls of the Brothers and Sisters of the Confraternity of the Blessed Virgin of Mt. Carmel after their death by Her continual intercession, by Her suffrages and merits and by Her special protection, especially on the day of Saturday which is the day especially dedicated by the Church to the same Blessed Virgin Mary."

The conditions for gaining the Sabbatine Privilege are that the wearer should (1) wear the brown scapular faithfully, (2) observe chastity according to one's state in life, and (3) recite the Little Office of the Blessed Virgin or, when permission to do so has been obtained, to pray five decades of the rosary daily.

At one time the scapular, even the small one, was required to be made of wool. Later, Carmelite regulations permitted the scapular to be made from any suitable brown material. The scapular medal may be substituted for this scapular after investiture only for good and serious reasons. Today, the brown scapulars are often imprinted with a picture of Our Lady of Mount Carmel handing the scapular to St. Simon Stock. On the back side, the scapulars sometimes contain the words, "Whosoever dies wearing this scapular shall not suffer eternal fire."

In the United States, the brown scapular is promoted by the Carmelites and by the Blue Army.

The Green Scapular of the Immaculate Heart of Mary
The Scapular of the Immaculate Conception
Badge of the Immaculate Heart of Mary

Although commonly called the green scapular, this sacramental is not the habit of any confraternity and is improperly styled a scapular, as it does not have a front and back part but only two pious images attached to a single piece of green cloth which hangs on a single string of the same color.

On one side of the cloth is a picture of the Blessed Virgin Mary. She is dressed in a long gown over which hangs a mantle. No veil covers her head, and her hair fails loosely over her shoulders; her feet are bare. Her hands are folded inward, and she holds her heart from the top of which brilliant flames issue. On the other side of the cloth is a picture of a heart ablaze with flames, pierced with a sword and dripping blood. The heart is surmounted by a cross and encircled by the words: "Immaculate Heart of Mary, pray for us now and at the hour of our death."

No special formula is required for blessing the green scapular and there is no investiture ceremony. All that is necessary is that the scapular be blessed by a priest and honored by the person wishing to benefit by its happy influences. It may be worn or carried. Additionally, if a person in need of grace is obstinate, the Green Scapular may be placed secretly upon his person or in his possession, and the giver should say the prayer for him. The prayer is that which encircles the heart, and should be said at least once daily.

The green scapular devotion was brought to the world through a series of private revelations to Sister Justine Bisqueyburu, a humble French sister of the Daughters of Charity of St. Vincent de Paul.

Sister Justine was born November 11, 1817, at Mauléon in the Lower Pyrenees. As a young child, she was sent to live with her maternal aunt and her husband. At the age of twenty-two, Justine asked permission to join the Daughters of Charity of St. Vincent de Paul. From the time of her novitiate, Sister Justine began to experience extraordinary graces. She kept these secret, however, speaking of them only to those charged with her direction. For over sixty-four years, Sister Justine appeared to the world as simply a dedicated and hard-working sister. Most of this time she served in various hospitals of the order. As a religious, she was extremely faithful to the rule, pious and evincing a strong devotion to Our Lady. She was a capable administrator and is remembered for her humility, fervor, and regularity.

On January 28, 1840, Sister Justine was making her entrance retreat for her novitiate. She was at prayer when suddenly the Blessed Virgin made herself visible to her eyes. Mary was dressed in a long white gown which reached to her bare feet, over which was a mantle of very light blue. Her hair hung loose, and she wore no veil. In her hands, she held her heart, from the top of which abundant flames gushed out. At the close of the retreat and another four or five times during the course of her novitiate, Sister Justine was privileged to see this same vision of Our Lady. At first these visions seemed intended only to increase the tender devotion of the young sister to Mary and her Immaculate Heart.

After receiving the habit, Sister Justine was sent to Blangy. Here, shortly after her arrival on the feast of the Nativity of the Blessed Virgin, she had another vision. The Mother of God appeared to her during meditation, holding in her right hand her heart surmounted by flames and in the left a kind of scapular. One side of the scapular, or cloth badge, contained a representation of the Virgin such as she had appeared to Sister Justine in previous apparitions. The other side contained, in Sister Justine's words, "a heart all ablaze with rays more dazzling than the sun, and as transparent as crystal." That heart, pierced with a sword, was encircled by an inscription of oval shape and surmounted by a gold cross. It read, "Immaculate Heart of Mary, pray for us, now and at the hour of our death." At the time of this vision, an interior voice revealed to Sister Justine the meaning of the vision. She understood that this picture was, by the medium of her order, to contribute to the conversion of souls, particularly infidels, and to obtain for them a good death. She also understood that copies should be made as soon as possible and distributed with confidence.

Sister Justine wrote to her novice mistress, begging her to keep her communication secret and telling her that she feared this was possibly the effect of her imagination. She asked if her novice mistress believed it necessary for her to speak of it to her spiritual director. The vision was repeated twice more in the next year, when Sister Justine at last confided it to her director Father Aladel. At first there was a delay in the making and distributing of these scapulars. The Virgin herself complained about the delay in later visions to Sister Justine. At last the scapulars began to be made and distributed. Formal permission and encouragement for the sisters to make and distribute the scapulars was given by Pope Pius IX in 1870.

Devotees of the green scapular say that great graces are attached to the wearing, or carrying, of this sacramental. These graces, however, are more or less in proportion to the degree of faith and confidence possessed by the user. The scapular is known for drawing forth devotion to the Immaculate Heart of Mary and for numerous conversions.

The White Scapular of Our Lady of Good Counsel

The origin of this devotion has a miraculous imprint. Before the advent of Christianity, there was a small town in Italy about thirty miles from Rome which was noted as a center for the cult of Venus, goddess of pagan love. After the conversion of Rome, Genazzano became a center for devotion to Our Lady, and about the fourth century a church was built here under the name of St. Mary, Mother of Good Counsel. About a thousand years later, in 1356, this church was given into the care of the Order of St. Augustine. By this time the church was in ruins, and it took another century to restore it.

These early Augustinian friars lived in near destitution, and a pious widow, Patruccia, sold all her property to begin the restoration on the church. Since there was not enough money to complete the restoration, she began to pray for the rest.

A strange prodigy happened on April 25, 1467. The town was in a happy mood, celebrating the feast of St. Mark the Evangelist, the patron of the town. While the celebration was in progress, someone noticed a strange cloud slowly moving toward the town. Finally, the strange cloud came to rest on the walls of the half-finished church. There the people found a striking picture of the Madonna with her child. The immediate effect of this miracle was that all banded together to complete the church.

Where did the picture come from? Two pilgrims from Albania arrived and declared they had been searching for this very picture which was missing from its customary place in the Albanian town of Scutari. The picture had been a great object of devotion there for a while, but the city was under siege by the Ottoman Turks, and thus she came to Genazzano.

Careful investigations made between 1957 and 1959 during restoration of the fresco have revealed something of its true origin. The image of the Madonna is about a foot wide and seventeen inches high. Today it is encased in an elaborate glass, metal, and marble framework. It is part of a larger fresco that once covered part of the wall now hidden by the baroque shrine altar. Art experts postulate that the fresco may be the work of the early fifteenth-century artist Gentile da Fabriano. The fresco was probably painted about the time of Martin V (1417-1431). At some later date before 1467, the fresco was probably covered over with plaster, and a terra-cotta image of the Madonna was hung on the wall. During the restoration by the friars and the pious widow and tertiary Petruccia, the image of the Madonna appeared and was taken to be a token of divine favor. Possibly when the stone ledge was being inserted into the wall, the plaster covering cracked and separated from the wall, revealing the fresco beneath. One striking aspect of the fresco is that the upper portion of the image is separated from the wall so that much of it is just a thin sheet of plaster. Yet the image has survived for centuries in such a precarious and fragile state through a number of earthquakes and even through the bombing of the town during World War II.

The initial approval of devotion to Our Lady under the title of Our Mother of Good Counsel was given by Pope Paul II. Later, other popes ratified this approval, and in 1682 the image was crowned with the approval of Pope Innocent XI. In 1753, Pope Benedict XIV established the Pious Union of Our Lady of Good Counsel. More than any other pope, Pope Leo XIII, who was himself a member of the Pious Union, was deeply attached to this devotion. He instituted the white scapular of Good Counsel, added the title Mother of Good Counsel into the Litany of Loreto, declared the shrine a minor basilica, and placed a copy of the image over the altar in the Pauline chapel in the Vatican.

From this picture came the front panel of the white scapular. This Madonna depicts the mother with her eyes closed and the Child's right arm around her neck. His left hand is at the neck of her garment. Mary is shown as a queen, and the Child's eyes are intent on her. The back panel of this scapular shows the papal coat of arms — the tiara and the keys of Peter. Underneath are written the words of Pope Leo XIII: "Son, follow Her counsel."

This scapular is worn by the members of the Pious Union of Our Mother of Good Counsel.

The Scapular of the Immaculate Heart of Mary

This scapular originated with the Sons of the Immaculate Heart of Mary in 1877. It was sanctioned by Pope Pius IX in that same year. It owes its origins to a heavenly inspiration given to Most Rev. Joseph Xifre. C.M.F., a co-founder and later superior general of the Missionary Sons of the Immaculate Heart.

The scapular is of white woolen cloth. The front part has a representation of the burning heart of Mary, out of which grows a lily. The heart is circled with a wreath of roses and pierced with a sword.

The Scapular of Our Lady of Ransom

St. Peter Nolasco (d. 1256) devoted his life to the rescue of captives from the Moors, who were then occupying much of Spain. With this aim in mind, he founded the Order of Our Lady of Ransom (Mercedarians) between 1218 and 1234.

The faithful, on entering the confraternity erected by this order, are given a small scapular of white cloth. On the front of the scapular is the picture of Our Lady of Ransom. The back part may contain the arms of the order.

Blue Scapular of the Immaculate Conception

Venerable Ursula Benicasa, foundress of the Order of Theatine Nuns, tells in her autobiography how the habit worn by her sisters was revealed to her in a vision. This habit was to be worn in honor of the Immaculate Conception, and in return Our Lord promised great favors to the order. Ven. Ursula then begged the same graces for all the faithful who would devoutly wear a small sky-blue scapular in honor of the Immaculate Conception and for the purpose of securing the conversion of sinners.

Ven. Ursula herself made and distributed the first of these scapulars, after having them blessed by a priest. The scapular usually bears a symbolization of the Immaculate Conception on one side and on the other the name of Mary. The scapular received papal approval in 1671 from Pope Clement X. In 1894, a confraternity, later raised to an archconfraternity, of the Immaculate Conception of the Blessed Virgin and Mother of God, Mary, was erected in the Theatine Church of St. Andrea della Valle at Rome. Members of the confraternity were invested with this blue scapular.

Scapular of the Blessed Virgin Mary
under the title of Mary, Help of the Sick

Today's universal symbol of aid and charity, the Red Cross, first appeared on the black background of the scapular of St. Camillus de Lellis. In 1576, this large, boisterous young man decided to serve the sick in the same hospital in Rome where he had previously been hospitalized for a painful infection of his leg. Eventually, he became the superintendent of this hospital. Seeing the deplorable conditions of the hospitals of his time, he gathered faithful companions to assist him in his work.

In 1584, Saint Camillus was ordained a priest. His companions formed the nucleus of a new order in the Church, the Ministers of the Sick, later called the Clerks Regular of the Order of St. Camillus. The scapular was originally part of the habit of this order. In the Church of St. Magdalene at Rome, there is a picture of the Blessed Virgin said to be painted by the celebrated Dominican painter Fra Angelico; it is specially venerated under the title Help of the Sick. Both panels of the scapular bear an image of this picture on one side and the red cross on the black field edged in red on the reverse. The original purpose of the red cross, which was approved by Pope Sixtus V in 1586, was to inspire the sick and dying with confidence and contrition by reminding them of the cross of Christ red with His blood shed for their redemption.

In 1860, a brother of the Order of St. Camillus, Ferdinand Vicari, founded a confraternity under the invocation of the Mother of God for the poor sick. At their reception, the members were given a scapular of black woolen cloth with the front portion bearing a copy of the famous picture and with the small red cross on the back portion.

This scapular is no longer available, and the confraternity has ceased to exist.

The Black Scapular of the Seven Dolors of the Blessed Virgin Mary

According to tradition, the Servite Order was founded and received their habit through private revelation made to seven noblemen of Florence who were later canonized. These wealthy young merchants were members of a Marian Confraternity known as the *Laudesi* ("Praisers"). In 1233, as they were meditating after ceremonies on the feast of the Assumption, Our Lady appeared to them and, promising her protection and help, told them to leave the world and live entirely for God.

At first, the seven retired to a life of prayer and solitude. Later, they were joined by others and their community evolved into a religious order, today known in many parts of the world.

On Good Friday 1240, the brothers were praying in their oratory, when suddenly they received a vision of the Mother of God surrounded by a radiant light. She was clad in a long black mantle and was holding a black habit in her hands. In this same vision, she gave the founders the name "Servants of Mary," presented them with the rule of Saint Augustine, and told them that their black habit would serve as a reminder of the sorrows she endured.

Shortly after Pope Alexander IV had sanctioned the Servite Order, many of the faithful began to associate themselves with the order in confraternities honoring the Seven Sorrows of Mary. In later times, the members of this Confraternity of the Seven Dolors of Mary also wore a scapular of black cloth.

Today's scapular of the Seven Sorrows is made of black cloth and usually bears a picture of Our Lady of Sorrows on the front panel. The back panel may also have a picture of Our Lady. Information about this

From top, a Cord Rosary, a Finger Rosary, the Decena, and the Irish Penal Rosary (see "Chaplets, Rosaries, Crowns, and Beads").

scapular as well as other devotions In honor of the Sorrowful Mother may be obtained from the Servite Order, the trustee of this cult.

The Scapular of the Sacred Hearts of Jesus and Mary

In 1900, the Sacred Congregation of Rites approved of a scapular of the Sacred Hearts of Jesus and Mary. One panel bears an image of the two Sacred Hearts in their traditional representations, the Heart of Jesus with the cross and fire, wreathed with thorns, and the Heart of Mary pierced with a sword. Beneath these are the instruments of the Passion. The other panel of the scapular usually bears simply a red cross.

A religious of the Daughters of the Sacred Heart in Antwerp, Belgium, convinced the Bishop of Marseilles of the supernatural origin of this scapular. He, along with Cardinal Mazella, protector of the community, petitioned the Holy See for its approval. The Missionaries of the Sacred Heart and the Oblate Missionaries have custody of this scapular.

The Sacred Hearts Badge

In his great encyclical on the Sacred Heart, *Haurietis Aquas*, Pope Pius XII enjoined the faithful to join devotion to the Immaculate Heart of Mary to that of the Sacred Heart of Jesus. His words echoed those of Our Lady at Fátima, "The Heart of Jesus wishes to be venerated together with the Heart of His Mother."

Devotion to the Sacred Heart has been practiced for centuries. Since the apparitions of Our Lady to St. Catherine Labouré in which she gave the pattern for a medal showing the two hearts, and since the messages of Our Lady at Fátima, the twofold devotion has increased in popularity. In 1793, Father Mary-Joseph Courdin founded the Congregation of the Sacred Hearts for its promotion.

The badge of the Sacred Hearts depicts pictorially and symbolically both the Sacred Heart of Jesus and the Immaculate Heart of Mary. It serves as a reminder of the great love Jesus and Mary have for us, and that we must love them in return. The badge reminds us that graces come from the Heart of Jesus through the Heart of His Mother.

Scapular of the Most Sacred Heart of Jesus

A scapular of the Sacred Heart was introduced in France in 1876. This scapular consists of two segments of white woolen cloth connected by two strings. One segment of the scapular bears the usual representation of the Sacred Heart, and the other bears a representation of the Blessed Virgin under the title of Mother of Mercy.

In 1876, a poor young woman named Estelle Faguette was dying of consumption in Pellevoisin, a small town in central France. Estelle had been the breadwinner for her family, who were distraught at the thought of her death. The last rites had been administered, and all preparations for her death were concluded.

As Estelle lay dying, she was visited with an apparition of Our Lady, who announced her complete cure in five days. Overcome with gratitude, Estelle begged to be allowed to enter a cloistered community. Our Lady answered, directing her to become a lay apostle instead and telling her, "One can be saved in every state. Where you are, you can publish my glory."

During the next year, Estelle received ten more apparitions of Mary. Each apparition emphasized something of importance. In one of the visits, Our Lady appeared to Estelle wearing a scapular which she asked Estelle to make known.

On one side of the scapular is an image of Mary Immaculate. On the other is the pierced heart of Jesus, ringed with thorns and flames burning from the top. The burning heart is surmounted with a cross.

The Bishop of Bourges appointed a commission to investigate, and in 1877 his report was taken to Rome. The Confraternity of Our Lady of Pellevoisin was established, and Pope Leo XIII gave approbation to the confraternity and to the scapular.

The Sacred Heart Badge

The most common token of the Sacred Heart is the Badge of the Sacred Heart, one of the most common of the Catholic sacramentals. This familiar badge owes its origin to St. Margaret Mary Alacoque.

St. Margaret Mary was a humble nun of the Visitation convent at Paray-le-Monial, France. She was favored in prayer by special revelations beginning in 1693 in which Our Lord called her to reveal to the world the love of his Sacred Heart. On one occasion when Christ appeared to her, He expressed the wish that those who loved Him should wear or carry a picture of His Sacred Heart. St. Margaret Mary made some little pictures which she and her friends carried. These are the first Sacred Heart badges.

In 1720, the city of Marseilles, France, was ravaged by the plague. Nearly a thousand persons a day were dying from the dread disease and the people were panicked with fear. The bishop requested the nuns of the city to make up thousands of badges of the Sacred Heart. He then consecrated the city to the Sacred Heart and distributed the little badges. No new cases of the plague were reported, and the people were wild with joy.

Over the centuries, the style of the badge has changed. Today, the Badge is an oval shape with a serrated-edge print showing Christ with His

Heart exposed on one side and the Heart itself on the other. The badge was brought to the United States by the Apostleship of Prayer and is used as an external sign of the union of the members with Christ. On the front of the badge are found the words "Apostleship of Prayer — League of the Sacred Heart." On the reverse are found two prayers: "Cease, the Heart of Jesus is with me," and "Sacred Heart of Jesus, Thy Kingdom Come."

Scapular of the Most Precious Blood

In Rome, members of the Confraternity of the Most Precious Blood were invested with a red scapular or a red girdle. No special indulgences were connected with the wearing of this scapular, and its use was optional with the members of the confraternity. As used in Rome, the scapular had on the front portion a representation of the chalice with the Precious Blood adored by angels. The back segment was simply a small portion of red cloth.

The Precious Blood Heart

American headquarters for the Confraternity of the Precious Blood is at the cloistered monastery of the Precious Blood Sisters in Brooklyn, New York. Its official emblem is a small heart made of red cloth. On one side is a reproduction of the mural behind the altar in the chapel of the Most Precious Blood in the monastery. A sunburst haloes the crucified figure of Our Lord. Above the crucifix is the name of the confraternity; about the foot are the words "We beseech Thee help Thy servants whom Thou hast redeemed with Thy Precious Blood." On the back of the heart is a red drop of the Precious Blood on a white background with the saying of Pope Pius IX, "Place on thy heart one drop of the Precious Blood of Jesus and fear nothing."

The Red Scapular of the Passion
(The Scapular of the Sacred Heart of Jesus
and of the Most Loving and Compassionate
Heart of the Blessed and Immaculate Virgin Mary)

The red scapular of the Passion was revealed in a series of apparitions of Our Lord to Sister Apolline Andriveau from July 26, through September 14, 1846.

A beautiful, intelligent, talented young Frenchwoman, Louise Apolline Aline Andriveau, at the age of twenty-three, joined the Sisters of Charity of St. Vincent de Paul. Here she blended with the other sisters, humbly dedicating her life to the service of the sick and the poor. On receiving the habit, Sister Apolline was sent to St. John's at Troyes, where

137

one of her duties was the care of the chapel. In the presence of the Holy Eucharist, she began to receive special graces from Our Lord.

"I went up to the Chapel before Benediction. I thought I beheld Our Lord; in his right hand he held a red scapular, the opposite ends of which were connected by two woollen strings of the same color. On one end of the scapular was represented our Savior crucified; the most painful instruments of the Passion lay at the foot of the cross. . . . Around the crucifix were inscribed these words: 'Holy Passion of our Lord Jesus Christ, save us!' On the opposite end of the scapular were represented the Sacred Hearts of Jesus and of His holy Mother. A cross seemed to rise between these two hearts — and the scapular at this end bore the inscription 'Sacred Hearts of Jesus and Mary, protect us!' "

The apparition of Jesus holding in His hand the scapular of His Passion was repeated frequently. On one occasion, Our Lord told Sister Apolline that those who wore the scapular would, on Fridays, experience a great increase of faith, hope, and charity.

When someone remarked that it would be a difficult matter to secure authorization for this devotion, Sister Apolline told them with confidence that as the devotion was wished for by Christ Himself, He would remove all the obstacles that usually oppose the introduction of new devotions. In fact, Pope Pius IX approved the scapular of the Passion in 1847, scarcely a year after the apparitions.

The front panel of the scapular pinpoints the central act of Redemption. In the center is a large oval of the crucifix, embellished with the other instruments of the Passion. A hammer and pincers in the upper left hand corner symbolize not only the tools used to drive and remove the nails, but also the hammer serves as a symbol of penance and the pincers remind us to pull out sin from ourselves and make room in our souls for the healing grace from the sacred wounds. In the upper right-hand corner three nails and the crown of thorns symbolize the mental and physical discipline that must go together for us to achieve integrity of spirit. Beneath the cross is a ladder whose steps symbolize the virtues by which we must ascend our own cross in union with the redeeming cross of Christ. The crowing rooster symbolizes that the time for repentance is at hand. The spear reminds us that we must pierce our own hearts and break them free from every attachment save God. Other symbols displayed are the scourges, the sponge and water pot, and Veronica's veil.

The last apparition to Sister Apolline took place just five days before the apparition of Our Lady of La Salette. The crucifix and passion instruments shown to Sister Apolline were similar to the crucifix which Our Lady wore on a chain around her neck at La Salette. The instruments of Christ's Passion teach us how to meditate on His many sufferings. By this daily remembrance we come to understand that if we hope to share the joys of His glory, we must first share His bitterness and humiliations in suffering.

The red scapular of the Passion is promoted by the Archconfraternity of the Holy Agony.

The Black Scapular of the Passion

Paul Francis Daneo, St. Paul of the Cross (1694-1775), received many graces from God indicating that he was to found a community to keep alive the memory of the Passion of Our Lord. The sacred habit of the religious order which he founded is represented in small reproduction by the black scapular of the Passion.

This scapular is made from black cloth and is oblong in shape. The emblem worn over the breast is the Passionist sign — the figure of a white heart surmounted by a cross with the inscription JESU XPI PASSIO (The Passion of Jesus Christ) and with three nails underneath the heart. The emblem is white on a black background. On the back part, there is the image of Jesus on the Cross. The instruments of the Passion are incorporated into the corners of each part: the chalice of Gethsemane, the veil with Christ's face imprinted on it, the crown of thorns, and the stone column at which Jesus was scourged. These symbols portray the main sorrowful mysteries. On the lower half of each panel is written *Sit Semper in Cordibus Nostris* ("May it [the Passion of Jesus Christ] be always in our hearts"). The two panels of the scapular are joined with black strings.

Those who are enrolled in the Black Scapular share in all the spiritual graces and indulgences of the Congregation of the Passion. Apparently, the Black Scapular was originally intended for, and restricted to, the Members of the Confraternity of the Passion, but in 1861 the privilege of being enrolled in this scapular was extended to all the faithful by Pope Plus IX. Additionally, the members of the confraternity are not required to be enrolled with this scapular, although it is strongly recommended.

Scapular of the Holy Face

There is a white scapular of the Holy Face which is worn by the members of the Archconfraternity of the Holy Face. On a piece of white cloth, this scapular bears the well-known Roman picture connected with the towel of St. Veronica. The members may wear the picture of the Holy Face on a medal or cross instead of the scapular which is merely one of the pious practices of the archconfraternity without any special indulgences.

Sister Marie de St. Pierre, a Discalced Carmelite nun of Tours, received special favors from Our Lord. Through her, He offered a number of promises to anyone who showed honor and reverence for His Holy Countenance. The wearing of this scapular is connected with this devotion.

The Small Passionist Emblem

Among the mystical lights that St. Paul of the Cross received before he founded the Congregation of the Passion was the sign or emblem of the order: a white heart, surmounted by a cross, bearing the title of the Passion of Jesus Christ.

The badges or emblems worn by the saint himself often seemed to have a special, miraculous power. He frequently gave away those he no longer wore. He sometimes allowed those persons for whom he was spiritual director to wear these signs secretly.

St. Paul himself explained the symbolism of the sign. The white color of the heart means that the heart which has the Passion imprinted on it ought to be already purified. He called the sign a "terror of hell" and a "sign of salvation." From this practice of the founder, the wearing of a small Passionist emblem gradually developed. The original emblems were of cloth; today the emblems are more commonly made of metal. The faithful who wear a small sign of the Passion are encouraged to recite the pious aspiration "Passion of Christ, strengthen me."

The Scapular of the Most Blessed Trinity

The scapular of the Most Blessed Trinity has its origin in a series of private revelations to St. John of Matha. The first of these revelations came as St. John was celebrating his first Mass. An angel clothed in a white garment appeared at the altar. Across his breast and shoulder was a cross of red and blue. His arms were crossed and held over what appeared to be two captives — a Christian and a Moor. St. John understood that he was to found an order for the redemption of captives, Christian and non-Christian alike.

St. John retreated to the desert, where he met St. Felix of Valois. Together the two men lived. for a time, the eremetical life, fasting and praying fervently for guidance in their mission. At last, after a number of other apparitions, the two traveled to Rome in 1198 to seek the counsel of the Holy Father. Pope Innocent III, while deliberating on their proposals, also had a vision of an angel wearing a red and blue cross. He approved the new institute and ordered it to be called the Order of the Most Holy Trinity for the Ransom of Captives. He gave the members a white habit with a red and blue cross.

This habit became the basis on which the scapular of the Blessed

Trinity was later made. This scapular is the badge of the members of the Confraternity of the Most Holy Trinity.

The Black Scapular of St. Benedict

The Benedictine scapular began in the early sixth century as a kind of apron worn over the standard habit to keep it clean while working. When the monks were not working, they wore a long, flowing choir robe called a cuculla. Later the scapular became a part of the habit as it is now worn.

The small scapular of the oblate is a reminder of the full habit worn by the monks. When a person becomes an oblate, he receives a small black scapular in the rite of investiture. In 1950, the Holy See gave permission for Oblates of St. Benedict to wear the medal of St. Benedict in place of the oblate scapular.

This scapular is a little larger than most of the small scapulars, being a little over two inches high and almost as wide. It is black with the image of St. Benedict as an abbot with staff and rule book on one side. The traditional chalice with the serpent symbolizes his deliverance from poison. On the other panel, St. Scholastica, Benedict's twin sister, is portrayed as a Benedictine abbess, with staff and book surmounted by a dove.

The Scapular of St. Dominic

The reception of the Dominican scapular by Blessed Reginald from the hands of Mary parallels the story of the brown scapular and St. Simon Stock. The small Dominican scapular was indulgenced in 1903 by St. Pius X, as often as the wearer devoutly kissed it. It is made of white wool, and was approved by the order as the usual form of affiliation with the community. No images are necessary, but the scapular as given in the house of the Dominican general at Rome has on one side the picture of St. Dominic kneeling before the crucifix and on the other that of Blessed Reginald receiving the habit from the hands of the Mother of God.

The Scapular of St. Joseph

Shortly after Pope Pius IX declared St. Joseph patron of the Universal Church in 1870, there began in the Diocese of St. Claude, France, the use of a scapular honoring St. Joseph. The devotion was founded by Mother Marie of Jesus, foundress of the Franciscan Sisters of the Immaculate Conception, and Father Peter Baptiste of Reims, O.F.M.Cap. The scapular was approved for the Universal Church by Pope Leo XIII in 1893, and its propagation was entrusted to the Capuchins.

The original scapular was white, but the one that was finally approved is made in the colors traditionally assigned, in Christian iconography, to St.

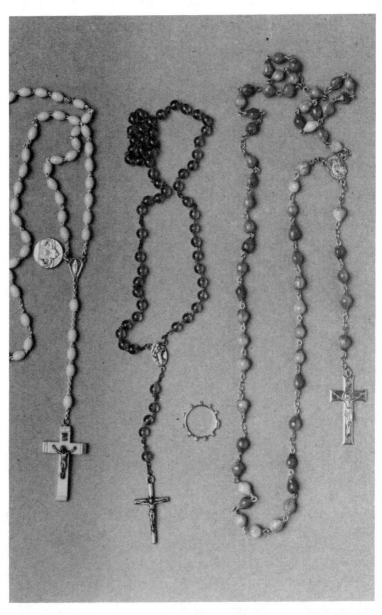

From left: Rosary of the Commemorative Medal, Yugoslav Rosary, Ring Rosary, Job's Tears Rosary (see "Chaplets, Rosaries, etc.").

Joseph — white, purple, and gold. The purple, which forms the base of the rectangular scapular, stands for Joseph's humility and modesty. On this are sewn two rectangles of yellow or gold, which stand for his justice and sanctity. The bands of this scapular are white, indicating Joseph's purity.

On the breast side of the scapular appears an image of St. Joseph bearing the Infant Jesus on his arm and carrying a lily in his other hand. Under this image is written, "St. Joseph, Patron of the Church, Pray for Us." On the other side of the scapular is the image of the papal arms (the tiara and two keys) with the dove as symbol of the Holy Spirit above it and a cross beneath. The inscription "The Spirit of the Lord is His Guide" is written in Latin beneath.

There are a number of purposes for this scapular, in addition to reminding the wearer of his dedication to St. Joseph. This scapular is intended to remind the wearer to imitate Joseph in his purity, humility, and justice. It serves as a reminder to invoke St. Joseph to strengthen, guard, and gladden holy Mother Church. By wearing this scapular, the wearer hopes to obtain at the time of his death the help of him whom the Church has also proclaimed patron of a happy death. A final purpose is to obtain from this saint the interior spirit, the fear of sin, and the grace necessary for the faithful fulfillment of one's state in life.

The Scapular of St. Michael the Archangel

A little-known scapular is that of St. Michael the Archangel, belonging to the archconfraternity of the same name. The confraternity was begun in the Church of St. Eustachius in Rome.

The two segments of cloth of this scapular are in the shape of a shield. One is blue and the other black, as are the bands. Both sides of the scapular have the traditional representation of the Archangel St. Michael slaying the dragon, carrying the inscription "Quis ut Deus?" (Who is like God?) These words are attributed to St. Michael in the great battle at or near the beginning of time when he and his heavenly host fell upon the army of Lucifer and cast them forth from the Kingdom of Heaven into the abyss of hell.

Scapular of St. Norbert

St. Norbert, the great eucharistic saint of his time, received the direction to found his order, an indication of the place where the order should begin, and the holy habit from the hands of the Blessed Virgin in a vision. St. Norbert and the Praemonstratensian Order which he founded became the wellspring of Eucharistic devotion which restored its place of primacy in Christian life.

Upon St. Norbert's true devotion to the Blessed Virgin and to the

Blessed Sacrament, he built the first "third order" for laymen in the church. In 1128, St. Norbert gave a little scapular of white wool to Count Theobald of Champagne and Blois as a proof and emblem of his union with the Norbertine family. Thus, the Norbertine scapular ranks as one of the oldest scapulars.

The Red Cross of St. Camillus

About three hundred years before the founding of the International Red Cross, the red cross had already become a symbol of organized charity and dedication to the sick. Saint Camillus de Lellis, the founder of the Camillians (Order of the Servants of the Sick), obtained the privilege of wearing a cross made of red cloth on the black habits of the order. It served as an inspiration for the sick by reminding them of the Passion, death, and resurrection of Our Lord. Additionally, it reminded the priests and brothers who wore the habit of their dedication and solemn commitment of service to the sick.

During the battle of Canizza in 1601, the Camillians were busily occupied with the wounded. The tent in which they had stored their equipment and supplies caught fire, and everything in the tent was destroyed except the red cross of one of the habits. Other miracles gradually increased devotion to the red cross.

Today, the Servants of the Sick carry on the work of St. Camillus in 350 houses, hospitals, clinics and other health facilities in almost thirty countries. They distribute small, simple red cloth crosses worldwide. A special blessing was inserted in the Roman Ritual for the crosses. From the sick who have received these crosses come many reports of a deepening faith in Christ the Healer, miracles, and conversions.

Chaplets, Rosaries, Crowns, and Beads

The practice of using a string of beads as an aid in meditation and prayer is an ancient one. Early monks, wishing to say a certain number of prayers, counted the prayers by moving small pebbles or stones from one container to another. Later, strings of beads were used for the counting. The Old English word bede, surviving today as the word bead, originally was a word for prayer.

During the Middle Ages, the Rosary which we know today as the Dominican Rosary evolved and became one of the most popular sacramentals of the Church. The word rosary is from the Latin *rosarium*, or rose garden. It signified a wreath or garland and was seen as a special favor of presentation to Our Lord and Our Lady. The word chaplet, from the Old French *chaplet*, and the Latin word *corona* also mean a wreath or crown.

Today, the words rosary, chaplet, corona, and beads are used interchangeably to refer to prayer devotions which use special strings of beads to aid the Catholic in meditation. Chaplets are intended to honor and invoke the members of the Holy Trinity, Our Lady, the angels or the saints. New chaplets are composed to honor and spread devotion to a particular saint or to reinforce devotion to a particular mystery or aspect of our religion. Some have been dictated by heavenly authors through private revelations.

The origins of many of the older chaplet devotions are clouded in history. The authors of even some of the more modern ones are unknown.

What all of the chaplet devotions using designated beads have in common is that they provide a tangible reminder of the spiritual.

The Rosary

Tradition holds that Our Lady gave the Rosary to St. Dominic Guzman in 1206 as a form of Gospel-preaching and popular prayer, although history seems to belie that tradition. Nonetheless, for more than seven centuries, the Rosary devotion has been one of the most popular devotional practices in the Church. Its combination of vocal and mental prayer have made it a prime tool for contemplation. Jesus is the author and source of grace; Our Lady's Rosary is the key to open the treasury of grace to us.

Although prayer beads had been popular before Dominic's time, he and his friars quickly adopted the rosary as an excellent way to teach the mysteries of Christianity to a largely illiterate European population. In

1470, Blessed Alan of Rupe founded the first rosary confraternity and thereby launched the Dominican Order as the foremost missionaries of the rosary. Through the efforts of Blessed Alan and the early Dominicans, this prayer form spread rapidly throughout Western Christendom.

Prayer beads have been found in many cultures and several religions. The earliest beads in Christian history were pebbles which monks moved from one pile to another as they repeated the Jesus Prayer. Later, they wove cords of knots, and this is the form that still prevails among Byzantine Christians. Strings of beads were first used as the layperson's psalter. Just as the literate monks and nuns chanted their 150 psalms, the illiterate recited 150 *Paternosters* (Our Fathers). In time, Scripture texts began to provide themes for meditation during the recitation of the Paters. Gradually the use of the angelic salutation began to replace or be mixed with the Paters. It was thus in the time of Dominic (thirteenth century), and the last half of the Hail Mary was not common until the Reformation.

The meditations on the fifteen mysteries serve as reminders of incidents in the lives of Christ and Mary, basic mysteries of our Christian faith. These are divided into the joyful, sorrowful, and glorious mysteries. Thirteen of the mysteries come from incidents in the New Testament. One, the assumption of Mary into heaven, comes from Sacred Tradition. The fifteenth, the Crowning of Mary as Queen of Heaven, is thought to be derived from images in the Book of Revelation.

The *mysteries of the Rosary* are as follows.

THE JOYFUL MYSTERIES

1. THE ANNUNCIATION — The angel Gabriel reveals the mysteries of the Divinity, saluting the Virgin Mother of God as full of grace.

2. THE VISITATION — Mary visits her cousin Elizabeth, who is pregnant with John the Baptist.

3. THE NATIVITY — The Word which from all eternity had proceeded from the Father is born as a mortal infant of a virgin mother.

4. THE PRESENTATION OF THE CHILD JESUS — The child is presented in the Temple; the Lawgiver obeys the Law.

5. THE FINDING OF THE CHILD JESUS IN THE TEMPLE — The joyful mother finds her lost son in the Temple, teaching the teachers.

THE SORROWFUL MYSTERIES

1. THE AGONY IN THE GARDEN — Jesus, the Redeemer, prays in the Garden of Gethsemane; sad and fearful, He grows faint and sweats blood.

2. THE SCOURGING AT THE PILLAR — God, delivered up by a traitor, is bound with rough cords and beaten with bloody scourges.

3. THE CROWNING WITH THORNS — The King of Glory is crowned with a crown of ignominy, made from thorns.

4. THE CARRYING OF THE CROSS — The Lord is forced to carry the instrument of torture to the place of execution.

5. THE CRUCIFIXION — Fastened with nails to a cross of shame, the guiltless hangs between the guilty. He breathes forth His spirit while praying for his persecutors.

THE GLORIOUS MYSTERIES

1. THE RESURRECTION — Death has been vanquished, and Christ the Conqueror comes forth from the grave, breaking the bonds of sin and opening the portals of Heaven.

2. THE ASCENSION — Having appeared to men, Christ ascends to Heaven and sits at the right hand of the Father.

3. THE DESCENT OF THE HOLY SPIRIT — The Holy Spirit showers down on the Apostles in fiery tongues of love.

4. THE ASSUMPTION OF OUR LADY — The Virgin is taken up to Heaven and welcomed with the jubilation of the heavenly hosts.

5. THE CORONATION OF MARY — The Virgin is crowned with a crown of twelve stars. Near the throne of her Son, she reigns over all created things.

Through the years. Our Lady has reaffirmed her approval of this devotion, and her pleasure in the title "Queen of the Rosary." Through Blessed Alan, she made fifteen promises to those who devoutly recite her beads. She told him that "immense volumes would have to be written if all the miracles of my holy Rosary were to be recorded." Our Lady's promises are:

"1. Those who shall have served me constantly by reciting the Rosary shall receive some special grace.

"2. I promise my special protection and great graces to all who devoutly recite my Psalter.

"3. The Rosary shall be a most powerful armor against hell; it shall destroy vices, weaken sin, overthrow unbelief.

"4. It shall make virtues and good works to flourish again; it shall obtain for souls abundant mercies of God; it shall win the hearts of men from the love of the world and its vanities, and lift them to a desire of things eternal. Oh, how many souls will be sanctified by this means!

"5. The soul which has recourse to me through the Rosary shall not perish.

"6. Whoever shall have recited the Rosary devoutly and with meditation on its mysteries, shall never be overcome by misfortunes, shall not experience the anger of God, shall not be lost by a sudden death: but if he be in sin he shall be converted; and if he be in grace, he shall persevere and be made worthy of eternal life.

"7. Truly devoted servants of my Rosary shall not die without the sacraments.

"8. It is my will that those who recite my Rosary have, in life and in death, light and the plenitude of graces; and in life and death, may participate in the merits of the saints.

"9. Every day I deliver from Purgatory souls devoted to my Rosary.

"10. True servants of my Rosary shall enjoy great glory in heaven.

"11. Whatever you shall ask through the Rosary, you shall obtain.

"12. I will assist in every necessity those who propagate my Rosary.

"13. I have obtained from my Son that all members of the Confraternity of my Rosary may have in life and in death all the blessed as their associates.

"14. All who recite my Rosary are my children and the brethren of my Only Begotten Son Jesus Christ.

"15. Devotion to my Rosary is a great sign of predestination."

Our Lady told Blessed Bartolo Longo to propagate the rosary and promised that those who would propagate this devotion would be saved. In 1884, Our Lady of Pompeii appeared at Naples to Fortuna Agrelli. who was desperately ill. She told Fortuna that the title "Queen of the Holy Rosary" was one which was particularly pleasing to her, and she cured Fortuna of her illness. At Lourdes, Our Lady told St. Bernadette to pray many rosaries. When Bernadette saw the beautiful lady, she instinctively took her beads in her hands and knelt down. The lady made a sign of approval with her head and took into her hands a rosary which hung on her right arm. As Bernadette prayed, Our Lady passed the beads of her rosary through her fingers but said nothing except the Gloria at the end of each decade. At Fátima, Mary told the children to pray the Rosary often.

Popes throughout history have loved the Rosary. Not a single Pope in the last four hundred years has failed to urge devotion to the Rosary. From Sixtus IV, in 1479, to the present day, the popes have urged the use of this devotion, and enriched its recitation with indulgences. Pius XI dedicated the entire month of October to the Rosary. Pope St. Pius X said, "Of all the prayers, the Rosary is the most beautiful and the richest in graces; of all it is the one most pleasing to Mary, the Virgin Most Holy." Pope Leo XIII repeatedly recommended the Rosary as a most powerful means whereby to move God to aid us in meeting the needs of the present age. In 1883, he inserted the invocation, "Queen of the Most Holy Rosary, pray for us!" into the Litany for the Universal Church. Pope John XXIII, who was particularly faithful to the daily recital of the whole Rosary, has said, "We can never sufficiently recommend the saying of the Rosary, not simply with the lips but with attention of the soul to the divine truths, with a heart filled with love and gratitude." Pope John Paul II tells us to "love the simple, fruitful prayer of the Rosary."

Many of the saints and a number of the religious orders have praised the Rosary. St. Charles said he depended on the Rosary almost entirely for the conversion and sanctification of his diocese. Founders of most religious orders have either commanded or recommended the daily recitation of the Rosary. The Benedictines speedily adapted this devotion in their ancient cloisters. The Carmelites were happy to receive the Rosary as well as their rule from the Dominicans. The Franciscans made their rosaries out of wood, and preached this devotion as well as poverty. Inspired by the example of their founder, the Jesuits invariably propagated the devotion. St. Francis Xavier used the touch of his chaplet as a means of healing the sick. St. Vincent de Paul instructed the members of his order to depend more on the Rosary than upon their preaching.

Our ancestors had recourse to the Rosary as an ever-ready refuge in misfortune and as a pledge and a proof of their Christian faith and devotion. St. Dominic used the Rosary as a weapon in his battle against the Albigensian heresy in France. In the last century, the Christian successes over the Turks at Temesvar and at Corfu coincided with the conclusion of public devotions of the Rosary. During the penal days in Ireland, the Rosary bound the Irish Catholics together as a church militant. When it was a felony to teach the Catholic Catechism, and death for a priest to say Mass, the Irish mothers used their rosaries to tell their little ones the story of Jesus and Mary, and thus kept the Faith green in the hearts of their children. St. John Vianney, the Curé d'Ars, declared emphatically that in the nineteenth century it was the Rosary which restored religion in France. Likewise, in the dark days of persecution in Mexico in our own century, the sturdy Mexican Catholics clung faithfully to their rosaries. The martyr Miguel Pro was allowed his last request before being shot by a firing squad — he knelt and prayed his Rosary.

A special society, the *Society of the Living Rosary*, was founded by the Venerable Marie Pauline Jaricot in the city of Lyons, France, in 1826. She formed bands of fifteen members who each said one decade of the Rosary daily. Thus, the entire Rosary was said collectively by the members of each circle daily.

Father Timothy Ricci, O.P., instituted the *Perpetual Rosary*, or Mary's Guard of Honor, in 1935. The aim of this devotion is to unite the members in such a way that some devoted watchers will ever be found in prayer and

Clockwise from left: Indian Corn-Bead Rosary, Ship's Engineers Rosary, Special Favors Rosary with charms, and Chaplet of the Infant of Prague (see "Chaplets, Rosaries, Crowns, and Beads").

praise at Our Lady's shrine, telling their beads for the conversion of sinners, the relief of the dying, and the succor of the dead. In Belgium, the Dominican nuns of the Third Order established a monastery for the express purpose of maintaining the Perpetual Rosary, so that there it became not merely the devotion of a society, but the distinctive work of a community. A number of shrines of the order are to be found in the United States. Here, the Rosary is said day and night by members of the community. Rosary processions are held, and pilgrims come to sing again and again the praises of their Heavenly Queen.

When reciting the Rosary, one begins by making the sign of the cross and reciting the Apostle's Creed on the crucifix. After an initial Our Father, three Hail Mary's are said, followed by the Glory Be to the Father. Then the first mystery is announced, after which one recites one Our Father and ten Hail Mary's while meditating on that mystery. The rosary is continued in this manner until all the mysteries have been contemplated, although often only five of the fifteen mysteries are recited at one time. Since the apparitions of Our Lady at Fátima in 1917, the prayer taught by Mary to the children has often been added to each decade: "O, my Jesus, forgive us our sins, save us from the fires of hell, lead all souls to heaven, especially those in greatest need." During the apparition of June 13, 1917, Our Lady made this agreement: "I promise at the hour of death to help with the graces needed for their salvation, whoever on the first Saturday of five consecutive months shall confess and receive Holy Communion, recite five decades of the rosary, and keep me company for fifteen minutes while meditating on the fifteen mysteries of the rosary with the intention of making reparation to me." The conditions of the *First Saturday devotion*, fathered from this and other apparitions include five decades of the rosary, a communion of reparation, reparatory prayer and some sacrifice made for the same intention. The devotion of the *Five First Saturdays* includes these conditions and adds confession and a fifteen-minute meditation on the mysteries of the rosary. Confession may be in the eight days preceding or following the Saturday, and the intention, if forgotten, may be made at confession on the first opportunity. The meditation may include one or all of the mysteries.

Rosaries have been manufactured from all materials, from precious gemstones to glass to wood to plastic. One rosary in the author's collection was crafted by American Indians from corn seed. Another, made for her by a ship's engineer, is fashioned of metal chain links. Yet another is made from seed known as "Job's tears." A descriptive folder accompanying this rosary reminds the user that Job's sufferings purified his love of God and points out that frequent use of these rosaries will make them shine more brightly.

Rosaries are made in all sizes, from tiny beads which fit entirely into one's palm to large *family rosaries* with beads over an inch in diameter. Sometimes, modifications have been made to rosaries for aesthetic or other reasons. Some wear a *rosary ring*, a single decade crafted as a ring which the wearer turns round and round to say successive decades. The Mexicans have a *decena*, a small single-decade rosary which is easily carried in a pocket. Another beautiful rosary from Mexico is called a *ladder rosary*. With the beads hung crosswise like rungs, it seems a symbolic ladder to Heaven.

A single decade *Irish penal rosary* was used during the dark years in Irish history when religious objects were forbidden to the Catholics. This rosary became not only a reminder of the fifteen mysteries, but a symbol of the Passion as well. The crucifix is lavishly embellished with symbols, front and back, to recall all the events of the Passion.

One of the loveliest and most practical rosaries available today is called the *special favor* or *symbolic rosary*. In place of the Our Father beads are sculptured metal symbols for each of the mysteries. This rosary is an excellent teaching tool because of its visible reminders of the mysteries.

Standard rosaries are often found with medals of particular saints or shrines attached to the centerpiece. Sometimes relics of saints or blessed (*beati*) are attached, or a single drop of holy water is caught in the centerpiece. These medals simply serve as a reminder of that particular person or place. It is a popular custom in many parts of the world to touch rosaries to the body or relics of saints. The rosaries thus become what are known as "*touch relics.*"

The *scriptural rosary*, as composed in the 1960s, is a modern version of the way the Rosary was once prayed throughout Western Christendom in the late Middle Ages. A different thought taken from Scripture is assigned to each Hail Mary bead. These Scriptures have been arranged so that the story of each mystery is told in consecutive steps. Popular versions of the scriptural rosary are available in Catholic bookstores.

A booklet called "Pray the Rosary" is distributed free by Word Rosary Intecessors, a Catholic intercessory prayer community based in South Bend, Indiana (see appendix). This Scripture-based Rosary was written by Martha Ortega. She and her husband have dedicated their lives to the awakening of the modern world to the power of the Rosary and the power of the Word of God to change lives. A faith experience which Mrs. Ortega believes cured her of an incurable illness led her to start thinking of the joy of God in everyday life, not just as something to experience after death. She wanted to share with others the blessings that come on a daily basis. After composing this Scripture-based Rosary in 1982, the Ortegas had a thousand copies printed for distribution. Mrs. Ortega says, "I thought a thousand copies were going to last forever." By May of 1988, they had distributed over 286,000 copies, and the booklet had been translated into a number of other languages. Missions all over the world have requested copies. The Ortegas' original idea to distribute the booklet to encourage people to pray the Rosary grew into a prayer community as well. In the solemn dedication of the ministry in 1988, the purpose of the mission was stated: "Through the Word Rosary Ministry, we hope to give You praise, honor, and glory, and to lift up Jesus the Living Word and to honor Your faithful servant Mary, the Mother of Jesus."

A beautiful trilogy of *meditational books* is published by the Friends of the Cross. These three books — *A Touch of Grace, Portrait of the Passion,* and *Crown of Glory* — are scriptural and pictorial in content and display the mysteries of the Life of Our Lord. The books present the major prophecies of the Old Testament pointing to the Messiah, and show, in Scriptures from the New Testament, how these prophecies are perfectly fulfilled in Christ. The books are perfect for meditation in conjunction with the recitation of the joyful, sorrowful, and glorious mysteries of the Rosary. They are available from the Friends of the Cross at a modest price (see appendix). This group is a pair of dedicated lay couples who have a special devotion to Our Lord's sufferings and who operate a small publishing apostolate.

Jesus Beads

"Lord Jesus Christ, Son of God, have mercy upon me, a sinner."

"Lord Jesus Christ, have mercy on me."

"Lord Jesus, have mercy."

"Jesus, Lamb of God Who take away the sins of the world, have mercy upon us."

The Jesus prayer takes many forms. Rooted in the Bible and accepted for centuries in the monastic life of Eastern Christianity, the Jesus prayer is a perfect prayer for modern Christians who want to follow St. Paul's advice to "pray constantly" (1 Thess 5:17). Short and simple to repeat, this prayer is heavy with meaning.

The Jesus prayer is directed to the Son. No one has ever seen God, but God has revealed himself in Jesus Christ. In seeking for the heart of the Father, we find him in and through the Son.

In biblical times, a person's name was not simply a way of identifying him. It was also a key to understanding the person — it had meaning. The meaning of the name Jesus is "one who saves." Christ is a Greek word, which means "the anointed one." During His lifetime on earth, Jesus was often referred to as "Rabbi" or "Teacher." After the Resurrection, he was most often called "Lord". Thus in the Jesus prayer we call on our Savior and King, acknowledging Him as Lord. In a spirit of humility, we recognize that we are sinners and call on our King for mercy.

Prayer can be defined as the heart's conversation with God. With unceasing prayer we can attain a unity with Christ that displaces our own selves and allows for Christ's indwelling in our hearts.

While Jesus still walked the earth, the Jesus prayer was prayed. People began to call to Him for mercy when they acknowledged him as the Son of God. The blind beggar outside the city walls of Jericho called out, "Jesus, Son of David, have mercy on me!" (Mk 10:47). The Canaanite woman cried out, "Have mercy on me, O Lord, Son of David" (Mt 15:22). The ten lepers said, "Jesus, Master, have mercy on us" (Lk 17:13).

From about the sixth century, the Jesus prayer was used in the monastery of St. Catherine on Mount Sinai. In the fourteenth century, Gregory of Sinai took the prayer to Mount Athos in Macedonia. He instructed the people in this prayer and the Holy Mount Athos became a center for the praying of the Jesus Prayer. Gradually a considerable literature on the use of this prayer developed. In the eighteenth century, many of these writings were collected and published in Venice under the title *Philokalia — the Love of the Beautiful*.

It was not until the middle of the twentieth century that this prayer made its way into the Western Church. Gregory of Sinai wrote little, but his teaching on prayer and the practice of mental prayer, silence and contemplation, had great impact in the Orthodox and Eastern churches. He emphasized the importance of physical aids such as rhythmical breathing to perfect concentration in mental prayer. The Jesus beads are another aid to concentration and to unceasing prayer.

The Jesus beads consist of a string of 100 beads connected at the ends by a crucifix. No prayer is said on the crucifix, although the beads may be begun by making the sign of the cross. The person then slowly and thoughtfully repeats the Jesus prayer on each bead.

The Little Crown of the Infant Jesus of Prague

Devotion to the Child Jesus under the title "Infant Jesus of Prague" has spread worldwide through its promotion by the Carmelite Order (see entry under "Images").

Venerable Sister Margaret of the Blessed Sacrament, a Carmelite

Sister of the Beaune Carmel who died in 1648, received a private revelation of Our Lord in which she was given a chaplet in honor of the Infant. The chaplet, known as the Little Crown, consists of fifteen beads. Three beads are in honor of the Holy Family: Jesus, Mary, and Joseph. On these the Lord's Prayer is recited. The other twelve beads are in honor of the Holy Childhood of Christ, and on them are recited twelve Hail Mary's. Before each of the Lord's Prayers one says, "And the Word was made flesh." Before the first of the Hail Marys, one prays "And the Word was made Flesh and dwelt among us." On the medal, one prays, "Divine Infant Jesus, I adore Thy Cross, and I accept all the crosses Thou wilt be pleased to send me. Adorable Trinity, I offer Thee for the glory of the Holy Name of God all the adorations of the Sacred Heart of the Holy Infant Jesus." In the revelations to Venerable Margaret, the Divine Infant promised special graces, above all purity of heart and innocence, to all who carried the chaplet on their person and recited it in honor of the mysteries of His holy infancy.

Rosary of Our Lady of Sorrows (the Servite Rosary)
The Rosary of the Seven Sorrows

The sorrows of Mary, as described in the Gospel, are not just a private experience — they are part of the history of salvation. In devout recitation of the Rosary of Our Lady of Sorrows, one realizes the sufferings of the Blessed Virgin and sees their continuance in the Church today. Mary becomes the symbol of the compassion of the Church which is called by God to stand with those who suffer. Contemplation of the sorrows of Mary leads to a compassionate, understanding share in human suffering as one stands "at the foot of those countless crosses where the Son of Man is still being crucified in His brothers and sisters in order to bring comfort and redemptive cooperation" (Constitutions, Order of Friar Servants of Mary. Rome: General Curia O.S.M., 1977. art. 290).

Devotion to the Sorrowful Mother began in the West about the twelfth century, promoted by such great saints as Anselm of Canterbury, Bernard of Clairvaux, and Bonaventure. The cultural climate of the time in which the Rosary of Our Lady of Sorrows developed was devoted to the Passion. Devotion to the Passion of Christ and the Sorrows of His Mother reached its pinnacle around the seventeenth century, although the rosary of the Sorrowful Mother evolved gradually from the sixteenth through nineteenth centuries.

During the Middle Ages, the ordinary Catholic no longer spoke the language of the official prayer of the Church. Thus, many other prayer forms and devotions developed. Of these, the greatest was the Dominican Rosary. The Servite Rosary is an adaptation of this prayer form.

The Dominican Rosary had been approved by papal bull of Sixtus IV in 1479. It swiftly became popular among the laity. The origin of the Servite Rosary probably falls in the decade between 1607 and 1617, as after the latter date historians for the order have found many references to it. Presumably this devotion applied the structure of the Dominican Rosary, which also was used in churches of the order, to the custom of the daily meditation on the seven sorrows of the Blessed Virgin. From the year 1698, members of the order wore the rosary on their belts; for all the Servants of Mary, priests, brothers, cloistered nuns, and sisters of congregations aggregated to the order, the beads became not only a part of the habit but also a sign of their esteem for this devotion.

The Servite rosary is a meditation on the mystery-events of God's love for us as reflected in the lives of Jesus and Mary. This rosary, like the Dominican Rosary, is a biblical prayer. The events of sorrow and salvation contemplated in it are taken from the Gospels themselves, and from the Church's interpretation of scriptural texts (*Rosary of Our Lady of Sorrows*, Chicago: Friar Servants of Mary, 1986. p.36).

Through the years, the Rosary of Our Lady of Sorrows grew in the esteem not only of the Servites, but also of the laity associated with them. At the same time, the esteem for the Dominican rosary was promulgated by the popes to such an extent that in 1885 the Prior General of the Servants of Mary made a bold request of Pope Leo XIII. He asked for the favor of substituting the Servite Rosary for the Dominican Rosary in churches proper to the order whenever the rosary was required in sacred functions. Additionally, he asked that in this case they might still enjoy all the indulgences and blessings granted to the use of the Dominican rosary at such times. This request was granted.

Today, the Rosary of Our Lady of Sorrows is often recited by an individual as a private devotion. It is also recited by groups of people gathered in church, especially those churches affiliated in some way with the Servite order.

The chaplet consists of seven groups of seven beads, each septet separated by a medal of one of the sorrows. Each mystery is introduced by a meditation to guide reflection as the Our Father and seven Hail Marys are prayed. The rosary is concluded with three Hail Marys as an added petition for true sorrow and a desire to model our lives on the example of the life and faith of Our Lady. At the end of the chaplet is a medal of Our Lady with her heart pierced with seven swords. A crucifixion scene is generally found on the obverse of this medal. When the rosary is recited in public by a group, the structure includes other elements, often including the Stabat Mater or the Litany of Our Lady of Sorrows.

The *seven sorrows* as traditionally listed are:

1. Mary accepts in faith the prophecy of Simeon (Lk 2:34-35).
2. Mary flees into Egypt with Jesus and Joseph (Mt 2:73-74).
3. Mary seeks Jesus lost in Jerusalem (Lk 2:43-45).
4. Mary meets Jesus on the way to Calvary (Lk 23:26-27).
5. Mary stands near the cross of her Son (Jn 19:25-27).
6. Mary receives the body of Jesus taken down from the cross (Mt 27:57-59).
7. Mary places the body of Jesus in the tomb, awaiting the Resurrection (Jn 19:40-42).

A new alternative form has been written which lists the mysteries under the biblical motif of rejection. This form is not intended to replace the traditional one, but to give an optional manner of saying the Rosary. The sorrows as listed for this new form are:

1. Jesus, the Son of God, is born in a cave: there was no room for his Mother at the inn (Lk 2:1-7).
2. Jesus, Savior of humankind, is a sign of contradiction (Lk 2:22-35).
3. Jesus, the newborn Messiah, is persecuted by Herod (Mt 2:13-18).
4. Jesus, Brother of all, is rejected by His neighbors (Lk 4:28-29).
5. Jesus, the Holy One of God, is arrested by the high priests and abandoned by His disciples (Mt 26:47-56).
6. Jesus, the Just One, dies on the cross (Jn 19:25-27).
7. Jesus, Master and Lord, is persecuted in His disciples (Acts 12:1-5).

Corona of Our Mother of Consolation (Augustinian Rosary)

Little is known of the origin of the corona of Our Lady of Consolation. Originally it was probably linked with the third order of St. Augustine. It does, however, have definite links with devotion to Mary under the title Our Mother of Consolation.

The tradition of asking the Mother of God for the gift of consolation dates back to the earliest centuries. The first written evidence of prayer to the *Theotokos*, Mother of God, is found on a scrap of Egyptian papyrus dating from between A.D. 300 and 450. In Greek is written: "Beneath the shelter of your tender compassion we fly for refuge, Mother of God. Do not overlook my supplications in adversity but deliver us out of danger."

The devotion to Mary under the title Mother of Consolation appears to come from two different sources. The first, treasured for centuries by the Order of St. Augustine, tells of St. Monica in the fourth century. Distraught with grief and anxiety for her wayward son, Augustine, Monica confided

From left: Kateri Tekakwitha Rosary (with staurolite cross) and Chaplet (broken chain), two St. Michael Chaplets, and Chaplet of the Precious Blood (see "Chaplets, Rosaries, Crowns, and Beads").

her trouble to the Mother of God, who appeared to her dressed in mourning clothes and wearing a shining cincture. Our Lady gave the cincture to St. Monica as a sign of her support and compassion, directing Monica to encourage others to wear it. Monica gave the cincture to Augustine, who later gave it to his community, thus instituting the order's wearing of the cincture as a token of fidelity to Our Mother of Consolation.

A second tradition, seemingly separate, dates from the fourteenth century and tells of a Roman nobleman in the Capitoline prison awaiting death. Reflecting on his approaching last moments, he dictated in his will that his son was to have a Madonna and Child painted and placed near the gallows for the consolation of all who would die in that place in the future. The son followed his father's wishes, and when in 1470 a youth who had been unjustly convicted was miraculously saved from the hangman's noose as his mother prayed before the picture, the place became a popular shrine. More miracles followed and a church was built. The painting was given the title Mother of Consolation. Because of the large number of pilgrims, the devotion spread rapidly over Europe.

Later, confraternities were established, but they ended in the nineteenth century because of political stress in Italy. The painting and the church remain under the care of the Capuchin Fathers.

In the twentieth century, we turn in hope to our luminous "sign of comfort," Our Mother of Consolation, whose joy is to bring to broken human hearts the fruit of the Resurrection, God's own consolation.

The corona expresses our faith as we find it written in the Apostles' Creed. The chaplet consists of thirteen pairs of beads. Two additional beads and a medal of Our Lady of Consolation are attached to the body of the corona. The corona begins by calling to mind the scene in the Cenacle when the Apostles devoted themselves to constant prayer. There were some women in their company, and Mary the mother of Jesus, and his brothers (Acts 1:14). The leader begins by making the sign of the cross, when reciting in public; after the announcement of each of the twelve articles of the Apostles' Creed, a brief reading is taken from the writings of St. Augustine or other writings of the Augustinian traditions on the articles of faith. After the reading there follows a silence, then the Lord's Prayer and the Hail Mary are prayed. When praying this corona in private, the readings may be omitted. The final Our Father and Hail Mary are said for the intentions of the Pope. The chaplet is ended by a recitation of the Hail, Holy Queen.

Passionist Chaplet of the Five Wounds

"He was wounded for our transgressions; he was bruised for our iniquities; upon him was the chastisement that made us whole, and with his stripes we are healed" (Is 53:5).

Traditionally it was to Blessed Angela of Foligno that Jesus revealed there was nothing to be done that would please Him more than devotion to His holy wounds. Speaking to Saint Gemma Galgani, Our Lord showed her His wounds and said, "These are works of love, of infinite love! They show to what extent I have loved you."

The Passionist chaplet of the Five Wounds was originated by the Most Reverend Father Paul Aloysius, C.P., the sixth superior general of the congregation, in order to stimulate devotion to the Passion of Christ through remembrance of the five holy wounds of Jesus in a simple way. This devotion also honors the mystery of the risen Christ, who kept the marks of the five wounds in His glorified body. Father Paul Aloysius presented the idea for the chaplet to Pope Leo XII, who approved it in 1823. Additionally, he transferred to the Passionist format the indulgences previously attached to an older chaplet which was introduced in Rome by the Jesuits at the beginning of the seventeenth century. From its inception, this chaplet has been one of the special devotional exercises of the Confraternity of the Passion.

The chaplet consists of five divisions of five beads each on which are said the Glory Be to the Father. Customarily, the sections are divided by medallions which represent the five wounds of Jesus in order — the wound in the left foot, the wound in the right foot, the wound in the left hand, the wound in the right hand, and finally the wound in the sacred side. At the end of each section of beads, a Hail Mary in honor of the sorrows of Mary is said. At the end of the chaplet, three additional Hail Marys are said in honor of Our Lady's tears. The medallion at the end of the final three beads shows an image of Our Mother of Sorrows.

The Chaplet of Mercy of the Holy Wounds of Jesus

"Now the men who were holding Jesus mocked him and beat him; they also blindfolded him and asked him, 'Prophesy! Who is it that struck you?' and they spoke many other words against him, reviling him" (Lk 22:63-65).

"Then Pilate took Jesus and scourged him" (Jn. 19:1).

"Then the soldiers of the governor took Jesus into the praetorium, and they gathered the whole battalion before him. And they stripped him and put a scarlet robe upon him, and plaiting a crown of thorns they put it on his head, and put a reed in his right hand. And kneeling before him they mocked him, saying: 'Hail, King of the Jews!' And they spat upon him, and took the reed and struck him on the head" (Mt 27:27-30).

"So they took Jesus, and he went out, bearing his own cross, to the place called the place of a skull, which is called in Hebrew Golgotha" (Jn

160

19:17). Jesus was nailed to the cross; He suffered and died. At last "one of the soldiers pierced his side with a spear, and at once there came out blood and water" (Jn 19:34).

After the resurrection, Jesus went to his disciples and wished them peace. After greeting them, "he showed them his hands and side. Then the disciples were glad when they saw the Lord." (Jn 20:20).

"Peace, this is the true gift of Jesus, through His wounds. Through them and through the blood they let flow, the reconciliation of the world with God was accomplished. This is the reason why the Savior gives it to his Apostles as a fruit of His wounds while presenting them His hands, His feet, and his side" (St. Thomas Aquinas).

Sister Mary Martha Chambon, a humble lay sister of the Visitation Convent of Chambéry, France, was given many graces by Our Lord. From Him she reported private revelations, in one of which He told her, "The executioners did well in piercing My side, My hands, and My feet, since they thereby opened a fountain whence will eternally flow the waters of My mercy. It is only sin, the cause of it, that must be detested. My Father is pleased with the offering of My sacred wounds and the sorrows of My blessed Mother. To offer them to Him is to offer Him His glory, to offer heaven to heaven. Behold how to pay for all debtors! For in offering to My Father the merit of My holy wounds, you satisfy for the sins of men."

In other visions, Our Lord presented His wounds as a source of grace for sinners, telling her that He had suffered as much for a single soul as for all souls together. He told her that it was His constant desire that men profit by the Redemption by corresponding to His graces. He instructed her to offer His wounds to God for the salvation of souls, especially those in Purgatory. Additionally, he asked for a Chaplet of Mercy in honor of His wounds, teaching her the aspirations that should be said.

This chaplet was approved in favor of the Institute of the Visitation in 1912, and by indult of the Sacred Penitentiary it was extended to all the faithful in 1924.

The Chaplet of Mercy in honor of the Holy Wounds may be said using the beads of a standard rosary. On the cross and the first three beads is said the beautiful prayer written by a Roman priest:

"O Jesus, divine Redeemer, be merciful to us and to the whole world. Amen.

"Strong God, Holy God, immortal God, have mercy on us and on the whole world. Amen.

"Grace and mercy, oh my Jesus, during present dangers; cover us with Thy precious Blood. Amen.

"Eternal Father, grant us mercy through the Blood of Jesus Christ. Thy only Son; grant us mercy, we beseech Thee. Amen. Amen. Amen."

On the small beads, say: "My Jesus, pardon and mercy, by the merits of Thy Holy Wounds."

On the large beads, say: "Eternal Father, I offer Thee the Wounds of our Lord Jesus Christ to heal those of our souls."

The Chaplet of Divine Mercy

The message of divine mercy is not new. The patriarchs and prophets proclaimed the mercy of God in the Old Testament. God told Moses His name: "The LORD, the LORD [Yahweh], a God merciful and gracious" (Ex 34:6). During His time on earth, Jesus Christ emphasized God's mercy and the covenant of love. He said, "Be merciful, even as your Father is merciful" (Lk 6:36). From the time of Christ, the Church and holy men and women have reaffirmed the love and mercy of God.

In our own century, God revealed His mercy to a humble Polish sister, Sister Faustina Kowalska, whom he called His secretary and Apostle of Mercy.

"The guiding thought of all the interior communications which she [had] received from Christ the Lord was the mystery of God's mercy and the obligation on our part to respond to it with a fullness of trust in Him" (Father Hyacinth Woroniecki).

During her short life in religion, Sister Faustina was apparently privileged to receive a number of instructions from Our Lord detailing a new form for devotion to His divine mercy. Our Lord gave, through Sister Faustina, special means of drawing on His mercy: an image of the Divine Mercy, a chaplet, a novena, a prayer at the hour commemorating His death, and the request for a Feast of Mercy.

From 1959 to 1976, there was a ban on spreading this devotion in the forms proposed by Sister Faustina. This ban was largely a result of a mistranslation of some of Sister Faustina's writings, which have all now been approved in the process for her beatification. The ban has been removed, and therefore there is no longer any prohibition to spreading the devotion in the form proposed by Sister Faustina. This declaration is not, however, the final official approval of the Church, nor is it the Church's official recognition that the revelations, believed on trustworthy human authority to have been granted to her, are of divine or supernatural origin. Private revelations such as those granted to Sister Faustina, even when finally approved by the Church, are considered as a special grace for the good of people but are not proposed for the obedience of faith, as are the public revelations of Scripture and tradition. Therefore, we are never obliged to follow those devotions which come to the Church from private revelations. On the other hand, new devotions can be of real value when they direct the soul to God, to Whom the worship of adoration is due. Therefore, until the Church's final, well-considered declaration regarding the devotion to the divine mercy in the forms proposed in the writings of Sister Faustina is made, we, the faithful, are permitted to practice this devotion if it leads us more securely to the love of God.

Two recent occurrences give hope that this devotion will one day, be stamped with the final, official approval of the Church. In 1980, the Sacred Congregation for the Sacraments and Divine Worship approved for use in Poland a votive Mass of the Mercy of God. Also in 1980, Pope John Paul II published an encyclical entitled "Rich in Mercy" (*Dives in Misericordia*), in which he set forth doctrinal and practical guidelines for a renewed understanding of, and recourse to, the God of Mercy in the Church.

What is the message of divine mercy? God is a merciful God. He is love itself, poured out for all mankind. God wants all to turn to Him with trust and love before he comes as the just judge. Turning to God's mercy is the answer to our troubled world. God wants us to live reconciled with Him and with one another.

Not only does God want us to receive His mercy, but He wants us to use it by being merciful to others. "Blessed are the merciful, for they shall obtain mercy" (Mt 5:7).

Helen Kowalska was born in 1905 in the village of Glogowiec, Poland. At the age of twenty, she entered the Congregation of the Sisters of Our Lady of Mercy, popularly called the Magdalene Sisters, whose major work is the education and training of girls who are morally and financially impoverished. Her name in religion was Sister Mary Faustina. She was accepted in the "second choir", and made perpetual vows in 1933. She died October 5, 1938, of multiple tuberculosis at the age of thirty-three.

As a religious, Sister Faustina was assigned to a number of the houses of her community, where she worked, for the most part, in the kitchen, the garden, at housekeeping and as porteress or gatekeeper. On the outside, she did not distinguish herself by anything in particular. She was conscientious in following her rule and in the performance of her duties. Few, even among those she lived with, realized the interior graces she received and the work to which God called her.

In 1934, in obedience to her spiritual director, Sister Faustina began keeping a personal diary which she titled "Divine Mercy in My Soul." This diary contains a detailed account of her profound revelations and extraordinary spiritual experiences.

The most fundamental element of the devotion to the divine mercy is complete confidence, or trust, in Jesus. In 1931, Sister Faustina received the first apparition of Jesus as The Merciful One. She described it thus:

"In the evening, when I was in my cell, I saw the Lord Jesus clothed in a white garment. One hand [was] raised in the gesture of blessing, the other was touching the garment at the breast. From beneath the garment slightly drawn aside at the breast there were emanating two large rays, one red, the other pale.

"In silence, I kept my gaze fixed on the Lord; my soul was struck with awe but also with great joy. After a while Jesus said to me:

'Paint an image according to the pattern you see with the inscription: Jesus, I trust in You. I desire that this image be venerated first in your chapel and [then] throughout the world.' "

Later, at the request of her confessor, Sister Faustina asked Our Lord about the symbolism of the rays and received, while at prayer, this clarification:

"The two rays denote blood and water — the pale ray stands for the water which makes souls righteous; the red ray stands for the blood which is the life of souls. These two rays Issued forth from the depths of My most tender mercy when My agonized heart was opened by a lance on the cross. These rays shield the soul from the wrath of My Father. Happy is the one who will dwell in their shelter, for the just hand of God shall not lay hold of him."

The first image of the Divine Mercy was commissioned by Sister Faustina's spiritual director, Rev. Michael Sopocko, and painted by Eugene Kazimierowski in Vilnius under Sister's direction. Sister Faustina complained to the Lord with tears, as she was not pleased with the way the painting was turning out, "Who will paint You as beautiful as You are?" In answer, she heard these words: "Not in the beauty of the color nor of the brush lies the sublimity of this image but in My grace" (I, 134). Thus Our Lord seems to be saying that in spite of the human work of the artist, the picture is to recall to mind His grace. He directed Sister Faustina to write down this short prayer: "O Blood and Water, which gushed forth from the Heart of Jesus as a fount of mercy for us, I trust in you."

There are at least fourteen passages in Sister Faustina's diary where Our Lord requests the establishment of a Feast of the Divine Mercy on the Sunday after Easter. Until final approval is given for such a feast for the entire Church, we can celebrate this feast privately by going to confession (within eight days before or after) and receiving Communion on that day. We can honor Divine Mercy by our prayers and works of mercy.

In preparation for the Feast of the Divine Mercy, Our Lord asked

Sister Faustina to make a novena praying the Chaplet of Mercy from Good Friday to the following Saturday. His simple instructions regarding the novena as a preparation for the Feast of Mercy are: "1. On each day you will bring to My Heart a different group of souls: 2. You will immerse them in this ocean of My mercy; 3. On each day you will beg My Father, on the strength of My bitter Passion, for graces for these souls."

Our Lord gave Sister Faustina a prayer for mercy. This chaplet is said on an ordinary set of rosary beads of five decades. It begins with the Our Father, the Hail Mary, and the Creed. Then, on the large beads, pray "Eternal Father I offer you the Body and Blood, Soul and Divinity of Your Dearly Beloved Son, Our Lord Jesus Christ, in atonement for our sins and those of the whole world." On the small beads, pray: "For the sake of His sorrowful Passion, have mercy on us and on the whole world." At the end, pray three times: "Holy God, Holy Mighty One, Holy Immortal One, have mercy on us and on the whole world."

As a final help in the devotion to Divine Mercy, Our Lord asked Sister Faustina for a daily remembrance of His passion at the very hour that recalls His death on the cross. "At three o'clock implore My mercy especially for sinners and, if only for a brief moment, immerse yourself in My Passion, particularly in My abandonment at the moment of agony. This is the hour of great mercy for the whole world. . . . In this hour I will refuse nothing to the soul that makes a request of Me in virtue of My Passion" (IV, 59).

Devotion to Divine Mercy can help us see God as He really is — a loving and compassionate God, waiting to forgive and welcome back repentant souls. This is the message of the Gospel, and of the Church throughout the ages.

Chaplet of the Precious Blood

Jesus said, "This is my blood of the covenant, which is poured out for many for the forgiveness of sins" (Mt 26:28).

"Unlimited is the effectiveness of the God-Man's Blood — just as unlimited as the love that impelled Him to pour it out for us, first at His circumcision eight days after birth, and more profusely later on in his agony in the garden, in his scourging and crowning with thorns, in his climb to Calvary and crucifixion, and finally from out that great wide wound in his side which symbolizes the divine Blood cascading down into all the Church's sacraments. Such surpassing love suggests, nay demands, that everyone reborn in the torrents of that Blood adore it with grateful love. This Blood, poured out in abundance, has washed the whole world

From left: Little Crown of the Blessed Virgin, Chaplet of the Little Flower, and Corona of Our Mother of Consolation (see "Chaplets").

clean. . . . This is the price of the world; by it Christ purchased the Church" (Pope John XXIII).

In the early 1800s, Saint Gaspar del Bufalo, with a deep personal appreciation of what Jesus did for us in His Passion and death, and seeing the need for positive actions in compassion to our neighbors in need, began to preach and widely spread the devotion to the Precious Blood. He did not consider worship of the Precious Blood simply another devotion, but as the summary of all religion. He said, "All the mysteries are summed up in the infinite price of Redemption, as the lines of a circle to the center which they have in common!" This apostle of the Precious Blood founded an order of missionary preachers, dedicated to this ideal, known as the Society of the Precious Blood.

Under St. Gaspar's influence, Blessed Maria de Mattias founded an apostolic order of sisters under the title of Adorers of the Blood of Christ. The spirit of the Congregation is based on Maria's words, "How beautiful is the Cross when it is carried in the heart with love." In the opening paragraphs of the Rule for this order, Blessed Maria has written: "For the triumph of His mercy and to show His infinite love for us, our divine Redeemer Jesus Christ shed all his Precious Blood with great suffering and humiliation, as price of salvation and of glory. He gave it all, He gave it for all, and He does not stop giving it." Since that time, thirteen more Institutes have been established in the Church under the title of the Most Precious Blood of Jesus.

The Feast of the Most Precious Blood (July 1) was instituted by Pope Pius IX in thanksgiving for his return to Rome from Gaeta after the revolution of 1848. In 1934, Pope Pius XI elevated it to the highest rank — first class — in order to commemorate the nineteenth centenary of the Redemption. In March of 1969, this feast was dropped from the new liturgical calendar, and it is no longer celebrated by the universal Church.

In 1960, Pope John XXIII approved the Litany of the Precious Blood, and through special indulgences encouraged its public and private recitation.

Before announcing the opening of the Second Vatican Council, he went to pray at the tomb of Saint Gaspar, calling upon him to intercede for the success of the council, and calling devotion to the Precious Blood of Jesus the "Devotion of Our Times."

"Glory to the Blood!" Mother Catherine Aurelie, a Canadian mystic, founded the Institute of the Sisters Adorers of the Most Precious Blood, a cloistered, contemplative order, dedicated to love, immolation, and reparation. She held the blood of Christ to be the source of grace. "O mysterious Blood! Though art all for us! Thou art our rest in weariness, our light in darkness! Thou art the source of all grace, an abyss of love, the vivifying fountain which springeth up to Heaven. It is the Blood of the Immaculate Lamb which gives to Christianity the strength to resist the tempests; to the earth, saints and, to Heaven, the elect."

Mother Catherine especially recommended to her sisters the recitation of the chaplet of the Precious Blood. Each bead of the Precious Blood Chaplet is, as it were, a chalice filled with the divine blood of Jesus, uplifted by Our Lady to the Eternal Father, imploring every grace necessary for your soul and body.

The Chaplet of the Precious Blood is divided into seven groups containing thirty-three "Our Fathers." These prayers are in honor of the thirty-three years of Christ's life on earth, when His blood flowed in human veins before it was poured out in reparation for our sins. After each group, the "Glory be to the Father" is said in thanksgiving for the gift of the Precious Blood. While reciting each group, the petitioner is to meditate on the seven bloodsheddings of Jesus. The seven mysteries are when Jesus shed His Blood in (1) the circumcision, (2) the agony in the garden, (3) the scourging, (4) the crowning with thorns, (5) the carrying of the cross, (6) the crucifixion, and (7) when His side was pierced.

Canon Francesco Albertini (1770-1819) is the author of the chaplet of the Precious Blood. A Precious Blood relic was kept on the side altar on the crucifix in the church of S. Nicola in Carcere. This relic was instrumental in building up a great devotion to the Precious Blood of Jesus in the heart of Canon Albertini. In 1808, at his suggestion, a Confraternity of the Precious Blood was instituted at this church; the newly ordained Gaspar de Bufalo was the preacher for this occasion, as Father Albertini was his spiritual director. Father Albertini urged the members of this pious association to meditate on the price of man's redemption as a means of stirring them to a generous response, and for this reason he composed the chaplet. The chaplet was approved in 1809 by Pope Pius VII.

As originally composed, the chaplet began with the invocation: "O God, come to my assistance. Lord, make haste to help me. Glory Be etc." Then followed a formal meditation written by Father Albertini for each of the seven mysteries. The mystery was followed by the invocation: "We beseech You therefore, help Your servants whom You have redeemed by Your Precious Blood." In 1843, Pope Gregory XVI approved and indulgenced a short form which omitted the formal mystery-meditation and merely announced the mystery and took for granted that the person continued to meditate as well as he could during the recitation of the thirty-three Our Fathers. Today, the Precious Blood Fathers use still a shorter form, reciting only one Our Father for each mystery. The history of when the beads for the chaplet began to be used with the prayers is shrouded; the beads were in existence, however, by 1893.

Chaplet of St. Anthony

The marvelous power of miracles conferred on St. Anthony by God has won for the saint the title of Wonder-Worker. In the ancient responsory of the Church, it is said, "If then you ask for miracles, go to St. Anthony."

Since his death in 1231 at the age of thirty-six, this humble Franciscan of Padua has become one of the most popular saints of the Church throughout the world. A gifted preacher, during life he was called the "Hammer of Heretics." He attracted large crowds wherever he went, and numerous miraculous events occurred during his lifetime. He was canonized less than a year after his death by Pope Gregory IX and is named as one of the Doctors of the church.

In 1263. the tomb of the saint was opened in order to transfer the remains to a new sanctuary built in his honor. Although the body had, in the natural course of events, fallen to dust, his tongue remained incorrupt as that of a living person. At this occasion, St. Bonaventure, then Minister General of the Franciscan Order, took the tongue in his hands and said, "O blessed tongue that never ceased to praise God and always taught others to bless Him, now we plainly see how precious thou art in His sight." These words of Saint Bonaventure now constitute the antiphon preceding the miraculous responsory, was also authored by Bonaventure.

The devotion known as the chaplet or beads of St. Anthony is practiced in honor of the thirteen miracles listed in the miraculous responsory. The chaplet is comprised of thirteen groups of three beads each, commemorating Anthony's thirty-six years of life on earth. On the beads are said one Our Father, one Hail Mary, and one Glory Be to the Father. The miraculous responsory is recited.

In one version, the person praying meditates on thirteen virtues of the saint. In another, he meditates on thirteen petitions which go along with the thirteen miracles in the responsory.

The Miraculous Responsory of St. Bonaventure

If miracles thou fain wouldst see
Lo, error, death, calamity,
The leprous stain, the demon flies,
From beds of pain the sick arise.
Resp.: The hungry seas forgo their prey,
The prisoner's cruel chains give way;
while palsied limbs and chattels lost,

Both young and old recovered boast.
And perils perish; plenty's hoard
Is heaped on hunger's famished board;
Let those relate who know it well,
Let Padua of his patron tell.

Resp.

To Father, Son, let glory be,
And Holy Ghost eternally.

Resp.

Pray for us O blessed Anthony, that we may be made worthy of the promises of Christ.

Let Thy Church, O God, be gladdened by the solemn commemoration of blessed Anthony thy Confessor: that she may evermore be defended by Thy spiritual assistance, and merit to possess everlasting joy. Through Christ our Lord. Amen.

The Rosary for the Dead

"My friends, let us pray much and let us obtain many prayers from others for the poor dead. The good God will return to us a hundredfold the good we do them. Ah! If every one knew how useful to those who practice it is this devotion to the holy souls in Purgatory, they would not be so often forgotten; the good God regards all we do for them as if it were done for Himself" (St. John Vianney, Curé d'Ars).

In the mid-nineteenth century, Abbé Serre of the Chapel of the Hôtel Dieu at Nismes, France, composed the rosary for the dead for the benefit of the poor suffering souls in Purgatory. The chaplet was promoted by the Archconfraternity of Notre Dame du Suffrage.

The chaplet consists of four decades of ten beads each which commemorate the forty hours Christ spent in Limbo, where He went for the purpose of delivering the souls of the holy persons who died before Him. The rosary has a cross and a medal of the Archconfraternity, representing the souls in Purgatory. The chaplet may also have five introductory beads as found on the Dominican rosary.

The *De Profundis* (Psalm 130) is said upon the cross, at the beginning and the ending of the chaplet. Anyone who is not familiar with that prayer may substitute an Our Father and a Hail Mary. The *Requiem Eternam* ("Eternal rest grant unto them, etc.") and the Acts of Faith, Hope, and Charity are said on the large beads, and on the small beads is said "Sweet Heart of Mary, be my salvation."

Franciscan Crown Rosary (Seraphic Rosary)
Rosary of the Seven Joys of the Blessed Virgin Mary

The Franciscan Crown, or the Rosary of the Seven Joys of the Blessed Virgin Mary, is an ancient sacramental treasured by the Franciscan order. Father Luke Wadding, a well-known Franciscan historian, dates the inception of this chaplet to 1422, the entrance date into the novitiate of the order of an unnamed pious young man. This young devotee of Mary had been accustomed, before his entrance, to decorate a statue of the Virgin with crowns of fresh flowers. This practice was forbidden to him in the novitiate, and fearing a lack of devotion to his Queen, he determined to leave the order.

In a vision, Our Lady appeared to him and told him, "Do not be sad and cast down, my son, because you are no longer permitted to place wreaths of flowers on my statue. I will teach you to change this pious practice into one that will be far more pleasing to me and far more meritorious to your soul. In place of the flowers that soon wither and cannot always be found, you can weave for me a crown from the flowers of your prayers that will always remain fresh."

Thereupon, Our Lady requested the young friar to say one Our Father and ten Hail Mary's in honor of seven joyous occasions in her life: (1) the Annunciation, (2) the Visitation, (3) the birth of Christ, (4) the adoration of the Magi, (5) the finding of Jesus in the Temple, (6) the resurrection of Our Lord, and (7) the Assumption of the Blessed Virgin into Heaven.

As the vision faded, the overjoyed novice began to recite the prayers as she had instructed him to do. While he was devoutly praying, the novice master passed by and saw an angel weaving a wreath of roses. After every tenth rose, he inserted a golden lily. When the wreath was finished, the angel placed it on the head of the praying novice.

The novice master demanded under holy obedience that the novice explain to him the meaning of the vision. The novice complied, and the novice master was so impressed with what he had heard that he immediately told his brother friars. The practice of reciting the Crown of the Seven Joys soon spread to the entire Order.

In later years, two Hail Mary's were added to make the total of the Hail Marys equal to seventy-two, the number of years that Our Lady is said by Franciscans to have lived on earth. A final Hail Mary and Our Father were added for the intention of the Pope. In the twentieth century, it has become customary to add a profession of faith such as the Apostles' Creed to the recitation of this crown. Additionally, since 1968 it has become customary to combine the former third and fourth mysteries and to add two other combined mysteries as the meditation for the fourth decade — the presentation of Jesus in the Temple and the purification of the Blessed Virgin.

Kateri Indian Rosary

Blessed Kateri Tekakwitha, the "Lily of the Mohawks," was born in 1656 at Ossernenon, near Auriesville, New York, a land watered by the blood of the martyred St. Isaac Jogues and his Jesuit companions. Her mother was a Christian Algonquin, and her father was the Iroquois chief of the Turtle tribe. When Tekakwitha was only four, her parents and younger brother died in a smallpox epidemic, which left Kateri with weak eyesight and marked with scars. Her pagan uncle then became Turtle chief and adopted Tekakwitha into his lodge.

Tekakwitha grew up innocent and industrious. Long before she knew Him through the teaching of the blackrobes, she learned to love Ra-wen-ni-io, God the Creator. At age eighteen, she begged Father de Lamberville, a French missionary, for baptism. Convinced of her sincerity, he allowed Tekakwitha to "take the Prayer" in 1676. It was then she was given the Christian name Kateri (Catherine).

From the time she became a Christian, Kateri was treated with contempt by her relatives and tribesmen. She bore all insults smilingly, with great patience. In 1677, through the intervention of her brother-in-law, Kateri fled to the Christian mission of Caughnawaga in Canada. Here she made her First Communion (1677) and made a long-cherished vow of perpetual virginity (1679), becoming the first of her people to make such a vow. She had hoped to form an Iroquois sisterhood in imitation of the French nuns, but fell ill and died in 1680, with the name of Jesus on her lips. Her cause for canonization was opened in 1939, and she was beatified by Pope John Paul II in 1980.

A chaplet has been composed by a member of the Tekakwitha League, in honor of Blessed Kateri.

The chaplet may be used as a private devotion to ask God to make Kateri a saint and to ask Kateri for her intercession for one's personal needs. The chaplet is rich in Indian symbolism and calls to mind Blessed Kateri's love for God's beautiful earth and all its creatures. The chaplet is made in two basic patterns; one begins with a cross and the other starts with a medal of Blessed Kateri and three beads.

The cross is made of staurolite, a crystal mineral which is naturally formed in the shape of a cross. There is an Indian legend that on the day that Christ died the woodland animals wept, and their tiny tears falling upon the earth crystallized into these small crosses.

The chaplet begins with making the sign of the cross and asking God to make Kateri a saint. There are twenty-four beads of the main rosary representing the twenty-four years Kateri lived on earth. The chaplet has three colors — crystal clear, red, and brownish gold.

Many Indians believe that the crystal-clear lakes and rivers are the tears of the Great Spirit. The Glory Be is recited on each of the crystal beads. We pray that the Holy Trinity, through the prayers of Kateri, whose name means "Putting all things in order" and "Moving all things before her" will restore the beauty of our waters, skies, forests, and air — the ecology of our entire world.

An Our Father is said on each of the brown or gold beads. Earth colors were popular with the Indians, and golden brown is the predominant color of the earth. God, Our Father, gave us the world in perfect order. Ask Blessed Kateri's intercession to set the earth, our minds, our bodies, and all our problems in order.

A Hail Mary is said on the red beads. Red, the traditional color of love, is also the color of the blood that flows in all mankind, transcending race and color. Red symbolizes the kind of love we must have for all mankind, accepting each person as our brother or sister, and the great love that Kateri had for Our Blessed Mother. Ask Kateri's intercession for Mary's help in forming this kind of love in our hearts.

Chaplet of St. Thérèse

"I am not dying, I am entering into life," wrote Sister Thérèse to a missionary friend in response to his expressed anxiety about her illness.

The young Carmelite nun, Sister Thérèse of the Child Jesus and the Holy Face, lay in agony. Tuberculosis had attacked not only her lungs but her entire body. Death was imminent. She indicated that with her death her true mission would begin: ". . . my mission of making God loved as I love Him, to give my little way to souls. If God answers my request, my heaven will be spent on earth up until the end of the world. Yes, I want to spend my heaven in doing good upon earth."

In her writing, Thérèse had developed a doctrine of abandonment and love. God did not require great deeds, only love. She discovered that love is to admit the need of love, and to express that need in prayer to Love itself, Christ. She teaches us that God puts within us the desire for Himself and only He can satisfy that desire. To accept any other source for human happiness leads only to despair (Father Boniface Hanley, *That Martin Girl.* Paterson, N.J.: St. Anthony's Guild, 1974, p. 29).

On Thérèse's death, copies of her autobiography, *Story of a Soul*, were circulated among the Carmelites and a few friends. Her doctrine of "the little way" was so startling, however, that more and more demand for its

173

From left: Franciscan Crown Rosary, Chaplet of St. Anne, and Chaplet of St. Anthony (see "Chaplets, Rosaries, Crowns, etc.").

teaching arose. Soon a cause for her beatification was entered in Rome, and in 1912, just six years later, the fame of her sanctity had spread to the United States. Pius XI canonized Thérèse in 1925. Had she lived, she would only have been fifty-two years old in the year of her canonization.

One of the greatest apostles of St. Thérèse in the New World was Father Albert Dolan. Gifted both as a preacher and as a writer, he introduced St. Thérèse and her "little way of spiritual childhood" to millions. He founded the Society of the Little Flower in 1923.

The chaplet of St. Thérèse stems from and is promoted by the Society. The chaplet is a private devotion which both honors the saint and invokes her intercession. There are twenty-four beads on the chaplet in honor of the twenty-four years of her life. One additional bead and a medal of the saint complete the chaplet. On the single bead, an invocation to St. Thérèse as Patroness of the Missions is said: "St. Thérèse of the Child Jesus, Patroness of Missions, pray for us." A Glory Be is recited on each of the 24 beads in thanksgiving to the Holy Trinity for having given us the young saint and her "little way." It is customary to recite the chaplet for a period of nine days or twenty-four days.

The Little Crown of the Blessed Virgin

"A great portent appeared in heaven, a woman clothed with the sun, with the moon under her feet, and on her head a crown of twelve stars" (Rev 12:1).

In a vision, St. John, the beloved disciple, saw a wonderful sign in the heavens. Scripture commentators interpret this as symbolic of Mary, with her virtues and privileges.

From this grew the devotion known as the Little Crown of Twelve Stars. The young Jesuit St. John Berchmanns and many other devotees of the Blessed Virgin made this devotion their daily favorite. St. Louis Mary de Montfort embellished the Little Crown by adding to each Hail Mary an invocation in praise of Mary's excellence, power, and goodness, ending with "Rejoice, O Virgin Mary! Rejoice a thousand times." St. Louis gave the Little Crown as a morning prayer to both of the religious families he started, the Montfort Fathers and the Daughters of Wisdom. It is one of the favorite devotions of the Confraternity of Mary, Queen of All Hearts.

This chaplet may be said with or without the use of the sacramental beads. The beads are arranged in three sets of four with a single bead before each group. The chaplet ends with a medal of Our Lady, Queen of All Hearts.

After an introductory prayer and an Our Father, four Hail Marys are recited in honor of Our Lady's crown of excellence. The invocations of this crown honor the divine maternity of the Blessed Virgin, her virginity, her purity, and her innumerable virtues. After the second Our Father is prayed, four Hail Marys are said in honor of the crown of power, honoring the royalty of the Blessed Virgin, her magnificence, her universal mediation, and the strength of her rule as Queen of Heaven. After the third and final Our Father, four Hail Marys are prayed with invocations which honor her crown of goodness: her mercy toward sinners, the poor, just, and the dying. The chaplet ends with a Glory Be to the Father and a final prayer.

The Little Rosary of St. Anne

Nothing much is known about the parents of the Virgin Mary, to whom the names Joachim and Anne are traditionally given. They are not mentioned in the Bible, and historically there is virtually no information available. The names derive from an early apocryphal writing called the Protevangelium of James, which professes to give an account of Mary's birth and life. This story bears a strong resemblance to the story of Hannah in 1 Samuel 1-2.

In the Middle East, the veneration of St. Anne can be traced back to about the fourth century. The Crusaders brought her name and legend to Europe, and it was printed in 1298 in the Golden Legend. From that time, popular veneration of her spread into all parts of the Christian world. A feast in her honor, celebrated in southern France as early as the fourteenth century, became universal in 1584 when Pope Gregory XIII prescribed it for the entire Church.

St. Anne soon became the patron of married women and was appealed to by the childless for help in obtaining children. According to legend, she was married three times, twice after the death of Joachim, and soon young women turned to her for help in finding a husband. All over Europe, young women appealed to her:

"I beg you, holy mother Anne,
Send me a good and loving man."

As gentle grandmother of Our Lord, she is invoked as a helper for various needs of body and soul. Many churches have been built in her honor, and have often become famous centers of pilgrimage.

Beginning in the eighteenth century, Anne, which means "grace," was used more and more as a favorite name for girls, and by the beginning of the nineteenth century it was the most popular girls' name in central Europe.

The chaplet, or little rosary, of St. Anne originated in the last quarter of the nineteenth century. It is a pious invention of one of her devout clients. The chaplet consists of three Our Fathers and fifteen Hail Marys. The chaplet is begun by making the sign of the cross and devoutly kissing the medal of St. Anne, praying "Jesus, Mary, Anne." The first section is recited to thank Jesus for His favors, to ask His pardon for sins, and to implore His future favor. The second part is recited in praise of Mary with a request that she present the current petition to St. Anne. The final set of prayers presents the petition to the good St. Anne. After each Hail Mary, the petitioner prays: "Jesus, Mary, Anne, grant me the favor I ask." At the end of each section, a Glory Be is recited as an act of praise to the Blessed Trinity.

The Sacred Heart Rosary
"Sacred Heart of Jesus, I trust in Your love."

The Sacred Heart Society began in 1980 when a group of people — priests, religious, and laity together — determined to strive by common effort to foster public worship of the Sacred Heart and to exercise works of piety and charity in the name of this same loving Heart of Jesus. Originally the group chose the name Heralds of Christ for M. III, as their work was directed to preparing the world for Christ's two-thousandth birthday and ushering in the third millennium. In the Encyclical *Redeemer of Man*, which Pope John Paul II issued in 1979, he asked all to prepare for the year 2000. His words called for a reawakening in us of the awareness of the key truth of faith as expressed in the Gospel: "The Word became flesh and dwelt among us." He asked the people of God to prepare for a great Jubilee. Thus, this private association of the Christian faithful (Canon Law, rev. 1983, canons 298 ff.) began to direct their efforts toward this goal of bringing Christ and the love of His Sacred Heart to the world.

As a means to promote interest in Christ's love, and to give people a practical aid to promote trust in His Love, they devised a rosary or chaplet in honor of the Sacred Heart with the Church's ejaculatory prayer, "Sacred Heart of Jesus, I trust in your love." This rosary offers a simple persistent prayer expressing to Jesus Christ our confident trust in His love for us. It is made up of thirty-three beads in honor of Christ's earthly life, and a Sacred Heart medal or emblem. On each bead, one prayerfully recites, "Sacred Heart of Jesus, I trust in Your love." Any other short prayer of trust may be substituted. The prayer is made especially for peace among peoples of the world, the needs of the Church, our families, all lovers of Christ, and the intentions of the Sacred Heart Society.

Anyone may copy and distribute this rosary, using any color or style of beads available. The chaplet should end with a medal or representation of the Sacred Heart. Cards explaining the makeup and purpose of this rosary are available from the Sacred Heart Society. The faithful who make and use this rosary should remember to have it blessed by a priest. Because of its simple design, the rosary is often strung on cord rather than having the beads separated by wire.

Chaplet of St. Raphael

The name Raphael comes from the Hebrew *rapha* ("to heal") and *El* (God). Thus, the name means "God heals" or the "Divine Healer." The story of the archangel Raphael is found in the Old Testament book of Tobit or Tobias. Raphael, one of the seven archangels who stand before God, is sent on a mission to aid Tobias because of his prayers. Raphael takes on the form of a beautiful young man but reveals himself at the end of the story. Some scholars also believe that Raphael is the angel of healing at the pool of Bethesda or Bethsaida (Jn 5:4). Catholic tradition assigns to St. Raphael the mission to assist and protect travelers, to cure men's ills, to arrange happy meetings, and to protect family life. St. Gregory calls Raphael the "Medicine of God."

The chaplet of St. Raphael is made up of a medal of the archangel and twelve beads. On the medal, the following verse is recited:

"You are Raphael the healer,
You are Raphael the guide,
You are Raphael the companion —
Ever at human sorrow's side."

The first three beads honor Our Lady as Queen of Angels, and three Hail Marys are said. The following prayer of praise is said on each of the nine beads to honor the nine angelic choirs:

"Holy, holy, holy Lord, God of Hosts.
Heaven and earth are full of Your glory!
Glory be to the Father;
Glory be to the Son;
Glory be to the Holy Spirit."

The angelic choirs are: Angels, Archangels, Principalities, Powers, Virtues, Dominions, Thrones, Cherubim, and Seraphim.

The chaplet is concluded with the aspiration "Raphael, angel of health, of love, of joy and light — pray for us."

Chaplet of St. Paul

St. Paul did not start his career as a follower of Christ; he was, instead, a fanatical persecutor of the Church of Jesus Christ. Our Lord, however, had great plans for this fiery enemy. On day while Paul, then called Saul, was on the road to Damascus, he was suddenly surrounded by a brilliant light and thrown to the ground. Then he heard a voice calling, "Saul, Saul, why do you persecute me?" (Acts 9:3-4).

After this stirring experience, Paul began to love Jesus with all the ardor that would send him thousands of miles over thirty years to tell the world about the Redeemer. He cheerfully faced every type of danger as he searched for souls in every corner of the then-known world. The tireless and powerful missionary to the Gentiles was, at the last, martyred in Rome. His thinking, expressed through his letters, has had a profound and enduring influence in the development of Christianity.

It has often been speculated that if St. Paul were alive today, he would use all modern means of communication to preach the Word of God.

In the early days of this century Rev. James Alberione, taking St. Paul as his mentor and example, began a great work of using modern communications to spread the Word of God. The member congregations of the Pauline family acknowledge him as founder, and carry out his ideas today in all parts of the globe. They use the modern media as an effective means to reach souls. Father Alberione composed the chaplet to St. Paul, prayed today by the member congregations especially for the intention of an increase of religious vocations. The chaplet has five petitions, each followed by a prayerful refrain.

"1. I bless You, O Jesus, for the great mercy granted to St. Paul in changing him from a bold persecutor to an ardent apostle of the Church. And you, O great Saint, obtain for me a heart docile to grace, conversion from my principal defect and total configuration with Jesus Christ.

"Jesus Master, Way, Truth and Life, have mercy on us.

Queen of Apostles, pray for us.

St. Paul the Apostle, pray for us.

"2. I bless You, O Jesus, for having elected the Apostle Paul as a model and preacher of holy virginity. And you, O St. Paul, my dear father, guard my mind, my heart and my senses in order that I may know, love and serve only Jesus and employ all my energies for His glory.

"Jesus Master. . . .

"3. I bless You, O Jesus, for having given through St. Paul examples and teachings of perfect obedience. And you, O great Saint, obtain for me a humble docility to all my superiors, for I am sure that in obedience I shall be victorious over my enemies.

"Jesus Master. . . .

"4. I bless You, O Jesus, for having taught me, by the deeds and by the words of St. Paul, the true spirit of poverty. And you, O great Saint, obtain for me the evangelical spirit of poverty, so that after having imitated you in life I may be your companion in heavenly glory.

"Jesus Master. . . .

"5. I bless You, O Jesus, for having given to St. Paul a heart so full of love for God and for the Church and for having saved so many souls through his meal. And you, our friend, obtain for me an ardent desire to carry out the apostolate of the media of social communication, of prayer, of example, of activity and of word so that I may merit the reward promised to good apostles.

"Jesus Master. . . ."

Chaplet of St. Michael

St. Michael the archangel is one of three angels named in holy Scripture. Christian tradition assigns four offices to him: (1) to fight against Satan; (2) to rescue the souls of the faithful from the power of the devil, especially at the hour of death; (3) to be the champion of God's people, and (4) to call away from earth and bring men's souls to judgment. He was venerated from earliest Christian times as an angelic healer.

The chaplet of St. Michael honors not only the great archangel but all the heavenly spirits. This chaplet originated in 1751 when St. Michael appeared to a devout Portuguese Carmelite, Antonia d'Astonac. He requested her to publish in his honor a chaplet of nine salutations, each one of which corresponds to one of the nine choirs of angels. One Our Father and three Hail Marys are said in conjunction with each of the salutations. The chaplet concludes with four Our Fathers honoring Sts. Michael, Gabriel, Raphael, and the Guardian Angel. He promised those who practiced the devotion faithfully that he would send an angel from each choir to accompany them when they received Holy Communion. He promised his assistance and that of all the holy angels during life to those who daily recited the chaplet, and to those faithful he also promised deliverance from the pains of Purgatory for themselves and the souls of their relatives. A group of Carmelite nuns who had experienced the spiritual benefits of this chaplet requested approval from Pope Pius IX, who indulgenced the chaplet in 1851.

The beads of this chaplet may be of a single color, usually black or white, or may be multicolored. One group of nuns made a nine-color chaplet based on the revelations of a German mystic. In the United States, the Oblates of St. Benedict distribute the chaplet, also made in nine colors but simply to separate the decades (the colors not having any special significance).

The chaplet is begun with an act of contrition and the recitation of the following invocation: "O God, come to my assistance. O Lord, make haste to help me. Glory be to the Father, etc."

The nine salutations are as follows:

"1. By the intercession of St. Michael and the celestial choir of Seraphim, may the Lord make us worthy to burn with the file of perfect charity.

"2. By the intercession of St. Michael and the celestial choir of Cherubim, may the Lord vouchsafe to grant us grace to leave the ways of wickedness to run in the paths of Christian perfection.

"3. By the intercession of St. Michael and the celestial choir of Thrones, may the Lord infuse into our hearts a true and sincere spirit of humility.

"4. By the intercession of St. Michael and the celestial choir of Dominions, may the Lord give us grace to govern our senses and subdue our unruly passions.

"5. By the intercession of St. Michael and the celestial choir of Powers, may the Lord vouchsafe to protect our souls against the snares and temptations of the devil.

"6. By the intercession of St. Michael and the celestial choir of Virtues may the Lord preserve us from evil and suffer us not to fall into temptation.

"7. By the intercession of St. Michael and the celestial choir of Principalities, may God fill our souls with a true spirit of obedience.

"8. By the intercession of St. Michael and the celestial choir of Archangels, may the Lord give us perseverance in faith and in all good works, in order that we may gain the glory of Paradise.

"9. By the intercession of St. Michael and the celestial choir of Angels, may the Lord grant us to be protected by them in this mortal life and conducted hereafter to eternal glory."

The chaplet is concluded with the following prayer: "O glorious Prince St. Michael, chief and commander of the heavenly hosts, guardian of souls, vanquisher of rebel spirits, servant in the house of the Divine King, and our admirable conductor, thou who dost shine with excellence and superhuman virtue, vouchsafe to deliver us from all evil, who turn to thee with confidence and enable us by thy gracious protection to serve God more and more faithfully every day. Pray for us, O glorious St. Michael, Prince of the Church of Jesus Christ, that we may be made worthy of His promises."

The Rosary or Crown of Our Lord (Camaldolese)

Blessed Michael Pini was born in Florence about 1440. As a young man he was a cupbearer at the court of Lorenzo de' Medici. His virtues were so outstanding that de' Medici had him ordained a priest. On a visit to the Sacred Hermitage of Camaldoli, he was so impressed by the sanctity of

Jesus Beads (crucifix with 100 beads) surrounding the Chaplet of St. Raphael the Archangel (see "Chaplets, Rosaries, Crowns, and Beads").

the life that he found there that he resolved to stay and take the habit of St. Romuald.

After the ancient custom of the Camaldolese, Blessed Michael eventually was granted a more solitary life, staying by himself in a cell at first for a year and later for the rest of his life. In his meditations, he often thought of the petitions of the Our Father. He asked himself how the faithful could best obtain spiritual benefits from this prayer. As he studied the prayer, through divine inspiration he wrote a chaplet in honor of Our Lord. He made a set of beads which he presented to his Superior. The chaplet was presented to Pope Leo X and received his approbation in a papal bull of 1516.

The Rosary of Our Lord instituted by Blessed Michael commemorates the thirty-three years Jesus spent on earth for our salvation. Thus, thirty-three Our Fathers are recited. Five Hail Marys are said in honor of the five wounds of the Redeemer and to remind us of Mary, our co-redemptrix.

The Rosary of Our Lord is divided into four parts commemorating His birth and hidden life, His public life, His passion and death, and His glorification. In order to keep the mind more recollected, a mystery is assigned as a meditation during the recitation of each of the prayers. When the rosary is recited in common, a preparatory prayer is recited, and the leader reads the mystery. When reciting privately, one can begin with any suitable mental or oral prayer. The Glory Be is said at the end of each decade, unless the rosary is being said for the dead, in which case one would pray, "Eternal rest grant unto them, etc."

Unlike most other chaplets which have a meditation for each decade or set of prayers, the Rosary of Our Lord has a meditation for each bead. The rosary begins thus:

"First mystery: the hidden life of Our Lord.

"The Angel Gabriel announced to the Blessed Virgin Mary the Incarnation of the word in her most pure womb. Hail Mary.

"1. The Son of God made man is born of the Virgin Mary in a stable. Our Father.

"2. The angels rejoice and sing Gloria in excelsis Deo. Our Father.

"3. He is adored by the shepherds who were informed by the angels. Our Father.

"4. On the eighth day He is circumcised and called by the most Holy Name of Jesus. Our Father.

"5. He is adored by the Magi, who offer Him gold, incense and myrrh. Our Father. etc."

The four parts of the chaplet as listed above are the most standard way of reciting this devotion. There is, however, an alternate set of mysteries which may also be used with this chaplet. This second set focuses primarily on the passion of Our Lord, and when recited with these mysteries is often called the Rosary of the Passion of Our Lord, when recited as the rosary of the Passion, the chaplet begins as follows:

"First mystery: Jesus says farewell to His Mother before giving Himself up to die for our salvation. Hail Mary.

"1. At the last supper, He washes the feet of His Apostles. Our Father.

"2. He institutes the Holy Eucharist and gives Communion to His Apostles. Our Father.

"3. Praying in the garden, He sweats blood and is consoled by an angel. Our Father.

"4. Betrayed by Judas, He is captured and bound. Our Father.

"5. Jesus is abandoned by all the disciples. Our Father.

"6. Led to Annas, He receives cruel buffets. Our Father. etc."

Finally, there is a short form of this chaplet which, instead of having a mystery or meditation for each prayer, presents instead a consideration for meditation before each decade. In this form, the first decade considers the life of Christ from infancy until He was twelve; the second considers the life of Our Lord from His youth until His Passion; the third considers the Passion of Our Lord; and the fourth, concluding portion considers His glorious resurrection and ascension.

The scope of this book does not allow for the printing of all of the mysteries of this beautiful chaplet. The reader who wishes to adopt this devotion should write to the Camaldolese hermits at their American foundation in California. The address is listed in the appendix, below.

Brigittine Rosary

The chaplet of St. Bridget was instituted, and its propagation begun, by St. Bridget of Sweden (1304-1373). St. Bridget was a widow and a mystic who was favored with numerous remarkable visions and revelations.

The chaplet consists of six decades of Hail Marys, each of which is preceded by an Our Father and ended by a Credo. After the six decades, an Our Father and three Hail Marys are added.

The chaplet therefore includes seven Our Fathers, sixty-three Hail Marys, and six Credos. The recitation of it is intended to honor, by the seven Our Fathers the seven sorrows and the seven joys of the Most Blessed Virgin; by the sixty-three Aves the sixty-three years which according to common custom the Blessed Mother lived on earth.

Fifteen of the mysteries of this chaplet are the same as the Dominican rosary. In each of the three divisions, there is a sixth mystery in the Brigittine chaplet. The first of the joyful mysteries is the Immaculate

Conception. The sixth of the sorrowful mysteries is the Dead Jesus in the arms of His Mother. The sixth of the glorious mysteries is the Patronage of Mary.

This chaplet is a favorite devotion of a number of religious orders, among them the Brothers of the Christian Schools.

The Chatky

The chatky is one of the major sacramentals of the Byzantine rite. In Greek, it is also known as the *konboskienon* or the *konbologion*. It's use began with the desert fathers in Egypt about the fourth century, and it became a part of the monastic habit. It was likened to the "sword of the spirit," blessed and presented to a monk when tonsured.

From the beginning, the chatky was adopted by the devout laity. It found its way to the West through the Russian émigrés who fled the communist revolution. The sacramental is worn about the neck among the Byzantines, and the Orthodox generally wear it on their belt.

The chatky is generally made of wool, although some are made of wooden beads. It consists of a varying number of knots, with the shorter and more common having one hundred and some of the longer ones three hundred. The knots are hand-tied, each made up of seven crosses, one tied atop the other. A cross tied with similar knots ends the chatky. On a new chatky, the bead-shaped knots are tight and close together. With use, the chatky lengthens considerably.

A single prayer is recited on the chatky — the Jesus Prayer: "Lord Jesus Christ, Son of God, be merciful to me, a sinner." Prayers on the chatky are the most common penance in the Byzantine rite, and it is customary to recite it and accompany the prayers with prostration.

Chaplet of the Holy Spirit (1)

Among the myriad devotions brought to the Catholic church by the spiritual children of St. Francis of Assisi is the Chaplet of the Holy Spirit. It was composed and promoted by John Mary Finigan of King's Lynn (1857-1931), a Franciscan Capuchin of the Great Britain province. This "apostle of the Holy Spirit" composed the chaplet in order to give the faithful an easy means of honoring the Holy Spirit. The chaplet was approved by the Vatican in 1900.

There are five mysteries of this chaplet. Each mystery is outlined with a scriptural meditation and a suggested practice for drawing grace into our own life. The chaplet begins with the sign of the cross, an Act of Contrition and the reciting of the prayer-hymn "Come Holy Ghost, Creator Blest." On the first two beads of the mystery the Our Father and the Hail Mary are recited. Then, seven Glory Be to the Fathers are recited. These prayers should be recited after reading the Scripture extract and meditating prayerfully on the suggested practice. The mysteries are as follows:

"1. Jesus is conceived by the Holy Spirit of the Virgin Mary. 'The Holy Spirit will come upon you, and the power of the Most High will overshadow you; therefore the child to be born will be called holy, the Son of God' (Lk 1:35).

"Pray often and fervently for the help of the Spirit of God and ask the Virgin Mary to intercede for you. In this way you will be formed in the image of Jesus Christ as a child of God.

"2. The Spirit of the Lord rests upon Jesus. 'And when Jesus was baptized, he went up immediately from the water, and behold, the heavens were opened and he saw the Spirit of God descending like a dove, and alighting on him' (Mt 3:16).

In Baptism, you received the marvelous gift of sanctifying grace. This life of God enables you to keep the promises then made for you, promises renewed each year publicly at the Easter Vigil. Use the gifts of faith, hope, and love Baptism gave you so that you may live as a follower of Christ. Thus you will be ready for your heavenly inheritance.

"3. Jesus is led by the Spirit into the desert. 'Jesus, full of the Holy Spirit, returned from the Jordan, and was led by the Spirit for forty days in the wilderness, tempted by the devil' (Lk 4:1-2).

"Always be grateful for the seven gifts of the Holy Spirit given to you in Confirmation — the spirit of wisdom and understanding, of counsel and fortitude, of knowledge, piety, and fear of the Lord. Be faithful to the Spirit, your divine guide, so you may surmount all the perils and temptations of life as a perfect Christian, a firm follower of Christ.

"4. The Holy Spirit in the Church. 'And suddenly a sound came from heaven like the rush of a mighty wind, and it filled all the house where they were sitting. . . . And they were all filled with the Holy Spirit . . . [speaking about] the mighty works of God' (Acts 2:2,4,11).

"Give thanks always that God guides His people, inspires and governs each of them by the same Spirit He sent at Pentecost. Hear and follow the Holy Father and the bishops who shepherd your souls, and love the Church, which is the pillar and ground of truth.

5. The Holy Spirit in the souls of the just. 'Do you not know that your body is a temple of the Holy Spirit within you, which you have from God? You are not your own' (1 Cor 6:19). 'Do not quench the Spirit' (1 Thess 5:19). 'And do not grieve the Holy Spirit of God, in whom you were sealed for the day of redemption' (Eph 4:30).

"Always be aware of the Spirit within you. Listen to His divine inspirations and heed them. So you will enjoy the twelve fruits of the Spirit, namely: charity, peace, joy and patience, kindness, goodness, long-suffering and meekness, faith, moderation, continence, and chastity."

The chaplet concludes with the Apostles' Creed followed by one Our Father and Hail Mary for the intentions of the Holy Father.

Chaplet of the Holy Spirit (2)

"We ought to pray and invoke the Holy Spirit, for each one of us greatly needs His protection and His help. The more we are deficient in wisdom, weak in strength, borne down with trouble, prone to sin, so ought we the more turn to Him who is the never-ceasing source of light, strength, consolation, and holiness" (Pope Leo XIII).

"The Holy Spirit was sent that He might continually sanctify the Church, and thus all those who believe would have access through Christ in one Spirit to the Father. He is the Spirit of Life, a fountain of water spring up to life eternal. To those dead in sin, the Father gives life through Him, until, in Christ, He brings to life their mortal bodies" (Vatican II, Constitution on the Church). Father Mateo Crawley-Boevey, SS.CC., called the "Modern Apostle of the Sacred Heart" by Pope Paul VI, also had a deep devotion to the Holy Spirit. He composed this chaplet of the Holy Spirit as a prayer of adoration to the Paraclete in honor of His Seven Gifts. He recommended that the chaplet be said often, especially if some important decision must be made, at certain grave moments, and when special spiritual help is needed. He proposed the chaplet as a means to grow in love for the Paraclete, the Consoler, the Advocate, and as a solid doctrinal devotion to help draw down the sevenfold gifts of wisdom, understanding, knowledge, counsel, fortitude, piety, and fear of the Lord.

The Chaplet of the Holy Spirit is said using a set of regular rosary beads. Begin by saying the Apostles Creed, the Glory Be to the Father, and an Our Father. Then the prayer is said, "Father, Father, send us the promised Paraclete, through Jesus Christ Our Lord, Amen." On the ten small beads, say, "Come, Holy Spirit, fill the hearts of Your faithful and kindle in them the fire of Your love." After the tenth bead say, "Send forth Your Spirit and they shall be created, and You shall renew the face of the earth." The other decades follow in the same manner, beginning with the Our Father. After the seventh and last decade, recite the Hail Holy Queen in honor of the Blessed Virgin, our Heavenly Queen, who presided in the Cenacle on the great Sunday of Pentecost.

Meditations for this chaplet may be made on seven glorious mysteries relating to seven wonderful operations of the Paraclete. These should be made briefly between the decades.

187

"1. Let us honor the Holy Spirit and adore Him who is Love Substantial, proceeding from the Father and the Son, and uniting Them in an infinite and eternal love.

"2. Let us honor the operation of the Holy Spirit and adore Him in the Immaculate Conception of Mary, sanctifying her from the first moment with the plenitude of grace.

"3. Let us honor the operation of the Holy Spirit and adore Him in the Incarnation of the Word, in the womb of the Virgin Mary, the Son of God by His divine nature and the Son of the Virgin by the flesh.

"4. Let us honor the operation of the Holy Spirit and adore Him proclaiming the Church on the glorious day of Pentecost.

"5. Let us honor the operation of the Holy Spirit and adore Him dwelling in the Church and assisting her faithfully according to the divine promise even to the consummation of the world.

"6. Let us honor the wonderful operation of the Holy Spirit creating within the Church that other Christ, the priest, and conferring the plenitude of the priesthood on the bishops.

"7. Let us honor the operation of the Holy Spirit and adore Him in the heroic virtues of the saints in the Church, that hidden and marvelous work of the 'Adorable Sanctifier.' "

Chaplet of Mary, Model for Mothers

This chaplet was written by the author of this book to honor Mary as model for mothers and to thank her for her daily assistance in the most difficult, important, and rewarding job any woman can have. No special beads are needed for the chaplet — ten fingers can serve as a reminder if needed. Each mystery is followed by a single Hail Mary, and the entire chaplet is concluded with the Memorare of St. Bernard.

"1. Annunciation — Mary, you were only about fifteen when the angel came to ask you to be the Mother Of God. You must have been frightened — alone and unmarried. Be with all those who today have found out that they are pregnant. For those who are not glad of the news, assist them to say 'yes' to the new life growing within them. Hail Mary. . . .

"2. Visitation — Mary, you hastened to your cousin to help her out during her pregnancy. Her preborn child recognized yours and leapt in his mother's womb. Take the preborn children who today will be pulled from their mothers' wombs by abortion into your tender and immaculate heart. Hail Mary. . . .

"3. Presentation — You followed the law and presented your Child in the Temple. Simeon told you that a sword would pierce your loving heart. In Baptism, I, too, have presented my children according to the law. I realize that I, too, will have swords of sorrow in my heart. Give me the strength to bear what is the difficult part of what is to come for my children. Hail Mary. . . .

"4. Finding in the Temple — How terrified you must have been, how worried, when you found Jesus was not where He was supposed to be. How overjoyed your heart felt when you found Him in the Temple! How proud you must have been to hear His words to the learned teachers, and how gratified that He went and was subject to you. Help me to trust that my children will be safe, yet understand my motherly worries and terrors. Help my children to be wise, and to be subject to me only in so far as I am subject to your Divine Child. Hail Mary. . . .

"5. The Wedding at Cana — His time was not come, He said; yet with the compassionate heart of a mother you understood the family's disgrace and made your request in perfect faith. May I live each day in perfect faith in the help of your Son. Hail Mary. . . .

"6. The Scourging — How did you bear to see your innocent Child broken and bloody? Help me to bear the hurts, the fears, the illnesses, and the anguish of my children. Help me to water their growth and comfort them with my prayers and my tears. Hail Mary. . . .

"7. The Road to Calvary — Jesus walked alone, dragging His heavy cross. You could not carry it for Him, although you gladly would have done so. How grateful you must have been to the Cyrenian for his assistance, and for the woman who compassionately wiped the face of Jesus. Help me to realize that I cannot carry my children's crosses for them, but that my love can be a support for them. Inspire me with gratitude for all those who assist my children — relatives, teachers, friends. Remind me to extend my love outward daily. Hail Mary. . . .

"8. The Crucifixion — Only a mother who has watched her child suffering and dying can begin to really comprehend your anguish at this dark hour. The pain must have felt as if your very heart were being wrenched from your breast. Remind me daily of all the suffering children of the world — from the starving child in the fourth world to the drug addict and the AIDS victim and the homeless in my own town — and of their sorrowful mothers. Hail Mary. . . .

"9. The Resurrection — Your faith was rewarded, and your Child returned from death. Before your heart was bursting with sorrow; now it seems to burst with relief and joy in the glorious miracle of renewed life. Fill my heart with the glorious mystery of the Resurrection, and admit me to the company of the Easter People. Hail Mary. . . .

"10. The Crowning as Queen of Heaven — Mary, you said 'yes' to God. Throughout your life, in sunshine and in shadow, you were His

From left: Rosary of Our Lady of Sorrows, small Passionist Emblems, and Sacred Heart Rosary (see "Chaplets, Rosaries, Crowns, and Beads").

faithful servant. After your falling asleep, you were taken to your Son, your Divine Master. Jesus said, 'Let not your hearts be troubled; believe in God, believe also in me. In my Father's house are many rooms; if it were not so, would I have told you that I go to prepare a place for you? And when I go and prepare a place for you, I will come again and will take you to myself, that where I am you may be also. And you know the way where I am going' (Jn 14:1-4). Dearest Queen, help me to say 'yes' daily to all that God asks of me in order that I may one day go to the place that He has prepared for me. Hail Mary. . . ."

The Memorare

Remember, O most gracious Virgin Mary, that never was it known that anyone who fled to thy protection, implored thy help, or sought thy intercession was left unaided. Inspired by this confidence, I fly unto thee, O Virgin of Virgins, My Mother. To thee I come, before thee I stand, sinful and sorrowful. O, Mother of the Word Incarnate, despise not my petitions, but in thy mercy hear and answer me.

Miscellaneous Other Sacramentals

When I first began work on this book, I was determined to do sufficient research to include a majority of all the sacramentals of the Catholic Church. After my preliminary work, however, I soon came to realize that I could spend many years on this research and still not cover all the sacramentals. Each bishop has the authority to approve sacramentals for use in his own diocese. Therefore, the number of sacramentals is not counted, and they cannot be listed. This book, then, contains only a few of the many and varied blessings, actions, and objects of devotion known and used in the Catholic Church. This final section contains information about some well-known and not-so-well-known sacramentals that did not easily fit into the previous categories. Hopefully, the text will have included for the reader sufficient information to display the beauty and variety of the sacramentals of the Catholic church . . . those things which, when well used, can provide for us a touch of faith.

Candles

Candles have been used from classical times in worship and in rites for the dead. Like other items which became sacramentals for the Christians, candles have a history that is secular or pagan in origin. Carrying tapers was one sign of respect for the high dignitaries of the Roman empire. The Church, from a very early period, took them into her service to enhance the splendor of religious ceremonials. These early candles were any kind of taper in which a wick, often made of a strip of papyrus, was encased in animal fat or wax.

The use of a multitude of candles and lamps was a prominent feature of the celebration of the Easter vigil, which dates almost from apostolic times. Their use was not confined to the hours when artificial light was necessary. St. Jerome, about the end of the third century, declared that candles were lit at the reading of the Gospel not to put darkness to flight but as a sign of joy. The great Paschal candle represents Christ the true Light, and the smaller candles represent the Christians who strive to reproduce the light of Christ in their lives.

Besides their use at baptism and funerals, candles were used in a number of other ways. They were constantly used in the Roman Ceremonial from the seventh century, and probably earlier. The candles were placed on the floor of the sanctuary and it was not until later that they were placed on the altar. Exactly when candles were moved to the altar has not been pinpointed, but the practice was well established by the twelfth century. Rubrics prescribe the number and use of candles for all Masses and other ceremonies.

The candles used for liturgical purposes are primarily made of beeswax. Historically the idea of the supposed virginity of bees was insisted on, and the wax thus was regarded as typifying in a most appropriate way the flesh of Jesus Christ born of a virgin mother. As a rule, liturgical candles are white, although some are made of unbleached wax and gilt, and paint may be added under some circumstances. It is fitting that these candles should be blessed, but that is not a regulation.

An elaborate blessing was performed on the Feast of the Purification, *Candlemas day*, which was followed by a distribution of candles and a procession. When the Pope was resident and performed the blessing, a number of the candles were thrown to the crowd and some were sent as special presents to persons of note.

The first historical description of the feast of the Purification is given about 390, when the feast was held in Jerusalem. From here, it spread into the other churches of the Orient. It first appears in the liturgical books of the Western Church in the seventh century. Pope Sergius I (701) first prescribed the procession with candles for this feast and for the other three feasts of Mary which were then celebrated in Rome. The ceremony of blessing for the candles originated at the end of the eighth century in the Carolingian Empire, as did most of the other liturgical blessings.

Candles were and are commonly used to burn before shrines toward which the faithful wish to show a special devotion. The candles burning their life out in front of a statue are symbolic of prayer and sacrifice. The custom may have begun with the practice of burning lights at the tombs of the martyrs in the catacombs. Here, lights were kept burning for lengths of time as a sign of unity with the Christians who remained on earth. The candles kept a silent vigil before the graves, and thus came to be known as *vigil lights*. One curious medieval practice was to offer a candle or candles equal in height to the person for whom some favor was asked. This was called "measuring to" such and such a saint. This practice can be traced from the time of St. Radegund (d. 587) through the Middle Ages. It was especially common in England and the north of France in the twelfth and thirteenth centuries.

In the past, candles were required on the altar for the solemn recitation of the Divine Office, for the celebration of Mass, and for other services. Candles were lit in ritual order to show reverence for the crucifix or tabernacle. At Benediction, twelve candles were lit. During ordination to the priesthood, the candidate used to present a candle to the bishop. Candles are also used during the dedication of a church, at the blessing of a baptismal font, at the churching of a new mother, at the singing of the Gospel, and during liturgical processions, among other occasions. During medieval times, after a sentence of excommunication was read, a bell tolled while the ritual book was closed, and a lighted candle was thrown to the ground to indicate the person's fall from grace. Today candles are principally used on or near the altar for the celebration of Mass.

Before Mass on February 2, candles are blessed in the church. Wearing a purple stole, the celebrant blesses the candles with prayers, sprinkles them with holy water, and incenses them before distributing them to the clergy and people as the *Nunc Dimittis* is being sung. Then a procession is formed with lighted candles and antiphons sung.

On the Feast of *St. Blaise*, the throat of the person to be blessed is centered between two crossed white candles while the person stands or kneels before the altar. The priest prays, "May God deliver you from trouble of the throat and from every other evil through the intercession of St. Blaise, bishop and martyr."

Oils

The use of oil for anointing far antedates Christianity. Historically, from the Hebrews to the primitive Church, it has stood for strength, sweetness, and spiritual activity. Pure olive oil is used for the Oil of Catechumens and of the Sick, and is an ingredient of holy Chrism. Olive oil is prescribed to be burnt in sanctuary lamps, but other, preferably vegetable oils may be substituted.

The Mass of the Chrism is solemnly celebrated in every cathedral on Holy Thursday. During this Mass, the bishop blesses the Oil of Catechumens and the Oil of the Sick and consecrates the Chrism.

The Oil of Catechumens is used in the anointing prior to Baptism.

The Oil of the Sick is used in sacramental anointings of the sick. The use of this oil is based on the injunction of St. James in his epistle: "Is any among you sick? Let him call for the elders of the church, and let them pray over him, anointing him with oil in the name of the Lord to heal him. And the prayer of faith will save the sick man, and the Lord will raise him up; and if he has committed sins, he will be forgiven" (Jas 5:14-15).

Chrism is a mixture of olive oil and balm (balsam). It is used in administering Baptism, Confirmation, Holy Orders, and in the consecration of churches. Anointing with chrism signifies the fullness and diffusion of grace. In the East, the consecration of the Chrism is a symbol of patriarchal authority. There, other ingredients including ginger, wine, and rose-water are added.

Oil of the saints is an oily or other liquid which has exuded from the relics of certain saints, an oil which has been poured over the relics of certain saints and collected as a sacramental, or an oil blessed in honor of a certain saint. This oil is used for anointing with prayer for the intercession of the saint and faith in God for health of the soul and body.

The word "*manna*" is often used in place of the word oil when describing the liquids which exude from the relics of some saints. Possibly this is due to the fact that the formation of this oil is as mysterious as was the formation of the manna supplied to the Israelites during their wandering in the wilderness in Old Testament times. The oil that has been observed originating from the relics of saints generally takes the form of a colorless, odorless, tasteless fluid and has occurred in different countries with various atmospheric conditions and circumstances (Cruz, *Relics*, p. 192). Three major saints with whose relics this phenomenon is associated are *St. Andrew*, who died in the first century; *St. Nicholas*, who died in the fourth, and *St. Walburga*, who died in the eighth. Medical science cannot explain why their bones secrete a liquid which still collects at certain times that would seem unfavorable for the formation of any liquid. The relics of *St. Gerard Majella* excluded a fluid for a time, although this has not continued to the present, and the first miracle accepted for his beatification involved the cure of a dying man who applied this mysterious oil and was restored to complete health. Other saints whose relics or bodies gave off a fluid include *St. Agnes of Montepulciano, St. Camillus de Lellis, St. Paschal Baylon, St. Julia Billiart, St. Mary Magdalene dei Pazzi, Venerable Mother Maria of Jesus, Blessed Matthia Nazzarei of Matelica,* and, in our own times, *St. Sharbel Makhlouf.*

St. Sharbel died in 1898, and a mysterious fluid was first observed coming from the body about four months after his death. This fluid appeared to come from the pores and seemed a mixture of blood and sweat. The fluid continued to exude for over half a century. At the ritual exhumation before beatification in 1965, the body had decomposed and the fluid had stopped its flow. There are numerous well-documented incidents of this phenomenon, but no natural explanation has been found for it.

From the middle of the fifth century, it was a custom to pour oil or water over the relics of martyrs and to collect this liquid as relics called *oleum martyris*. The custom was later extended to the relics of saints who were not martyrs. *St. Paulinus of Nola* and *St. Martin of Tours* are examples of saints whose relics have been thus treated.

In the fifth and sixth centuries, the tomb of the martyr *St. Menas* became a popular place of pilgrimage. As a souvenir, flasks of oil and water were given to the pilgrims. The water probably came from a well near the tomb; the oil was taken from that burned in lamps before the tomb. This practice has continued as a part of the cultus of a number of saints through modern times. A special prayer for the blessing of oil in honor of *St. Serapion, Martyr*, was found in the Roman Ritual. Originally this blessing had been reserved to the Order of Our Lady of Ransom.

Agnus Dei *(Lamb of God)*

"Lamb of God, who takes away the sin of the world, have mercy on us" (cf. Jn 1:29).

In addition to the words spoken by St. John the Baptist to Our Lord, repeated as an invocation before communion in the Mass, *Agnus Dei* (Latin for "Lamb of God") is also the name of one of the oldest sacramentals of the Church. It is a small disc of wax stamped with a lamb which represents Our Lord as victim. Sometimes the lamb is shown with a halo and cross or pennon (streamer). The wax is taken from Paschal candles or candles blessed by the Pope on Candlemas Day.

The Agnus Deis originated from the custom of using bits of the paschal candle as articles of devotion. These sacramentals are often encased in silk or leather to protect the image and are often ornately embellished with embroidery, lace, or other fancy stitchery. They were generally made in convents. The Pope solemnly blessed them on the Wednesday of Holy Week in the first and every subsequent seventh year of his reign. In the prayers of blessing, the dangers of fire, flood, storm, plague, and childbirth were referred to. When the discs of wax were brought to the Pope, he dipped them into a vessel of water mixed with chrism and balsam while he recited the consecratory prayers. The distribution of the Agnus Deis took place on Easter Saturday when the Pope, after the Agnus Dei of the Mass, put a packet of the sacramentals into the inverted miter of each cardinal and bishop who came up to receive them.

This sacramental is sometimes worn about the neck, much as we would wear a medal, and is used as a reminder to seek God's protection in trouble. During the reign of Queen Elizabeth, the Agnus Dei was among the things especially forbidden to be brought into England. As in the case of the Paschal candle, the wax of the Agnus Dei symbolizes the virgin flesh of Christ; the cross associated with the lamb suggests the idea of the victim offered in sacrifice. As the blood of the paschal lamb of the Old Testament protected each household from the destroying angel, the purpose of these sacramentals is to protect those who use them from all malign influences. The efficacy of this sacramental is not, of course, from the wax, the balsam, or the chrism; the efficacy of the Agnus Dei is from the blessing of the Church and the merits of the "Lamb of God, who takes away the sins of the world."

Blessed Roses

A pious custom in Dominican and some other churches on the Feast of the Holy Rosary is the blessing of roses. The rose is seen as a figure of the rosary and its mysteries.

The green leaves represent the Joyful Mysteries; the thorns of the bush stand for the Sorrowful Mysteries. The Glorious Mysteries are seen in the flowers.

The formula in the Roman Ritual for the blessing of the roses reads:

"O God, Creator and Preserver of mankind, deign to pour out Thy heavenly benediction upon these roses, which we offer to Thee through devotion and reverence for Our Lady of the Rosary. Grant that these roses, which are made by Thy Providence to yield an agreeable perfume for the use of men and women, may receive such a blessing by the sign of Thy holy cross that all the sick on whom they shall be laid and all who shall keep them in their houses may be cured of their ills; and that the devils may fly in terror from these dwellings, not daring to disturb Thy servants."

One of the most famous oil wells in Texas is the Santa Rita No. 1. This well, drilled on state-owned lands, opened the field that pumped riches into the University of Texas, where the original pump is displayed today in Austin. The name originated with a group of Catholic women from New York, who had invested in stock sold by the driller. They asked that the well be named for *St. Rita*, as patron of the impossible. After the driller completed the derrick over the well, he climbed to the top, sprinkled dried rose petals which had been blessed in the saint's name and given him by the investors, and christened the well (*Texas Highways*, September 1989, p. 55).

St. Anthony's Bread

Saint Anthony's bread is not a sacramental, but rather a pious custom of those devoted to St. Anthony of Padua. Charity is a wide avenue to the favors of heaven, and St. Anthony loves the poor now as he did in life.

Often, those who appeal to the Wonder Worker accompany their request with a promise that if the saint grants the favor they request at the expiration of a certain length of time, they will donate a sum of money in his honor to the needy. The alms may be given to any charity or for the education of a poor seminarian who aspires to the priesthood.

Clockwise from left: Little Sachet (Gospel of the Holy Name),
blessed rose petals and leaves, Agnus Dei in container, and "My
Ticket to Heaven" booklet (see "Miscellaneous Sacramentals").

Blessed Dresses

In the 1950s and '60s, it was a pious custom for young ladies to wear blessed dresses as a promise or to obtain some special favor. The most commonly used blessed dresses were those in honor of our Lady of Lourdes, our Lady of Sorrows, the Immaculate Conception, of Carmel, of Mary Help of Christians, of St. Anthony, and of St. Joseph. The color of the dress indicated in whose honor it was worn. The dress of Our Lady of Lourdes was white with a blue sash tied in front. That of Our Lady Help of Christians was coral pink with a powder blue sash tied in a bow at the left side. All blessed dresses were to be modest with long sleeves and closed necklines.

Via Matris (The Way of the Sorrowful Mother)

In 1233, Our Blessed Lady appeared to seven noblemen of Florence and instructed them to establish a religious order which would preach her sorrows to the world. In another apparition, she gave them instructions for a habit, a rule, and a name — Servants of Mary. The order became the last of the five mendicant orders of the Church.

The seven saints retreated to Monte Senario and built the first monastery of the new order. From here began a wave of devotion to Our Mother of Sorrows that spread throughout the civilized world. The *Via Matris* is among the many devotions which grew out of the fervent preaching of the Servites. One historical study indicates that the devotion existed as early as the fourteenth century in Flanders.

Patterned on the Stations of the Cross, the Via Matris is a set of seven stations commemorating the seven sorrows of Our Lady. The stations are canonically erected in churches; although the blessing and erection of these stations used to be reserved to the Servite Order, since Vatican II any priest may perform the ritual. They were first indulgenced by Pope Gregory XVI.

The stations of the Via Matris are as follows:

1. The Prophecy of Simeon

"Simeon blessed them, and said to Mary his mother, 'Behold, this child is set for the fall and the rising of many in Israel, and for a sign that is spoken against (and a sword will pierce through your own soul also), that thoughts out of many hearts may be revealed' " (Lk 2:34-35).

2. The Flight Into Egypt

"Now when they [the wise men] had departed, behold, an angel of the Lord appeared to Joseph in a dream and said, 'Rise, take the Child and His mother, and flee to Egypt, and remain there till I tell you; for Herod is about to search for the child, to destroy him.' And he rose and took the child and his mother by night, and departed to Egypt, and remained there until the death of Herod" (Mt 2:13-14).

3. The Loss of Jesus in the Temple

"And when the feast was ended, as they were returning, the boy Jesus stayed behind in Jerusalem. His parents did not know it, but supposing him to be in the company they went a day's journey, and they sought him among their kinsfolk and acquaintance; and when they did not find him, they returned to Jerusalem, seeking him" (Lk 2:43-45).

4. Mary Meets Jesus on the Way to Calvary

"And there followed him a great multitude of the people, and of women who bewailed and lamented him" (Lk 23:27).

5. Jesus Dies on the Cross

"But standing by the cross of Jesus were his mother, and his mother's sister. . . . When Jesus saw his mother, and the disciple whom he loved standing near, he said to his mother,'Woman, behold, your son. Then he said to the disciple, 'Behold your mother' " (Jn 19:25-27).

6. Mary Receives the Dead Body of Jesus in Her Arms

"Joseph of Arimathea, a respected member of the council . . . took courage and went to Pilate, and asked for the body of Jesus . . . and he bought a linen shroud, and taking him down, wrapped him in the linen shroud" (Mk 15:43-46).

7. Jesus Is Laid in the Tomb

"Now in the place where he was crucified there was a garden, and in the garden a new tomb where no one had ever been laid. So because of the Jewish day of Preparation, as the tomb was close at hand, they laid Jesus there" (Jn 19:41-42).

Novenas

A novena is a prayer extended over a period of nine days, and said for some special petition. The word comes from the Latin word *novenus*, meaning a set of nine. Various reasons have been advanced for the choice of nine days, but basically the custom seems to have been taken over from Roman paganism. Originally the novena was made for the repose of the soul of a dead person, and the term novena is still used for a novena of Masses said after the death of a pope.

The first novena of the Church was held by the Apostles and disciples, who along with our Blessed Lady awaited the coming of the Holy Spirit. After the Ascension, the Apostles, together with Mary and the disciples, men and women numbering about 120 persons, gathered in the Cenacle, the upper room in Jerusalem where the Last Supper had taken place. There they spent the time in prayer, awaiting the fulfillment of the Lord's promise: "Stay in the city, until you are clothed with power from on high" (Lk 24:49).

Following the example of the Apostles, the faithful make novenas directly to God or to Him through one of the saints to obtain spiritual or temporal favors. Any suitable prayers may be used in making a novena, but it is preferable to hear Mass and receive Holy Communion daily as practices of the novena.

Public novenas are made in churches, often in preparation for a specific feast. Other elements of the novena services may include the Stations of the Cross or the Via Matris; litanies, hymns, and the novena prayers may be followed by Benediction. A perpetual novena is one which is held regularly on the same day, such as every Friday, in a church, like the popular novena to Our Lady of Perpetual Help. Attending the devotions nine times consecutively constitutes a novena. Novenas may be made privately by individuals also.

Many beautiful novena services have been composed through the years. Some have been composed by the saints, and at least one, that of the Queen of the Holy Rosary, was begun at the direction of Our Lady in a vision.

Quinceañera

The *Quinceañera* is a Catholic celebration familiar to those in the Southwestern United States and wherever those of Spanish descent reside. It is the traditional celebration when a young lady turns fifteen.

The service and Mass are quite beautiful. In it, the girl renews the promises made for her at baptism. The priest reminds her that she has become a woman, and is now the traditional age Our Blessed Mother was when she became the Mother of God. The girl promises to remain faithful to God and to follow His will for her life, whether as a married woman, a single woman, or a religious. She asks that God's graces not be wasted in her. Then she asks Our Lady to present her offering to the Lord, and to be her model of a valiant woman, her strength, and her guide.

The girl is traditionally dressed in a long dress almost as elaborate as a wedding gown, but in her chosen colors. She wears a long lace mantilla. She has fifteen attendants representing her fifteen years, and these range in age from about five years old to older girls who are usually the girl's best friends. During the ceremony, the priest blesses gifts for the girl such as a Bible, a rosary, a cross, a medal, and the crown. The mantilla is removed, and the girl is crowned with a jeweled tiara.

After the Mass, a joyous fiesta is held, with mariachi musicians serenading the birthday girl. The refreshments are ample, including an elaborate cake. The girl celebrating her *quince años* begins the dancing by granting the first dance to her father or closest male relative. Then all, from youngest to oldest, join in the fun and festivities.

Sacred Heart Auto Emblem

In 1954, Father Gregory Bezy, S.C.J., was inspired to initiate a league of "prayerful, careful, and reparative drivers." While praying in the Sacred Heart Church in Walls, Mississippi, Father Gregory recognized that thousands of people were being killed or maimed in automobile accidents yearly. He firmly believed that if he could convince people to turn the chore of driving into a prayerful activity, drivers would become more alert and avoid accidents. He also felt that driving could be a worthwhile time for people to make reparation for the lack of courtesy displayed by so many drivers on the roads.

The Sacred Heart Fathers and Brothers had been invited by the bishop to come to northern Mississippi to help in the evangelization of his diocese. The diocese was poor, and the congregation needed to support their mission work financially. Father Bezy had been appointed by the provincial superior to raise the funds needed for the missionary work, and he had already begun the Sacred Heart League and the Sacred Heart Southern Missions to solicit contributions for the work through direct mail.

To remind people that driving time could be prayer time, Father Gregory had a statue of the Sacred Heart designed which could be placed on the dashboard of cars and other vehicles. When dashboards were metal, a small magnet in the plastic statue was used to hold it in place. The statues were mailed to millions of people across the United States in an effort to get them to join the "apostolate of prayerful, careful, and reparative driving." Excess contributions collected were used to support the home-mission effort in northern Mississippi.

In the late '60s, Father Gregory and his assistant, Roger Courts, designed a symbol of the Auto League which was more appealing to post-Vatican II Catholics, a Sacred Heart dashboard medal. The medals were mailed out nationwide in an effort to continue and expand the Auto League and the other apostolic works of the Sacred Heart League and Southern Mission. As with any item that is mass-produced and widely distributed, the dashboard medal lost its popularity as had the statue. Therefore, the league currently distributes a membership key ring.

Highway death tolls have increased vastly since 1954. There is still a need for careful and prayerful driving. These small Sacred Heart auto emblems can and should serve as a valuable reminder to today's drivers. As in the past, excess funds collected are used in the home missions in northern Mississippi, providing health, education, and social services to thousands of residents. Additionally, the Apostolate of the Printed Word is a work of the Sacred Heart League begun in 1976 to design, publish and distribute religious and devotional materials to encourage and enhance the spiritual life of the recipients. These materials are distributed to friends and benefactors of the Sacred Heart League free of charge, and quantities of them are made available to bona fide ministries and institutions. Nearly two million Good News New Testaments have been distributed to date, along with other publications. This Apostolate of the Printed Word fulfills one of the main purposes of the *Sacred Heart League* — to promote devotion to the Sacred Heart of Jesus.

Enthronement of the Sacred Heart

The great modern apostle of devotion to the Sacred Heart, especially of priestly and family consecration, was Father Mateo Crawley-Boevy (1875-1960). A priest of the Sacred Heart Fathers, he founded the Catholic University of Valparaiso, Chile, and then requested Pope St. Pius X to allow him to devote himself to bring the "entire world, home by home, family by family," to the Sacred Heart. Instead of granting permission, the Pope commanded Father Mateo to dedicate his life's work to this aim. Father Mateo spoke five languages fluently. He traveled worldwide and organized the crusade for the Enthronement of the Sacred Heart (Kern, p.123).

The Enthronement ritual is a paraliturgical family celebration in which Jesus Christ is proclaimed the Lord of the home. Father Mateo wrote, "The Enthronement can be defined as the official and social acknowledgment of the sovereignty of the Heart of Jesus over a Christian family, an acknowledgment made tangible and permanent by a solemn installation of the picture of the Divine Heart in the place of honor, and by an act of consecration."

Father Mateo saw the sanctification of the family as the ultimate goal of the apostolate. He believed the enthronement fulfilled all of the requests of the Sacred Heart made to St. Margaret Mary at Paray-le-Monial. To him, the family as a social cell must be the living throne of the King of Love.

In the Enthronement ceremony, a representation of the Sacred Heart is installed in a prominent place in the home. Preferably, this is done by the father or the head of the household. Then, the family is consecrated to the Heart of Jesus, Lord. In their voluntary dedication, they are set aside as something holy and pleasing to the Lord. The consecration is a covenant or pact that the family freely makes with the Heart of Jesus. It is like a collective renewal of the baptismal commitment made by each member of the family.

The Little Sachet (Gospel of the Holy Name)

"When JESUS was named — Satan was disarmed. . . . He [Jesus] made me understand the glory it gives Him to celebrate His victory in those words, for they cause the demon to tremble with rage; and He promised to bless all who wear this Gospel, and to defend them against the attacks of Satan."

Sister St. Pierre, a Nun of the Carmel in Tours France, in 1847 made known the devotion to this "little sachet" to all who came to her monastery seeking help, cures, and consolation. It consists of a leaflet on which are printed the Gospel passage from Luke which mentions the giving of the name of "Jesus" to our Savior, a picture of the Christ Jesus, the initials I.H.S., and some invocations to inspire confidence, together with the line "When Jesus was named, Satan was disarmed." The leaflet is folded into a small square, encased in a pouch, and carried or worn about the person as a reminder of the power of the Most Holy Name of Jesus.

The faithful are encouraged to recite the doxology (Glory be to the Father) five times and say the ejaculation "Blessed be the Most Holy Name of Jesus without end" frequently while wearing the sachet.

Spiritual Communion

Nothing can really compare with receiving Our Lord in Holy Communion. A spiritual communion, however, can be offered often. St. Thérèse of Lisieux said, "To communicate spiritually . . . is extremely profitable, and afterwards you may practice inward recollection . . . for this impresses upon us a deep love of the Lord. If we prepare to receive Him, He never fails to give, and He gives in many ways that we cannot understand."

One suggested form of spiritual communion is as follows: "O Lord Jesus, since I am unable at this time to receive You in the Holy Sacrament of the Eucharist, I beg You to come spiritually into my heart in the spirit of Your holiness, in the truth of Your goodness, in the fullness of Your power, in the communion of Your mysteries, and in the perfection of Your ways. O Lord, I believe, I trust, I glorify You. I'm sorry for all my sins. O Sacrament most Holy, O Sacrament divine, all praise and all thanksgiving be every moment Thine."

My Ticket to Heaven

In 1982, Father Paul Thomas, a priest of the Altoona-Johnstown diocese (Pennsylvania), told his congregation, "I have been telling people how to get to heaven for forty years. I am going to put it in a nutshell for you."

Father Paul then sat down and composed a meditation that begins, "Lord Jesus, Your holy will be done . . . first, last, and always. But it is Your holy will that I go to heaven when I die. Therefore, may this be my ticket to Heaven."

Father Paul then had his office girl mimeograph copies of the meditation, which he attached to his Sunday bulletin for the three hundred families of his parish. He never dreamed it would go outside his own congregation. A retired high school principal from a distant town attended Mass at Father Paul's parish that weekend, and wrote him a letter commending him on the meditation, and expressing the fact that many people needed the type of uplift that the meditation contained. Father Paul thought that perhaps he should make it available to others, and had his local printer make five thousand copies. These were gone before he knew it, so he had them reprinted. As of 1989, nearly two and a half million copies from over twenty-six printings of the little meditation had been distributed all over the world.

The demand for the booklets is steady, and there is no charge for them, although many have sent donations to help in the cost of reprinting. The meditation, which is a straightforward presentation of the cardinal mysteries of the Christian faith, includes a number of biblical references. The booklet is not copyrighted, and those who receive them have permission to reproduce them, or translate them into other languages.

Appendixes

Correspondence

My special thanks to these and the many other persons who helped so much in the research for this book, by their prayers, their interest, and their information.

Ms. Anne Marie Adach, Tekakwitha League, Auriesville, N.Y.

Father Alban, O.F.M., Franciscan Mission Associates, Mt. Vernon, N.Y.

Association of the Miraculous Medal. Perryville, Mo.

Augustinian Fathers, Villanova University, Villanova, Pa.

Sister Mary Beard, Director, Marian Center, Emmitsburg, Md.

Rev. Alfred Boeddeker, O.F.M., President, Sacred Heart Society, San Francisco, Calif.

Rev. Conrad Borntrager, O.S.M., Provincial Historian, Basilica of Our Lady of Sorrows, Chicago, Ill.

Rev. John Boscoe, C.S.B., Our Lady of Guadalupe Church, Rosenburg, Tex.

Ms. Eleanor Breurles, Corresponding Secretary, Scandanavian Catholic League, New York, N.Y.

Rev. Mark Brummel, C.M.F., National Shrine of St. Jude, Chicago, Ill.

Rev. Blaine Burkey, O.F.M. Cap, Communications Office, Capuchin Province of Mid-America. Hays, Kan.

Byzantine Sisters, St. Basil's Center, Houston, Tex.

Patricia Carter, Office Manager, Christian Life Communities, St. Louis, Mo.

Rev. John Catoir, Director. The Christophers, New York, N.Y.

Father R. Charest, S.M.M., *Queen of All Hearts* Magazine, Bay Shore, N.Y.

Rev. Thomas H. Clancey, S.J., New Orleans, La.

Crosier Community. Onamia, Minn.

Ms. Joan Carroll Cruz, New Orleans, La.

Msgr. Luigi de Magistris, Regent, Sacred Apostolic Penitentiary, Rome, Italy.

Rev. Msgr. Alan F. Detscher, Associate Director, Bishop's Committee on the Liturgy, Washington, D.C.

Discalced Carmelite Nuns, New Orleans, La.

Dismasians, Honolulu, Hawaii

Dominican Nuns, Monastery of the Infant Jesus, Lufkin, Tex.

Rev. Jack Dowling, S.S.S., Provincial Superior, Congregation of the Most Blessed Sacrament, Cleveland, Ohio

JoAnn Dykes, Rose Scapular Co, Oxnard, Calif.

F. Harry Faulhaber, Miraculous Lady of the Roses, Hickory Corners, Mich.

Mrs. Ruth Flere, Secretary, National Shrine of St. Dymphna, Massillon, Ohio

Most Rev. Harry J. Flynn, Bishop of Lafayette, Lafayette, La.

Renee Fuller, Houston, Tex.

Franciscan Friars of Marytown, Libertyville, Ill.

Rev. James Gaunt, C.S.B., University of St. Thomas, Houston, Tex.

Sister Maria Goretti, A.P.B., Secretary, Monastery of the Precious Blood. Brooklyn, N.Y.

Mary Ellen Hall, Houston, Tex.

Sister M. Lea Hill, D.S.P,. Vice Provincial Superior, Boston, Mass.

Rev. William A. Holt, O.P. Dominican Friars' Guilds, New York, N.Y.

Juanita Hoppe, Catholic Leaflet Apostolate, Toledo, Ohio

Heather Horn, Houston, Tex.

Sister Julia Hurley, R.S.C.J., Albany, N.Y.

Linda Isley, For Fathers Only, Culver City, Calif.

Ms. Elizabeth Jacobs, Akwasasne Home, St. Regis, Quebec, Canada

Sister Helen Kallus. Oblates of St. Benedict. Naperville, Ill.

Mary Grace Larsen, Secretary, Sacred Heart Archdiocesan Center, Chicago, Ill.

Rev. Jerome LeDoux, S.V.D., Vice Provincial, Society of the Divine Word, Bay St. Louis, Miss.

Rev. Albert C. Louapre, S.J., Assistant to the Provincial, New Orleans Province, Society of Jesus, New Orleans, La.

Raymond L. Lovasik, Tarentum, Pa.

Rev. Robert Lynch, O.F.M., Director, The Way of the Cross, Boston, Mass.

Rev. Luigi Magistris, Regent, Sacred Penitentiary Apostolic, Vatican City

Very Rev. Gerard M. Mahoney, C.M., Provincial Superior, Congregation of the Mission, Philadelphia, Pa.

Mariannhil Fathers. Dearborn, Mich.

Rev. Sebastian MacDonald, C.P., Provincial Superior, Passionist Community, Chicago, Ill.

Rev. Kevin Mackin, O.F.M., St. Anthony's Guild, Paterson, N.J.

Rev. Robert J. McAllister, S.J., Director, Apostleship of Prayer, New Hyde Park, N.Y.

Rev. Ray McKee, C.SS.R., Marian Devotions, St. Louis, Mo.

Rev. Michael Miller, C.S.B.,Vice President for Academic Affairs, University of St. Thomas, Houston, Tex.

Rev. James Moeglein, O.S.C., Assistant to the Provincial, Crosier Fathers and Brothers, Minneapolis, Minn.

Rev. Norman J. Muckerman, C.SS.R., Liguori, Mo.

Rev. Joseph T. Muller, M.S.C., Missionaries of the Sacred Heart, Aurora, Ill.

Rev. Thaddeus Murphy, O P., Director, St. Martin de Porres Guild, New York, N.Y.

Rev. Joseph Phan Nam, C.M.C., Secretary, Congregation of the Mother Co-Redemptrix, Carthage, Mo.

Rev. Leo Neal, O.F.M. Conv., Director, Albanian Catholic Information Board, Santa Clara, Calif.

Rev. Reggie Nesvadba, St. Mary's Seminary, Houston, Tex.

Office of Worship, Diocese of Galveston-Houston

Mrs. Martha Ortega, Word Rosary Intercessors, South Bend, Ind.

Very Rev. Richard O'Donnell, O.S.Cam., Provincial, Order of St. Camillus, North American Province, Milwaukee, Wis.

Passionist Nuns. Owensboro, Ky.

Mrs. Silvia Pena, *Texas Catholic Herald*, Houston, Tex.

Doris M. Poisson, Secretary, Pro Maria Committee, Lowell, Mass.

Rev. Charles J. Polifka, O.F.M Cap., Provincial Minister, Capuchin Province of Mid-America, Denver, Colo.

Rev. Andrew Pollack, C.PP.S., Cincinnati Province, Precious Blood Fathers, Carthagena, Ohio

Gary Prince, Holy Rosary Apostolate, Zurich, Ontario, Canada

Mark Ratay, Publications Department Manager, The Sacred Heart League, Walls, Mich.

Bill Reck, The Riehle Foundation. Milford, Ohio

Sister Mary Reginald, D.M., Villa Rosello, Newfield, N.J.

Rev. Christopher Rengers, O.F.M. Cap., Capuchin College, Washington, D.C.

Father Robert, Prior, Immaculate Heart Hermitage, Big Sur, Calif.

Father Robert, C.M.F., National Shrine of St. Jude, Chicago, Ill.

Rev. Msgr. Dan Scheel, Chancellor, Diocese of Galveston-Houston, Houston, Tex.

Victor Shoemaker, Marian Movement of Priests, St. Francis, Maine

Jimmy Sicking, President, St. Louis Senatus, Legion of Mary, St. Louis, Mo.

Rev. Anthony Skurla, O.F.M., Superior, Byzantine Franciscans, Sybertsville, Pa.

Mrs. Barbara Smith, Administrative Secretary, World Apostolate of Fátima, Washington, N.J.

Sisters of Charity, St. Joseph's Provincial House, Emmitsburg, Md.

Rev. Al Seichepine, C.S.SP., Cornwells Heights, Pa.

Mary-Eunice Spagnola, Mary Productions, Middleton, N.J.

Brother David Tejada, F.S.C., Santa Fe, N.M.

Rev. Paul Thomas, Patton, Pa.

Alice Venturini, Staten Island, N.Y.

Rev. Anselm Walker, St. Basil's Church, Houston, Tex.

Sister Grace Waters, M.S.C., Provincial Councillor, Missionary Sisters of the Sacred Heart of Jesus, Chicago, Ill.

Sister Gabrielle Woytko, O.P., Slovak Cultural, Educational, and Literary Center, Oxford, Mich.

Edward Zych, Hohenwald, Tenn.

Bibliography

Attwater, Donald, Ed., *A Catholic Dictionary*. New York: Macmillan, 1941

Ball, Ann, *A Litany of Mary*. Huntington, Indiana: Our Sunday Visitor Books, 1988

___, *Holy Names of Jesus*. Huntington, Indiana: Our Sunday Visitor Books, 1990

Barry, William T., C.SS.R., Trans., *Enchiridion of Indulgences, Norms and Grants*. New York: Catholic Book Publishing Co., 1969

Boase, Rev. Leonard, S.J., *Catholic Book of Knowledge*. Chicago: Catholic Home Press, Inc., 1962

Breen, Rev. Stephen P., *Treasure Wrapped in Cloth*. Wilmington, Delaware: Apostolate of Christian Action, 1961

Burkey, Father Blaine, O.F.M. Cap., "The Scapular of St. Joseph: a Capuchin Devotion." *Annals of the Capuchin Province of St. Augustine*, Feb. 1961. p.35

Cacella, Joseph, *How Fátima Came to America*. New York: St. Anthony's Welfare Center, 1957

Christopher, Rev. Joseph P., and Spence, Very Rev. Charles E., Trans., *The Raccolta*. New York, Benziger Brothers, Inc., 1943

Cruz, Joan Carroll, *Relics*. Huntington, Indiana: Our Sunday Visitor Books, 1984

Doheny, Msgr. Wm. J., C.S.C. *The Life of Saint Birgitta of Sweden*. Rome: Private Publication, 1980

Eckel, Rev. Frederick L., *A Concise Dictionary of Ecclesiastical Terms*. Nashville, Tennessee: Abingdon Press, 1960

Green, Louisa Meigs, *Brother of the Birds*. Philadelphia: David McKay Co., 1929

NA (no author), *Great Heart of Joseph, The*. Washington, D.C.: St. Joseph Medal, 1971

Hanley, Boniface, O.F.M., "That Martin Girl." *The Antonian*, Patterson, N.J.: St. Anthony's Guild, 1974

Hebermann, Charles G., Ed., *The Catholic Encyclopedia*. New York: Robert Appleton and Co., 1912

Hodge, Larry, "Taming the West." *Texas Highways Magazine*, Vol. 36. No. 9, September, 1989

Huels, John M., O.S.M., *Father Keane, Servant of Mary*. Berwyn, Illinois: Servite Press, 1979

Husslein, Rev. Joseph, S.J., *Heroines of Christ*. Milwaukee: Bruce Publishing Co., 1949

NA: *Little Treasury of St. Anthony, The*. Patterson, New Jersey: St. Anthony's Guild, 1979

Longpré, Anselme, R.C., *The Holy Wounds of Jesus*. Montreal: Companions of Jesus and Mary, 1986

NA: *Manual of Piety of the Brothers of the Christian Schools*. New York: LaSalle Bureau, 1951

Mead, Rev. Jude, C.P., *St. Paul of the Cross, A Source/Workbook for Paulacrucian Studies*. New Rochelle, New York: New Don Bosco Publications, 1983

Montfort, St. Louis Marie de, *The Secret of Mary*. New York: Montfort Publications, 1984

Morrow, Most Rev. Louis, S.T.D., *My Catholic Faith*. Kenosha, Wisconsin: My Mission House, 1966

Mott, Marie Edouard, C.M., *The Green Scapular and Its Favors*. Emmitsburg, Maryland: Marian Center, 1961

Nevins, Albert J., M. M., *The Maryknoll Catholic Dictionary*. New York: Grosset and Dunlap, 1965

NA: *New Catholic Encyclopedia*. New York: McGraw Hill, 1967

NA: *Orate Fratres, A Manual of Prayers for Divine Word Missionaries*. Manila: Arnoldus Press, 1977

Osborn, D.E.W., Comp., *Euchologion (Trebnyk), A Byzantine Ritual*. Hamtramck, Mich.: Byzantine Catholic Church, 1978

Parente, Fr. Pascal P., *Beyond Space*. Rockford, Illinois: TAN Books, 1973

NA: "Passion Scapular." *Bulletin of the Archconfraternity of the Holy Agony*, Vol. 101, No. 4: Winter 1988, p. 18

NA: *Perpetual Help Story, The*. Liguori, Missouri: Liguori Publications, 1976

NA: *Pieta Prayer Booklet*. Hickory Corners, Michigan: Miraculous Lady of the Roses, 1986

Plaku, Palok. "The Holy Legend of Our Lady of Shkodra." *Albanian Catholic Bulletin*, Vol. IX, 1988. p. 12

Quintiliani, Patricia S., *Treasury of Chaplets*. Cambridge, Massachusetts: Ravengate Press, 1986

NA: *Rosary of Our Lady of Sorrows*. Chicago: Friar Servants of Mary, 1986

NA: "St. Joseph, the 'Now' Saint." *Immaculata* Magazine Vol. 22, No. 10: March 1971, p. 13

NA: *St. Joseph Today*. St. Louis: The Capuchin Troupe, 1974

NA: "The Scapular of the Passion." *Annals of the Archconfraternity of the Holy Agony of Our Lord Jesus Christ*, Vol.2., No. 2: Spring, 1893

Shaughnessy, Patrick, O.S.B., *Twenty-Four Rosaries and Chaplets*. St. Meinrad, Indiana: Grail Publications, 1954

Simcoe, Mary Ann, Ed., The Liturgy Documents. Chicago: Liturgy Training Publications, 1981

NA: *Sister Mary Martha Chambon and the Holy Wounds of Our Lord Jesus Christ*. Montreal: Companions of Jesus and Mary, 1986

Sjogren, Per-Olof, *The Jesus Prayer*. Philadelphia: Fortress Press, 1975

NA: *Stations of the Way of the Cross, The*. Paterson, New Jersey: St. Anthony's Guild, 1936

NA: *Take My Advice*. Villanova, Pennsylvania: Augustinian Press, 1987

NA: *Vademeci, S.V.D.*. Rome: General Council, Society of the Divine Word, 1962

Walton, Paul H., *Dali/Miro, Masters of Surrealism*. New York: Tudor Publishing Co., 1967

Weiser, Francis X., *Handbook of Christian Feasts and Customs*. New York: Harcourt Brace, 1958

Weller, Philip T., S.T.D., *The Roman Ritual*. Milwaukee: Bruce Publishing Co., 1964

Sources for Information

The list of addresses below is intended to give the reader a resource for further information about many of the sacramentals in this book. In addition, addresses for a number of confraternities, pious unions, and other organizations are included and listed topically. For a more extensive listing of such organizations, the reader is referred to the *Catholic Almanac*, published annually by Our Sunday Visitor Books.

Agnus Dei: Discalced Carmelite Nuns, 1611 Mirabeau Ave., New Orleans, LA 70122

Alcoholism: The Calix Society, 7601 Wayzata Blvd., Minneapolis, MN 55426

Beauraing, promotion of the apparitions of: Pro Maria Committee, 22 Second Ave., Lowell, MA 01854

Chaplet of St. Michael: Oblates of St. Benedict, 24 W. 350 Maple, Naperville, IL 60540

211

Chatky: Byzantine Sisters, St. Basil's Center, 1815 Parker Rd., Houston, TX 77097

Cord of St. Joseph: St. Joseph's Union, 108 Bedell St., Staten Island, NY 10309

Cross, The Way of the: Franciscan Apostolate of the Way of the Cross, 103 Arch St., Boston, MA 02107

Cross, Your, prayer cards: Catholic Leaflet Apostolate, 2740 West Central Ave., Toledo, OH 43606

Devotion to Bd. Kateri Tekakwitha: Tekakwitha League, Auriesville, NY 12061

Devotion, Divine Mercy: Congregation of Marians, Stockbridge, MA 01263

Devotion, Holy Face: Holy Face Association, P.O. Box 1, St. Henri Station, Montreal, Canada H4C 3J7

Devotion, Holy Ghost: Archconfraternity of the Holy Ghost, Holy Ghost Fathers, Cornwells Heights, PA 19020

Devotion, Holy Wounds: Companions of Jesus and Mary, P.O. Box 84, Opelousas, LA 70570

Devotion, Infant of Prague: National Shrine of the Infant Jesus of Prague, P.O. Box 488, Prague, OK 74864

Devotion, Mother of Perpetual Help: The Director, Our Mother of Perpetual Help, Liguori Publications, One Liguori Drive, Liguori, MO 63057

Devotions, Passionist: Passionist Nuns, 1420 Benita Ave., Owensboro, KY 42301

Devotion, Precious Blood: Monastery of the Precious Blood, Fort Hamilton Parkway and 54th St., Brooklyn, NY 11219

Devotions, Queen of All Hearts: Montfort Missionaries, 26 S. Saxon Ave., Bay Shore, L.I., NY 11706

Devotions, St. Anthony of Padua: St. Anthony's Guild, 508 Marshall St., Paterson, NJ 07503

Devotions, St. Dymphna: National Shrine of St. Dymphna, 3000 Erie Street S., P.O. Box 4, Massillon, OH 44648

Devotions, St. Joseph: The Work of St. Joseph, Capuchin College, 4121 Harewood Rd. N.E., Washington, DC 20017; Sacred Heart Archdiocesan Center, 110 W. Madison St., Chicago, IL 60602-4196

Devotion, St. Martin de Porres: St. Martin de Porres Guild, 141 E. 65th St., New York, NY 10021-6699

Devotion, St. Jude: National Shrine of St. Jude, 205 West Monroe St, Chicago, IL 60606

Devotion, St. Thérèse of Lisieux: Society of the Little Flower, 1313 Frontage Rd., Darien, IL 60559

Devotions, Servite: Servite Development Office, 1439 South Harlem, Berwyn, IL 60402

Devotions, Slovak: Slovak Cultural, Educational and Literary Center, 775 W. Drahner Rd., Oxford, MI 48051

Enthronement of the Sacred Heart: (see Sacred Heart, National Enthronement Center)

Holy Spirit: (see devotion, Holy Ghost)

Literature, distribution of Catholic: The Riehle Foundation, P.O. Box 7, Milford, OH 45150; Catholic Leaflet Apostolate, 2740 West Central Ave., Toledo, OH 43606; My Ticket to Heaven, Rev. Paul Thomas, R.D. 2, Box 51-H, Patton, PA 16668

Little Sachet: (see *Agnus Dei*)

Medal, Miraculous: The Association of the Miraculous Medal, St. Mary's Seminary, 1811 West St. Joseph St., Perryville, MO 63775; Knights of the Immaculata, National Center Militia Immaculatae, Franciscan Friars of Marytown, 1600 W. Park Ave., Libertyville, IL 60048

Medal, Our Lady of Confidence and Maria Goretti: Pro Trinitas, 6322 N. Keating, Chicago, IL 60646

Mental Illness: (see Devotions, St. Dymphna)

Motherhood, Christian: Confraternity of Christian Mothers, 220 Thirty-seventh St., Pittsburgh, PA 15201-9990

Night Adoration in the Home: (see Sacred Heart, National Enthronement Center)

Passion of Our Lord: (see Devotions, Passionist)

Peace Movement, National Catholic: Pax Christi U.S.A., 348 East Tenth St., Erie, PA 16503

Persecuted Church, Holy Wounds, Prayers for the: St. Dismas, P.O. Box 23243, Honolulu, HI 96822

Prayer, Apostleship of: Apostleship of Prayer, 3 Stephen Ave., New Hyde Park, NY 11040

Rosary, Confraternity of the Most Holy: Dominican Friars' Guilds, 141 E. 65th St., New York, NY 10021-6699

Rosary, Ladder: Linda Brown, 806 W. Durink, St. Mary's, KS 66536

Rosary, Meditational Books for: Friends of the Cross, 1833 Montclair, Fort Worth, TX 76103; Word Rosary Intercessors, Inc., 1330 Helmen Dr. South Bend, IN 46615

Rosary of Our Lord: Camaldolese Monks, Immaculate Heart Hermitage, Big Sur, CA 93920

Rosary, Special Favor: Special Favor Rosary Guild, 321 Barrack Hill Rd., P.O. 165, Ridgefield, CT 06877

Sacred Heart: Apostleship of Prayer (see Prayer, Apostleship);

International Institute of the Heart of Jesus, 7700 W. Blue Mound Rd., Milwaukee, WI 53213; National Enthronement Center, Three Adams St., Fairhaven, MA 02719; Sacred Heart League, Walls, MI 38686;

Sacred Heart Society, 135 Golden Gate Ave., San Francisco, CA 94102

Sacred Hearts (Jesus and Mary): Sacred Heart Archdiocesan Center, 110 W. Madison St., Chicago, IL 60602-4196

Sacred Heart, Our Lady of the: League of Our Lady of the Sacred Heart, Missionaries of the Sacred Heart, P.O. Box 270, Aurora, IL 60507

Scapular, Brown: World Apostolate of Fátima (The Blue Army), Washington, NJ 07882

Scapular, Green: Marian Center, St. Joseph's Provincial House, 333 S. Seton Avenue, Emmitsburg, MD 21727

Scapular, Red: Archconfraternity of the Holy Agony, St. Joseph's Provincial House, Emmitsburg, MD 21727

Scapular, White: Pious Union of Our Mother of Good Counsel, Director of the Pious Union, P.O. Box 338, Villanova, PA 19085

Service and Evangelization: Legion of Mary, St. Louis Regional Senatus. Box 1313, St. Louis, MO 63788

Seven Sorrows of the B.V.M.: (see Devotions, Servite)

Staurolite: John B. Kachinsky, Lathrop's Gem Shop, 6702 Ferris St., Bellaire, TX 77401

Suffering, The Apostolate of: (see Sacred Heart, National Enthronement Center)

Water, Lourdes: The Lourdes Center, Marist Fathers, Box 575, 698 Beacon St., Boston, MA 02215

Water, St. Odilia: Shrine of St. Odilia, Crosier Fathers, Onamia, MN 56359-0500

Index